The Guide to **Jewish Interfaith Family Life**

To Bob,

Thanks for making our family feel so welcome.

I hope you find this book a valuable resource.

Jim

The Guide to Jewish Interfaith Family Life

An InterfaithFamily.com Handbook

Edited by Ronnie Friedland & Edmund Case

Foreword by Anita Diamant, author of *The New Jewish Wedding*

Preface by Rabbi Kerry M. Olitzky,
Executive Director, The Jewish Outreach Institute

Introduction by Dr. Paula Brody, LICSW

For People of All Faiths, All Backgrounds

JEWISH LIGHTS Publishing

Woodstock, Vermont

The Guide to Jewish Interfaith Family Life:
An InterfaithFamily.com Handbook

Library of Congress Cataloging-in-Publication Data
The guide to Jewish interfaith family life : an InterfaithFamily.com handbook / edited by Ronnie Friedland and Edmund Case; foreword by Anita Diamant ; preface by Kerry M. Olitzky ; introduction by Paula Brody.
p. cm.
Includes bibliographical references.
ISBN 1-58023-153-5 (pbk.)
1. Interfaith marriage. 2. Interfaith families. 3. Children of interfaith marriage.
4. Jewish families—Religious life. I. Friedland, Ronnie. II. Case, Edmund, 1950–
HQ1031 .G85 2001
306.84'3—dc21
2001003467

10 9 8 7 6 5 4 3 2 1
Manufactured in the United States of America

For People of All Faiths, All Backgrounds
Published by Jewish Lights Publishing
A Division of LongHill Partners, Inc.
Sunset Farm Offices, Route 4, P.O. Box 237
Woodstock, VT 05091
Tel: (802) 457-4000 Fax: (802) 457-4004
www.jewishlights.com

To my children, Joshua and Rebecca, sources of boundless joy, and to the Little family, who so graciously accepted my wish to raise my children as Jews.

—R.F.

To Wendy, my inspiration, and all of the sojourners who ask her question—*yes,* there *is* a place for you in Judaism.

—E.C.

Contents

Ronnie Friedland is editor of InterfaithFamily.com. She has co-edited two parenting books, *The Mothers' Book* and *The Fathers' Book*. She has two grown children, Joshua and Rebecca, and was in an interfaith marriage for nearly twenty years.

How to Use This Book

RONNIE FRIEDLAND

The Guide to Jewish Interfaith Family Life is written for:

- Interfaith couples.
- Interdating couples.
- Parents and relatives of interfaith couples.
- Children of interfaith parents.
- Jews-by-Choice who have non-Jewish relatives.
- Jewish and non-Jewish relatives of Jews-by-Choice.
- Jewish and non-Jewish friends who want to better understand interfaith couples and Jews-by-Choice.
- Jewish or interfaith couples who have adopted a non-Jewish child.
- Professionals and lay leaders in the Jewish or any other faith community who work with interfaith couples or Jews-by-Choice.
- Members of the Jewish or any other faith community who are concerned about interfaith marriage and who want to better understand interfaith families and choices made by interfaith couples.

This guidebook—and the Internet magazine it has grown from—offer much-needed resources and fill a notable gap in our contemporary Jewish community. Although a high proportion of Jewish families include intermarried members, until today no handbook for interfaith families exploring Jewish life was available.

Our goal for this book is twofold: to help families as they journey through interfaith life, and to gently encourage them to make Jewish choices. Our perspective is that it is best if parents choose one religion for their children, while always treating the other partner's religion and family members with the utmost respect. Although each family has to work out what best meets its unique needs, we hope that the religious choice will be Judaism.

The articles in this book were originally written for the online magazine InterfaithFamily.com. Published by Jewish Family & Life! (a member of the Jewz.com Media Network), InterfaithFamily.com has become a lively home for interdating and intermarried couples and their families—a place where they feel warmly welcomed to the Jewish community, where their unique needs are addressed, and where they can engage in meaningful online discussions with others in similar situations. Readers of this book who wish to discuss issues raised here will find special online forums for that purpose on InterfaithFamily.com.

As a guide for couples from different religious traditions, and for their parents, children, and extended families, the book is organized around the interfaith couple's journey together: the wedding, relationship issues, choosing a religious identity for children, sharing that choice with parents, deciding on birth ceremonies for the child, dealing with the challenges of raising a child whose religious identity is different from that of one of his or her parents, extended family relations, handling holiday celebrations, creating a comfortable *Bar/Bat Mitzvah* in an interfaith family, discussing interfaith dating with children, and death and mourning issues. The book also includes chapters on divorce and stepfamily issues, adoption, gay interfaith relationships, and grandparenting children who have interfaith parents.

Most chapters begin with an "expert" offering advice on a particular topic, followed by interfaith family members discussing their own personal experiences with that issue. We hope that interfaith families who may feel isolated will find support in the practical suggestions and personal stories from individuals whose experiences resonate with their own.

As interfaith couples journey through life together, many partners gradually adopt a religious culture and life that they would not have anticipated when they first married. Although some choose to convert before marriage, increasingly others come to this decision—if they come to it at all—over time, after reaching a level of comfort with the religion in which they have raised their children, celebrated holidays, and attended religious services. Many other partners agree to raise their children Jewish and support that process by participating in Jewish life—yet choose not to convert. These partners, we believe, should be honored for their commitment to raising Jewish children, not made to feel inferior because, for whatever personal reasons, they did not convert. Their support of their children's religion strengthens rather than harms the Jewish community. The chapters on synagogues and conversion address these issues and others as well.

Professionals—religious educators, outreach workers, and clergy who work with interfaith families—and indeed anyone who wants to understand the growing phenomenon of Jewish interfaith family life will learn from listening to the voices of our writers.

We hear a great deal about the issue of interfaith families from the Jewish community. Now it is time for the Jewish community to listen to the voices of the interfaith families themselves.

Anita Diamant has written six guides to contemporary Jewish practice, including *Choosing a Jewish Life: A Handbook for People Converting to Judaism and for Their Families and Friends* (Schocken).

Foreword

ANITA DIAMANT

This is a book about my family. And about your family, too. But truly, this is a book about the entire Jewish community and its future.

My daughter spent a semester of her sophomore year in high school studying Jewish history and Hebrew in Israel, while her grandmother, my mother-in-law, attended church every Sunday. Your family has its own tales of contradiction and connection. Taken together, all of our stories tell the tale of the collective family known as the Jewish people.

There is a tendency to think of "interfaith families" as a recent phenomenon.

And it is true that the Jewish people survived—against impossible odds—in large part because Jews maintained distinct practices that clearly defined the difference between "us" and "them." However, there are other reasons for our unlikely continuity on the world stage. And one of these is the permeability of our boundaries.

Our non-Jewish family members—referred to in the Bible as "the strangers within your gates"—have been a secret source of our community's health and vibrancy throughout history. Usually without fanfare, often informally, sometimes even secretly, "they" have become part of "us," and in the process enriched the cultural, spiritual, and genetic fabric of the Jewish people. Jews have always accepted the stranger among us who wished to convert, even when it was against the law and dangerous to do so. We have also always quietly adopted foundlings and married our maids and our neighbors, incorporating the strangers within our gates into our hearts, into our families. This helps explain why we Jews are so genetically diverse: blue-eyed, brown-skinned, red-headed, kinky-haired. And this opening to others has renewed and revitalized the Jewish people.

The fact that "they" are "us" is widely advertised as a "Problem," sometimes even trumpeted as a "Mortal Threat" by strident voices within the Jewish establishment. But the professional hand-wringers, whatever statistics they marshal, seem completely cut off from the people and families in question. They ignore the Talmudic injunction "Find out what the Jews are doing." (Brachot 45b)

I grew up in an extended interfaith family. My Uncle Teseo did not attend church but felt he couldn't convert while his mother was alive. My Aunt Pia remained a devout Catholic all her life. Another aunt, Aunt Dory, converted to Judaism before her marriage to my uncle.

My brother married a non-Jew, and their children have no religious affiliation or connection whatsoever. I, too, fell in love with a non-Jew, but he converted to Judaism a week before our wedding, and is now an active member of our congregation, our movement, our community.

All of this is my daughter's Jewish legacy, and the legacy that she will hand down, God willing, to her children.

A generation ago, my family constellation might have been seen as an aberration. Today we are typical. Which is why this book is so timely, and so important. The essays in this book describe the life and challenges of the Jewish family at the start of the twenty-first century. And although there are dilemmas and problems on these pages, there are also helpful strategies and spiritual epiphanies. There is wisdom, and humor, and hope.

Once, while driving my grade-school-age daughter to Hebrew school, I asked if she thought it was important to marry someone Jewish. Emilia thought about my question for approximately twenty seconds and then listed three categories of acceptable marriage partners: people who were born Jewish, people who converted to Judaism, and people "like Marisa's father." Marisa, a Hebrew school classmate, is the daughter of a Jewish mother and a non-Jewish father who fully supports his family's Jewish observance and affiliation.

Emilia's religious requirement for a life partner was someone willing to share a Jewish home. It strikes me that my daughter had given voice to an emerging reality within the Jewish world.

The overwhelming majority of North American Jews count non-Jewish relatives in their nuclear and/or extended families: spouses, parents, in-laws, cousins, nephews, children. The lines between "us" and "them" have not been this fuzzy since Abraham (himself not born to Jewish parents) took his motley household to live in a distant land and discover a radical new relationship to the sacred.

The current permeability of Jewish boundaries does challenge the distinctiveness of the Jewish people in some ways. There is no denying that certain forms of Jewish culture are edging toward extinction. While this is a melancholy reality, it is not a threat to Jewish continuity. There have been many variants of Jewish culture, most of which are long gone: Alexandrian recipes we will never savor, Castilian jokes we will never hear. Yet, the Jews persist, writing new melodies for ancient prayers.

Judaism is a sacred culture that embraces many ethnicities. It is a tradition founded on muscular questions about God and humanity and grounded in optimism. Nurtured by our faith in the goodness of life and in the power of community, a gateway to meaning and holiness, Judaism grows and changes. Open from its very beginning to seekers and sojourners, our house is sturdy, and we have room inside for multitudes, for contradictions, and certainly for our non-Jewish parents and children.

Rabbi Kerry M. Olitzky is executive director of the Jewish Outreach Institute, the only national organization dedicated to providing a network of programs and services to intermarried families and children. His most recent books are *Jewish Paths toward Healing and Wholeness: A Personal Guide to Dealing with Suffering* and, with Rabbi Lori Forman, *Restful Reflections: Nighttime Inspiration to Calm the Soul, Based on Jewish Wisdom* (both from Jewish Lights).

Preface

RABBI KERRY M. OLITZKY

This book is about choices. It is also about personal freedom. And it is about forging a pioneering path in Jewish religious and communal life—even when doing so requires a great deal of effort in a community that often seems unwelcoming, and especially when the Jewish community seems unfriendly. For these reasons, I feel privileged to add my name to the many serious spiritual seekers whose words are included in the pages of this volume. The authors of too many books talk about Jewish life—practice and observance—as if it exists without people who are willing to move from idea into reality. This book is about real people doing real things, having integrated the practice of Judaism into their daily lives and those of their children and families.

Jewish life has to reflect the ideas that those who practice it hold dear. This book succeeds in making sure that each idea, each practice, and each personal struggle are not anonymous or just an exercise. Instead, these articles are real, and each idea has a real person's name attached to it. As we learned long ago in our history, "Judaism is with people"—and how they live their lives within the context of Jewish communal life.

In this new Jewish community that is emerging, people have made their many choices and continue to do so, following a pattern that they themselves are creating as they move through the life cycle. The choices are varied and colorful. Each choice helps to weave a beautiful tapestry of a richly hued Jewish community, one that is flexible, open, and encouraging of new ideas while respectfully committed to its past. Some have chosen to in-marry. Others have chosen to intermarry. Some have remained single. Some have chosen same-sex partners. Others have chosen to live in multi-generational and blended families. Still others—perhaps too vast a number—have chosen to simply opt out.

Opting out of religious life should be the real concern of those who care about the future of Judaism. I believe this deeply concerns those whose voices are heard reverberating throughout the articles in this book. Regardless of who they are and the life choices they have made, they remain passionate about the opportunity to express themselves Jewishly. The people in this book, and the families in which they live, have all chosen to lead Jewish lives, as they define them, fully recognizing that this definition is fluid and evolving—and that it has to meet their own special needs. It is the dynamism of this flexible definition that provides us with a profound sense of optimism for the Jewish future. Like a precious stone with many facets, Judaism's glow continues to be bright regardless of the particular angle from which you encounter its light.

Our experience in the past fifty years suggests that each individual approaches religious life with the right to make personal choices about his or her own life. And when individuals become parents, this right extends to decisions we make regarding our young children. We who subscribe to this view must affirm the right of individuals to make such choices even when they are not consistent with our own, even when we may disagree with them. We make these choices every day and in every aspect of our lives. So why are we so surprised when individuals extend this principle into Judaism?

The Jewish community is large enough so that it need not be reluctant or afraid to open its borders to all those who would come and dwell within it, even those not born within it who have not chosen to convert and leave behind the religion into which they were born. This is not counter-intuitive. It is simply what we call the "facts on the ground." Judaism is strong and vibrant. If the Jewish community is not willing to grow beyond its ancient borders, then it will implode into itself, having made no room for new ideas to move it forward. This book is proof that such dire consequences do not have to happen as a result of interfaith marriage. In fact, the opposite can be—and often is—true. Interfaith marriage can help grow the Jewish community.

In some respects, this book and the lives that it represents are an experiment, because, in general, it relates the experiences of those who are members of interfaith families who have chosen to lead Jewish lives. The varieties of Jewish life that are described here meet the needs of individual families whose complexities even the ancient rabbis who thought of so much did not anticipate. An honest study of Jewish history reveals that each time the Jewish community made progress, it had to take quantum jumps. Future models for Jewish life were seldom anticipated. That is what made it so exciting, and that is what breathed such profound optimism into it.

The phenomenon of intermarriage is certainly not new. And experimentation with practice and observance within families is also not new, particularly on an individual basis. What is new and what is demonstrated in this book is the collective experimentation of large groups of people. The strength of this volume and what it represents is clearly seen in the numbers of people who have contributed to it and the webzine from which these articles are taken—InterfaithFamily.com. Interfaith marriage by Jews is not a passing phenomenon that can easily be written off. According to the data we have available, we are talking about one million households led by at least one head of household who was not born Jewish and one who was born Jewish. We are all Jews-by-Choice, and the authors of many of the articles in this book have *chosen* to be Jewish and lead a Jewish life. While some may want to write these families out of the Jewish community, this book comes to tell us that they do not choose to be written off. It comes to tell us about the transformative power of Judaism to raise ordinary everyday life to a level of sacredness for literally hundreds of thousands of families who will not be defined by antiquated inherited standards and definitions—families whose voices will neither be silent nor be silenced.

Acknowledgments

We want to thank the co-founder of Jewish Family & Life!, Yosef I. Abramowitz, for seeing the need to support and reach out to interfaith families on the Internet, and having the courage and will to create InterfaithFamily.com to serve them. Yossi is a true visionary and an extraordinarily kind and supportive colleague.

We also want to thank Paula Brody, director of Outreach Programs and Training for the Northeast Council of the Union of American Hebrew Congregations (UAHC, the Reform Movement). In producing InterfaithFamily.com, we have relied greatly on her wisdom, sensitivity, and experience. Paula advised us as to the tone, content, and organization of both the magazine and this book, and recommended many of our topics and writers. She has had a profound impact on countless interfaith couples through the years, and has trained both clergy and outreach workers, as well as us, on how to be sensitive to their needs.

We are extremely grateful to our institutional funders, without whom InterfaithFamily.com would not exist. In particular, we are grateful to Robyn Lieberman and her colleagues at the Walter & Elise Haas Fund, which provided the initial funding that made InterfaithFamily.com a reality; to Robert Gamble and his colleagues at the Richard & Rhoda Goldman Fund, which provides very generous ongoing support that allows us to continue to grow; and to Judith Krell and her colleagues at Combined Jewish Philanthropies of Boston, whose support enables us to offer current, continually updated information about programs and welcoming organizations in the Jewish community. We also want to thank Judith Ginsberg and her colleagues at the Covenant Foundation for its support of Jewish Family & Life! during the time that InterfaithFamily.com was launched.

All of our colleagues at Jewish Family & Life! have helped to brainstorm, argue about, and support the development of InterfaithFamily.com and this book. We are especially grateful to Audrey Beth Stein for her design and webmastering help; to Susan Berrin, editor of the journal *Sh'ma*, who helped create InterfaithFamily.com and who was its initial co-editor; to Rabbi Sue Fendrick, editor of SocialAction.com; to Judith Bolton-Fasman, editor of JBooks.com, for editorial help; to Gabriella Soble, editor of JVibe.com and MzVibe.com, and Rachel Simonds for suggesting friends who contributed to this book; to Erica Ernst for her administrative support; and to the rest of the diverse and creative group of employees at Jewish Family & Life!, with whom we so enjoy working. We also want to thank Mac and Marti McCuller of Agassa Technologies, our outside technology consultants, for all of their important background work on the website.

This book, of course, would not exist without our writers. We are grateful to Anita Diamant, who generously gave her much-demanded time to this project, reading and commenting on the manuscript, writing the Foreword, and allowing us to include several articles she wrote for InterfaithFamily.com. We are also indebted to the many members of interfaith families whose lives fill this book. We feel privileged to have been allowed to share their very personal stories. We find their willingness to be frank and forthright both moving and incredibly helpful to others. And we are fortunate to include the contributions of so many skilled professionals, whose wisdom and experience will greatly benefit our readers. It has been a privilege to work with people who are truly inclusive and welcoming of interfaith families.

We are indebted to the Jewish Outreach Institute (JOI), its co-founder Egon Mayer, and its executive director, Rabbi Kerry Olitzky, for their groundbreaking work in promoting a Jewish community that is inclusive of intermarried families.

We owe special thanks to Stuart Matlins, publisher of Jewish Lights, for recognizing the importance of this book and the entire team at Jewish Lights Publishing for making it a reality.

And finally, to the Jewish community, we want to say: We're here. We are part of you. Please welcome us as we are.

Paula Brody, Ed.D., LICSW, is director of Outreach Programs and Training for the Northeast Council of the Union of American Hebrew Congregations (UAHC, the Reform Movement), where she develops and coordinates a wide range of programs and services to welcome interfaith families into Reform congregations. She is a consultant to, and the "Dear Dr. Paula" columnist for, InterfaithFamily.com.

Introduction

PAULA BRODY

Over the last thirteen years, I have worked with hundreds of interfaith families as the director of Outreach Programs and Training for the Northeast Council of the Union of American Hebrew Congregations (UAHC, the Reform Movement). My extensive work on the cutting edge of outreach to interfaith families has sensitized me to the multiple complex issues inherent in interfaith family life. I am so very pleased that InterfaithFamily.com is publishing this collection of real-life experiences of interfaith families. It is my hope that this guidebook will enable readers to address and resolve issues they are facing in their own lives.

Interfaith families have always been part of the fabric of Jewish life. Since biblical days, the very first Jewish families blended religious perspectives. Indeed, if InterfaithFamily.com's website or this guidebook had been available in biblical times, it would have been very helpful! Virtually all the issues listed in the table of contents of this book—interfaith relationships, choosing a religious identity for children, telling parents about religious choices, relationships with the extended family, growing up in an interfaith family, grandparenting, step-parenting, and the many other contemporary interfaith family issues—are encountered in the Bible.

In the Book of Genesis, we learn that Abraham and Sarah, biblical foreparents to the world's monotheistic religions, chose a different religious path from their parents, who worshipped idols. How do you think their parents felt when Abraham and Sarah's faith journey carried them far away from their home, and from the belief system and traditions in which they were raised? Their son Isaac married Rebecca, who was actually a cousin from their homeland. Isaac and Rebecca had two sons, Esau and Jacob. When Esau intermarried with the Hittites, his mother Rebecca despaired, sounding somewhat like a contemporary parent, "If Jacob marries from among the native women, what good will life be to me?" (See Genesis 28:5–9). Although Jacob did not marry out, however, his beloved son Joseph did, choosing Asenath, the daughter of an Egyptian priest. Imagine the issues they faced deciding how to raise their two sons, Ephraim and Manasseh. (Interestingly, the traditional *Shabbat* blessing for sons, "May you grow up to be like Manasseh and Ephraim," invokes the names of these two sons of Joseph and his Egyptian wife Asenath—a biblical interfaith family.)

Most of the narratives included in this book are written from the point of view of people who, while struggling with issues and decisions, have made Jewish choices for their children. However, part of what makes this book refreshing is the inclusion of the Christian partners' perspectives on these interfaith family decisions. Thus, the reflections of Jim Keen (my son-in-law), Cheryl Opper, and Andrea King, among others, are especially valuable in providing a thoughtful look at how feelings and needs evolve over years in an interfaith family. From these reflections, we learn that the passage of time is a key to gaining comfort with traditions that may have been uncomfortable or unfamiliar initially. Christians acknowledge that living an ostensibly Jewish family life is not something they would have ever predicted for themselves. These writers also acknowledge that experiencing another faith's rituals, even while maintaining their own religious traditions, has brought new meaning into their lives.

Although this book offers the insights of many rabbis and professionals within the Jewish community who care deeply about interfaith families, it also brings a priest's understanding to complex family decisions. Father Walter Cuenin's article "Is Heaven Denied to an Unbaptized Child?" will bring comfort to couples wrestling with birth-ceremony decisions. Catholic grandparents will also appreciate Father Cuenin's point of view.

This book honestly presents the complicated loyalties and unresolved issues that shape religious identity. In my experience, most individuals in an interfaith family experience several challenges as they attempt to untangle the knotted threads of religious identity tied to parents and extended family. Our religious backgrounds are often as complicated as our families. Feelings and needs associated with our religion are indelibly linked to powerful childhood memories of holiday celebrations and significant life-cycle moments.

Opening a dialogue about our religious beliefs is difficult even for couples of the same faith. When was the last time you had a deep discussion with a close friend or family member about your belief in God? It is, therefore, understandable that interfaith families might experience a communication gap when discussing different belief systems or how these beliefs are to be passed on to children. Interestingly, interfaith families talk more about faith issues than most other families do. Finding words for these meaningful conversations about deep theological differences, however, is never easy. This book may enable you to bridge those chasms in communication and to find words to talk about God, religious belief, and worship. The experiences of others who have addressed these questions may inspire you to begin important conversations about religious differences.

Remember, as a member of an interfaith family, you are not alone. Many have traveled this road, including the biblical families who lived thousands of years ago. We can learn much from the lives and stories of those who have found a roadmap for this journey. This book chronicles these journeys. May it be a guidebook for you and your family as you find your own path—a path that, I hope, will be filled with an abundance of life's blessings.

1. Interfaith Weddings

Anita Diamant has written six guides to contemporary Jewish practice, including *Choosing a Jewish Life: A Handbook for People Converting to Judaism and for Their Families and Friends* (Schocken).

You Don't Need a Rabbi to Have a Jewish Wedding

ANITA DIAMANT

You're in love? That's terrific!

You're getting married? Congratulations!

Even though one of you isn't Jewish, you've decided to raise your children as Jews, and you've talked about joining a temple someday? Wonderful!

You want a rabbi to officiate at your wedding? Uh-oh.

Interfaith couples who want an unambiguously Jewish wedding often have a hard time finding a rabbi willing to stand up with them. Indeed, it's nearly as hard as finding a rabbi willing to co-officiate at an explicitly interdenominational ceremony.

A small number of rabbis perform intermarriages as hired guns, charging a lot of money just to show up at the wedding. Other rabbis make their decisions on a case-by-case basis, meeting with a couple several times and agreeing to officiate only when they believe there is a real commitment to creating a Jewish home. However, the majority of rabbis—from all Jewish denominations—say "No." Even when they say it nicely, it feels like a personal rejection. And it can hurt.

It helps to understand why most rabbis refuse to officiate. According to Jewish tradition, the core of the ceremony is the ritual statement made by the groom to the bride: "By this ring, you are consecrated to me according to the laws of Moses and Israel."

It's the "laws of Moses and Israel" part that's problematic; if both parties aren't bound by those laws, the commitment has no legal teeth, and the marriage has no Jewish standing. Most rabbis who officiate at intermarriages do not include this statement, which is referred to as the *harah aht* (for the first two Hebrew words). But most rabbis (and cantors) refuse because, regardless of what is or is not said, their very presence makes it appear that the marriage has Jewish standing.

The truth is, nobody needs a rabbi to have a Jewish wedding, and that includes couples where both people are Jewish. For a Jewish wedding to be "kosher," according to Jewish law, all that is required is a bride and groom, two witnesses who are not related to either of them, and a ring—or indeed, any object of modest value that the bride accepts from the groom.

Of course, it's more complicated than that. Over the centuries, the Jewish wedding has incorporated many other traditions that are now "standard" and expected. Prayers such as the *sheva brachot* (seven wedding blessings), and customs such as breaking the glass, are what make Jewish weddings unique and beautiful. The presence of a rabbi has become traditional as well, both as the bearer of the Jewish community's blessing and now as a duly appointed representative of the secular authorities, who signs the state marriage license.

But, in fact, you can create a beautiful, meaningful wedding that celebrates your love for each other and your authentic commitment to Judaism without a rabbi. It happens every day. Here's how:

STUDY JEWISH WEDDING CUSTOMS
AND TRADITIONS

Learn as much as you can about the hows, whys, and wherefores of the Jewish wedding. Talk to rabbis, cantors, and other couples who have had Jewish weddings. Read everything you can get your hands on. (My book *The New Jewish Wedding* has been helpful to lots of interfaith couples, and is widely recommended by Reform, Conservative, and Reconstructionist rabbis.)

Once you have a handle on the tradition, decide what elements are most meaningful to you and make them your own by, for instance, creating an original *chuppah* (wedding canopy) or writing a non-traditional *ketubah* (marriage contract). Explain your choices to your families in advance, and to your guests in a wedding booklet that defines Hebrew words and describes customs that may be unfamiliar.

FIND A THOUGHTFUL JUSTICE OF THE PEACE (OR JUDGE) TO OFFICIATE

Some justices of the peace (JP) specialize in intermarriages, and know how to help you craft your ceremony with sensitivity and skill. Ask around for recommendations; some rabbis may be able to suggest a name. Both members of the couple should interview the justice of the peace or judge, and both of you should be comfortable asking him or her questions. Be clear with the judge or JP about the kind of ceremony you have in mind.

OR HAVE A FRIEND DEPUTIZED FOR A DAY

In most states, individuals can petition for the right to perform wedding ceremonies for a day, so some couples ask a knowledgeable Jewish friend or family member to officiate. This is a great honor, and most people are very moved when asked. Your officiant will probably want to study Jewish customs and laws, and may help plan the ceremony with you.

This is a more personal alternative than hiring a JP, and a practice that seems to be growing in popularity.

HONOR YOUR NON-JEWISH FAMILY

Every wedding is a joining of two families as well as of two individuals. Making the ceremony Jewish can seem like a rejection of the non-Jewish family, so it's important to make both sides feel equally cherished and honored. Parents and siblings might be asked to read a poem during the ceremony. Some couples feature the non-Jewish family's customs and traditions at the party or reception that follows the wedding ceremony. This can mean serving ethnic food, wearing traditional clothing, and/or celebrating with music and dancing, toasts and roasts, that have special meaning to the non-Jewish relatives.

Whatever you choose, *l'chaim* (to life)!

Jim Keen is a freelance writer based in Ann Arbor, Michigan. He has fifteen years of experience in an interfaith relationship. He is married with two children.

Our "Jewish-ish" Wedding

JIM KEEN

Unless you elope to Vegas, chances are planning your wedding won't be easy. My wife and I made things even more difficult by having an interfaith wedding. We took on the task of trying to appease my Protestant family and Bonnie's Jewish family, while also remembering to take care of our own needs in the process. In interfaith weddings, families don't just battle over seating arrangements, they are often torn apart by the issues of marrying outside the religion.

Looking back, the first difficulty we ran into was the impossibility of not offending any member of either family. My parents had their own visions of how a proper wedding should be. These were probably ideas that had been cooking in their heads for years. Basically, Protestant weddings are plain and simple. There is no "Protestant culture" that is an integral part of the ceremony or reception (unless you count the garter toss—I don't know who thought that one up). You walk down the aisle, a minister marries the bride and groom, maybe a song or poem is recited, you walk back up the aisle, and then there is a party afterward.

In the Jewish wedding, however, there are countless elements of Jewish traditions, many of which Bonnie's parents considered important. For instance, you've got the *chuppah* (wedding canopy) under which the couple are married, the breaking of the glass by the groom for good luck, the blessing over the wine, the blessing over the *challah* (braided bread), dancing the *hora* (Jewish circle dance), etc.

Bonnie and I had the task of somehow trying to make sure nobody felt uncomfortable on our special day. Stop right there. Did you see what I just wrote? "Our special day." Somewhere along the way, we remembered that it was important for us to make sure our day went the way we wanted it to go. Don't get me wrong. Our parents were very cooperative and had our best interests at heart. But we were the only two people who could plan our wedding the way we wanted it to go.

Okay, what exactly did we want? As we were new at planning weddings, we weren't sure what we did want. We started by making a list of all the things that were important to us. Bonnie had been to many of her cousins' Jewish weddings and was accustomed to seeing the traditional Jewish elements that I mentioned earlier. She had always felt that these features would be there when she, herself, became a bride. I, because I'm a typical guy, never really thought much about weddings. I hadn't even been to that many and didn't know of any burning cultural items that I just had to have. Although I'm of Scottish descent, I felt that kilts would be a little too much. So you can pretty much guess how I felt about the flower arrangements and dessert menus.

Between the two of us, however, there was one thing for which we both had strong feelings. We each wanted to have God as part of our ceremony. After all, God is a big part of our lives. So would we have a minister marry us? What about a rabbi? Wait, that wouldn't be fair to one of us. How about a co-officiated wedding? I think the word "officiated" is very appropriate. With all the negotiating we were doing, I expected a guy in a black-and-white striped shirt and yellow flag to marry us. It would be hard to find two clergy who would agree to jointly conduct a wedding service. There aren't many out there who see co-officiating as proper. Although we felt that we could eventually find the right two people, we decided that this approach, although fair, didn't make us comfortable. With the ceremony divided into a Jewish part and a Christian part, we just couldn't envision there being any flow to the service. It may work for some couples, but it was not our style.

On the other hand, Bonnie said that having a minister perform the ritual would make her feel like we were having a Protestant wedding. Likewise, a rabbi would give the service an overly Jewish tone for me. Although we decided that we would raise our children Jewish, it was still not possible for us to have a true Jewish wedding. For this, you need both the bride and groom to be Jewish. One out of two doesn't cut it. Then there was the issue of where to hold the wedding. For the same reasons, we didn't feel it would be fair to one of us if the ceremony were held in a church or temple.

Wow! We could see why everyone told us that interfaith marriages were difficult. Sometimes it crossed our minds that we had to be crazy to even attempt such a feat, but our love for each other kept us determined. Then one day, we found the perfect solution. A friend of Bonnie's mom, named Sheila, was a justice of the peace who performed civil ceremonies. She also happened to be a cantor. She specialized in officiating at weddings between interfaith couples and happily agreed to involve God. As a bonus, we found someone to perform the songs in our wedding.

Sheila had suggested a nice hotel as a warm and friendly neutral location to hold the service. This worked out extremely well for the reception, too. We were able to incorporate some Jewish elements, such as the *chuppah* and the breaking of the glass. We even danced to a traditional Jewish tune called the *"Fralich."* I was worried that my Protestant friends and family would be lost. But to my surprise, this dance really energized the crowd and set a festive tone for the rest of the afternoon. Because these were mostly cultural details, my family did not feel threatened. As important as it was that Bonnie and I plan the wedding for our tastes, we also felt that it was a family affair and that everyone should be made to feel welcome, if possible. Luckily, my family said it was the greatest wedding they'd ever been to. "No more boring Protestant weddings!" my mom declared. I think they really enjoyed the change of pace.

Not everyone we had invited agreed to attend the wedding. My wife comes from a Conservative Jewish family. However, many of her relatives were Orthodox and did not approve of our marriage. Her great-uncle politely declined our invitation. At first, I was upset—no, angry. I thought it was insulting. However, after having thought about it, I came to understand his position. Her great-uncle was deeply rooted in his faith, which told him that intermarriage was not appropriate. Although we missed him, I now had a sudden respect for this man, who stood for what he thought was right.

Fortunately, my family had no problems with our interfaith marriage. They had gotten to know Bonnie over the previous five years and had developed a loving relationship with her. I knew this didn't always happen, so I thanked my lucky stars. My parents did have concerns, though. While we were dating, my mom and dad warned me that we would be facing some very difficult issues in the future. They weren't kidding!

Our biggest wedding-related problem was that Bonnie's grand-mother was undecided as to whether or not she would come. To Bonnie, a wedding without her *bubba* (grandmother) would be like apples without honey on Rosh Hashanah (Jewish New Year), only on a much larger scale. Ever since my wife had broken the news to her grandmother that we were getting married, *Bubba* said that she wished her well, but was not sure she would come to the wedding.

Thanks to some heart-to-heart talks with Bonnie's stepmom, *Bubba* decided that what was most important was her grand-daughter's happiness. She came to the wedding. She even danced with me that wonderful summer afternoon. And while the Bo Winnaker Band played Benny Goodman's "Memories of You," I'll never forget what she said to me: "Jim, you're my grandson now."

Rabbi Neil Kominsky graduated from Harvard College and the Hebrew Union College–Jewish Institute of Religion in Cincinnati. He has served since 1995 as rabbi of Temple Emanuel of the Merrimack Valley in Lowell, Massachusetts, and as Jewish chaplain of Phillips Academy in Andover, Massachusetts.

"Why Do You Do This?" A Rabbi's Experience with Interfaith Marriage

NEIL KOMINSKY

It usually starts with a phone call. The voice on the line is very tentative, afraid of being rebuffed or giving offense: "Somebody gave me your name and...umm...do you officiate at interfaith marriages?"

My reply, "Sometimes. Can you tell me a little about your situation?" elicits a sigh of relief, followed by a torrent of information, feelings, and concerns. Once we've worked through the preliminaries on the phone—the rabbi will be the only officiant; I don't do weddings on *Shabbat* (the Jewish Sabbath), and yes, that includes Saturday at 7:30 in June; the date and place are viable for me—we schedule an appointment so that I can meet face to face with both partners and talk.

We meet and have an excellent conversation. After an hour or so of careful questions and answers, and if it becomes clear to me that this is a relationship that will support a Jewish future, one I can say a blessing over, I will agree to do the wedding. Just as we're finishing up, that anxious tone reappears in one of their voices: "Do you mind if I ask you one more question?"

"Not at all."

"We've been turned down by a dozen rabbis all over the state. How come you're willing to do interfaith marriages and they're not?"

It's a fair question, one I've been asked repeatedly over twenty-eight years as a rabbi. Why do I officiate when so many of my colleagues do not? The answer comes in two parts. The first question is, can I officiate at such a marriage? Only if that question is answered in the positive, does the second question arise, should I?

Whether a rabbi feels that he or she can officiate has to do with *halakha* (traditional Jewish law) and the rabbi's relationship to it. *Halakha* simply does not recognize the possibility of marriage between a Jew and a non-Jew; there is no such category in Jewish law. You could line up seventy rabbis, perform all the required actions, and pronounce all the required words, and it would still not be a marriage within the rules of this system. The couple is simply not eligible to marry each other.

Obviously, if one accepts the *halakhic* definitions, the conversation stops right there. Orthodox and Conservative rabbis, who hold *halakha* to be binding, can't officiate. Reform and Reconstructionist rabbis have a more liberal approach to Jewish law, but that does not automatically mean that they believe they can officiate, either. Some would say that a rabbi's authority to officiate at a marriage assumes a Jewish marriage, and, following the traditional definition, a Jewish marriage requires two Jews. If so, again, the conversation is over. Others of us, however, would say that our mandate as rabbis in the contemporary world involves serving the needs of Jews and Jewish life in some ways that the tradition never envisaged. If so, then officiation at a marriage where only one partner is a Jew can become possible.

But even if one can, should one officiate? I believe—and this language will drive some of my more traditional colleagues crazy—that it is a *mitzvah* (a religiously mandated act) to do so under the proper circumstances. I base this position on several premises. The first is that a deeply rooted, mutually nurturing love relationship is a gift of God, deserving of acknowledgment and blessing. The second is that all marriages are, in some sense, mixed marriages.

Any two human beings who pair up will have some areas in which they are a perfect fit and others where, having grown up in different circumstances—whether economic, political, cultural, interpersonal, geographical, or religious—their assumptions and internal maps will differ in ways that challenge them to find common approaches with which both partners can live. Any viable relationship must look these differences in the face and figure out how to deal constructively with them. I see this as a major agenda in premarital counseling. Religion, you will have noted, is simply one of these areas, and one which, like the others, can usually be addressed in ways that will strengthen the relationship. When a couple approaches a rabbi to officiate at their marriage, they are already making a statement about where they think viable common ground can be found. (I exclude here the "we don't care, and it will keep my mother from having a heart attack" argument, which is not very frequent and which does not, in my view, justify rabbinic officiation.)

Very often, in my experience, non-Jewish partners who, for any of a number of very good reasons, do not see themselves converting to Judaism—at least in the foreseeable future—can be very comfortable about supporting the Jewish partner's religious identity, living in a home that identifies with a welcoming Jewish community, and bringing up Jewish children. Such a couple, in my opinion, represents a positive contribution to the Jewish future, and I am glad to assist them with a ceremony which carries the resonances of Jewish tradition while making those changes in wording which permit it to reflect the couple's situation with integrity.

Thus, I would not use the traditional formula "according to the laws of Moses and Israel" for such a couple, as traditional Jewish law does not accord with this ceremony. On the other hand, to affirm, as I do, that the commitment is "according to Divine and human law" spreads a more universal and, I believe, accurate umbrella over the proceedings. Nearly three decades of experience have taught me to rejoice in the opportunity to offer blessings over such a relationship and the future it promises.

Alice Waugh works as an editor at the Massachusetts Institute of Technology and lives in Brookline, Massachusetts.

How I Honored My Non-Jewish Parents at My Jewish Wedding

ALICE WAUGH

My marriage to Ben, in July 1998, brought together two families with very different backgrounds and cultures. Ben's parents are both the children of Russian/Ukrainian immigrants, while mine are from white Anglo-Saxon Protestant families who've mostly been in America since colonial days. My father has many Jewish colleagues and is comfortable with the American Jewish culture, but my mother is a bit less familiar with it, having grown up outside the United States and lived in England since 1972. She doesn't know some of the Yiddish words that have crossed over into mainstream American lingo, and I'm pretty sure she's never tasted a bagel. However, they are both quite used to interacting with people from many nations and have respect for cultures different from theirs.

Most importantly, though, my parents so genuinely shared my happiness and were so fond of Ben (and I think his parents felt the same way about me) that whatever we wanted to do was pretty much okay with them. Perhaps because we were in our mid-thirties, Ben and I also knew what we wanted, and we planned and arranged almost everything ourselves, without parental assistance (though they were very generous in helping to pay for our two-day social event in the woods of northeastern Massachusetts).

Before meeting Ben and considering the whole issue of religion, I had been essentially an atheist. During our engagement, my religious beliefs began evolving (which they continue to do). After taking some classes to learn more about Judaism, I decided to convert and did so a month before our wedding. So we had a Jewish wedding ceremony, but that still left us with a lot of decisions.

What Ben and I did was to create a ceremony with many of the traditional Jewish elements, including a *chuppah* (wedding canopy), Hebrew blessings, a broken glass at the end, and, of course, a rabbi—but one who was modern, inclusive, and open to alternative interpretations wherever possible. Ben and I wanted to make everyone—his parents and our guests as well as my non-Jewish parents—feel comfortable and honored.

You'll notice I refer to my parents as "non-Jewish" rather than "Christian." I guess if they had to be pigeonholed into any religious category, it would be Christian (their own parents were some sort of non–church-going Protestants), but in fact they're both staunch atheists. So we were fortunate that we didn't have to worry about trampling on religious beliefs or traditions that were in conflict with those of Judaism. They were going to participate in our ceremony, and it probably would have made them uncomfortable if they had had to say things that indicated a belief in God—any God.

We had our rabbi, Moshe Waldoks, recite the *sheva brachot* (seven wedding blessings) in Hebrew, but we then had seven friends and relatives read translations by Rabbi Daniel Siegel that we found in Anita Diamant's book *The New Jewish Wedding*. For example, Diamant notes that a fairly traditional translation of the second blessing is "You abound in blessings, *Adonai* our God, you created all things for your glory." But we chose Rabbi Siegel's alternative, which says, "We acknowledge the Unity of all within the sovereignty of God, realizing that each separate moment and every distinct object points to and shares in this oneness."

Ben and I like this concept of oneness or unity, as opposed to the notion of a God who is a separate, sentient being who "created" the universe. And, of course, it's an easier concept for two people like my parents, who are firm believers in evolution and reject any literal reading of the Bible's creation story.

In addition to the seven blessings, we also had friends and relatives give us seven "best wishes" they had written themselves. Most had humorous elements, but they reflected the speakers' individuality and were very touching in their affection for Ben and me.

Finally, we included the traditional blessings that parents give their children. Ben's parents repeated the Hebrew after Rabbi Waldoks, and then added their own thoughts in English. My parents followed, omitting the Hebrew but again offering their own warm thoughts and wishes for our happiness. Likewise, when Ben and I exchanged rings, we said the traditional Hebrew ("by this ring you are consecrated to me in accordance with the traditions of Moses and Israel") and then spoke vows in English that we had written ourselves.

Before the breaking of the glass, there were remarks by Rabbi Waldoks. He is the rather non-traditional rabbi of Temple Beth Zion in Brookline, Massachusetts, which is now unaffiliated with a particular movement of Judaism but is being shaped by his own inclusive style and that of the growing congregation.

The best way to honor people in an unfamiliar setting, I believe, is to give them a role in what's going on, explain what's happening, and refrain from making them do or say anything that would make then uncomfortable. This is what Ben and I tried to do while still retaining traditional elements and being true to our own beliefs, and I think we succeeded.

Rabbi Devon A. Lerner is the author of *Celebrating Interfaith Marriages* (Owl), a book that helps couples create their own sensitive and meaningful interfaith wedding ceremony.

One Rabbi's Approach to Interfaith Wedding Ceremonies

DEVON A. LERNER

"Rabbi, how can we create a wedding ceremony that includes aspects of both of our traditions without offending anyone?" The answer: "It is not only possible, but it is easier to achieve than you might think."

During the last twenty years, I have officiated at hundreds of interfaith ceremonies that were very well received by both sides of the family. The key to creating a sensitive and beautiful interfaith ceremony involves (1) knowing a little about the basics of wedding ceremonies, (2) identifying which customs and traditions are important to you and your families, and (3) having some freedom to participate in creating your ceremony.

About the basics: both Christian and Jewish wedding ceremonies have certain elements in common, including a welcoming of your guests, a blessing of you as a couple, your exchange of vows and rings, the pronouncement of your marriage, and a closing prayer or benediction. Of course, each tradition handles these elements differently.

Christian and Jewish wedding ceremonies also include their own distinctive features. Some of the unique elements of a Jewish ceremony include Hebrew prayers, the blessing over the wine as a symbol of joy, a special set of seven wedding blessings, the breaking of the glass, and the presence of a *chuppah* (wedding canopy). Some of the unique features of a Christian ceremony may include Hebrew scripture and New Testament readings, the lighting of a unity candle, the reading of the Lord's Prayer, and the declaration of intent or consent. How you combine the different elements and customs depends on your own beliefs and connection to your respective traditions.

Some couples prefer a Jewish-style ceremony, which I define as a ceremony that is primarily Jewish, with very few, if any, Christian elements. Couples who choose this style are usually those in which the Jewish partner is very strongly connected to his or her Judaism, and the Christian partner has little, if any, involvement with the church. Brides and grooms who have strong connections to both of their traditions often want a more equal balance of Jewish and Christian elements in their ceremony.

Almost any mix of Jewish and Christian elements can create a sensitive and beautiful interfaith ceremony, if you follow a few basic principles:

1. Choose words that reflect your own beliefs and feelings.
2. Choose a neutral setting for your wedding.
3. Include explanations of the various elements of your ceremony.
4. Avoid saying prayers in Jesus' name.

When you choose words that are meaningful to you, it shows, and your joy is felt by everyone. By choosing a neutral setting, you avoid any appearance that one family's heritage is more important than the other's. When you include explanations of the different traditions in your service, you help everyone feel included in your ceremony; and when you avoid saying prayers in Jesus' name, you are addressing an issue that can be sensitive for both Christians and Jews.

For many Christians, a service without Jesus is hard to imagine. Since Jesus is the foundation of Christianity, this is very understandable. For many in the Jewish community, however, the figure of Jesus evokes painful memories of persecution and anti-Semitism. Years of Christian-Jewish dialogue continue to help heal the wounds of the past; but because of this history, most priests and ministers understand and accept the practice of saying prayers in God's name, not in Jesus' name, in interfaith settings.

If you follow the basic guidelines I have outlined above, you can create a lovely ceremony that is appreciated by both sides of your family.

Jeffrey K. Salkin, senior rabbi of The Community Synagogue, Port Washington, New York, is a noted author and teacher, best known for his book *Putting God on the Guest List: How to Reclaim the Spiritual Meaning of Your Child's Bar or Bat Mitzvah* (Jewish Lights). He served as the co-chair of the Outreach Commission for the Union of American Hebrew Congregations (UAHC, the Reform Movement) and as the chair of the Central Conference of American Rabbis' Reform Jewish Practices Committee.

What's Jewish about the Jewish Wedding?

JEFFREY K. SALKIN

Ask any rabbi—or anyone seriously involved in synagogue life—and they will tell you that the most difficult issues in contemporary Judaism revolve around the life cycle.

With the exception of the Days of Awe, Jewish spirituality has shifted from the festivals to the life cycle. It is the life cycle that exercises our souls and forces us to confront the big issues of life. The questions we ask about those life-cycle rituals are at the center of Jewish identity and the quest to be human.

In our time, the most controversial Jewish life-cycle ceremony is the Jewish wedding. As a ritual, there is no better way to understand the sacred flow of Jewish history and theology. To paraphrase Robert Fulghum, almost everything you need to know about Judaism you can learn at a Jewish wedding. Why do I say that? Because there is far more to the Jewish wedding than what meets the eye. On one level, it is a beautiful ritual—the coming together of two people, two families, two sets of stories. On yet another level, the Jewish wedding is a sacred drama, an allegory of the relationship between God and the Jewish people. The Jewish wedding is a covenantal ceremony. It is a covenant between a man and a woman. But the term "covenant" *(brit)* carries within it the echo of the *brit* between God and Israel. The Jewish imagination deliberately merges those two covenants. Husband and wife, Israel and God—believe it or not, it is all basically the same. Each covenant mirrors the other.

You can chase this sacred covenantal mirror all over our sacred literature. In a famous *midrash* (teaching story), God holds Mount Sinai over the heads of the Jewish people. Will the mountain be our *chuppah* (wedding canopy)—or our tomb? On the holiday of Shavuot, our "wedding day" with God, celebrating God giving the *Torah* (the first five books of the Hebrew Bible), some Jewish communities actually set up a *chuppah* on the *bimah* (podium) and write a *ketubah* (wedding contract) between Israel and God. The ancient rabbis re-imagined the erotic Song of Songs as an allegory about the relationship between God and Israel. Several of the prophets, most notably Hosea, imagined that covenantal failure (idolatry) was like marital failure (adultery).

What is the purpose of both covenants? To create and celebrate *kedusha* (holiness), which is connected to the Hebrew word for marriage, *kiddushin*. Like *mitzvah* (commandment), "holiness" is a Hebrew term that is virtually untranslatable. It means to be sanctified, set apart, lifted above the animal-like and the mundane, touched by God. Judaism presents us with a living vocabulary and grammar of holy places (*Eretz Yisrael*, Jerusalem, the home, and the synagogue), holy times (the life cycle and the festival cycle), and holy relationships, such as God and the Jewish people, parent and child, and the "holy of holies" of human relationships—marriage. When we perform an otherwise neutral act in a holy manner, we affirm that we are made in God's image, and we elevate that act into something higher and holier. Holiness is a "bottom line" term for Jews. It means that something has been invested with Jewish value and meaning.

How does the Jewish wedding ceremony serve as a mini-course in holiness? Walk through it with me. Something profound is happening here.

WE CREATE HOLY SPACE

The wedding begins with the sanctification of space. First, as the couple enters, we create private holy space. The bride and groom stand beneath the *chuppah*, which symbolizes the Jewish home. Therefore, in the midst of the wider community (the assembled guests, who represent the entire Jewish people—past, present, and future) we delineate an island of private holy space. To use a larger metaphor, the couple is now standing in its own "Holy of Holies" in the midst of a larger "Jerusalem."

Then the rabbi or cantor reads or chants certain Psalms: "Blessed are those who come here in the name of God; we bless you from the house of God." "Serve God with gladness, come before God with rejoicing." Those psalms recall the entry of the Israelites into the ancient Temple in Jerusalem. The home (symbolized by the *chuppah*) and the ancient Temple (symbolized by the psalms) are sacred. Marriage is the Holy of Holies of relationship. The *kiddushin* of relationship is like the *kedusha* of place and time. That is why many Jews prefer to celebrate wedding ceremonies in one of Judaism's sacred spaces—at home or in the synagogue—and not in a place like a restaurant, country club, or catering hall.

WE CREATE HOLY TIME

The contemporary Reform wedding ceremony then moves on to the *Shehecheyanu* (prayer giving thanks for having lived to this day), the sanctification of this sacred moment. Though the inclusion of this blessing in the wedding is not traditional, it "works" because it underscores the crucial importance of the sanctity of this moment in the life of the couple, the family, and, by extension, the Jewish people.

WE CREATE A HOLY RELATIONSHIP

There are two sections of the wedding ceremony: *birchot erusin*, the engagement blessings, and *birchot nisuin*, the wedding blessings. The engagement blessings begin with the blessing over the wine, and then move to this blessing: "We praise You, *Adonai* our God, Ruler of the Universe, who hallows us with *mitzvot* and consecrates this marriage." God has permitted us to marry certain people through *chuppah* and *kiddushin*. The larger implication is clear from a complete rendering of the Hebrew that one would find in a traditional service—that there are both permitted relationships, and forbidden (adultery, incest, and those who are already engaged to someone else) relationships.

We then move to the statement that epitomizes the wedding ceremony. The bride and groom exchange rings and say these words: *Hare at mekudeshet* (said by the male) or *attah mekudash* (said by the female) *li betaba'at zo k'dat Moshe v'Yisrael*. It is difficult to translate this blessing. Most would translate it this way: "With this ring you are consecrated to me as my wife/husband in accordance with the law of Moses and the people Israel." It is the word *mekudash* (feminine, *mekudeshet*) that is most historically and Jewishly charged. At that moment, the couple declares that each is holy to the other. It is as if they were saying, "As *Shabbat* (the Jewish Sabbath) is to Jewish time, and as Jerusalem is to Jewish space, you will be to me."

The current edition of *Rabbi's Manual of the CCAR* (Central Conference of American Rabbis, the Reform rabbinical association) adds a text for the couple to read: "I betroth you to me forever; I betroth you to me with steadfast love and compassion; I betroth you to me in faithfulness" (Hosea 2:21–22). The couple is echoing God's words to the Jewish people. Once again, the Jewish wedding mirrors the covenant. How God feels about us, and how we feel about God, is the way that we feel about each other.

WEDDING BLESSINGS

We move to the *birchot nesuin,* the wedding blessings themselves. Here we find one of the masterpieces of Jewish liturgy—the *sheva berachot* (seven blessings) which form the liturgical centerpiece of the wedding ceremony and are the essence of Judaism.

Consider, first, the number of blessings. The seven blessings invoke the seven days of creation. Note how the blessings unfold.

1. "We praise You, *Adonai* our God, Ruler of the universe, Creator of the fruit of the wine." Judaism is not a puritanical faith. Pleasure is good. It is sanctifiable.
2. "We praise You...Creator of all things for Your glory." God did not create the world to be a void. The world is a reflection of God's goodness. It is therefore endowed with overarching meaning.
3. "We praise You...Creator of man and woman." As Rabbi Samuel Dresner noted, the wedding is the moment when people become complete and therefore truly *adam*—fully human. Creation itself waits for this moment.
4. "We praise You...Who creates us to share with You in life's everlasting renewal." The Jewish wedding celebrates the potential of the human being acting not only in God's image, but as God's partner because God created us to recreate life. Pro-creation is re-creation of the world.
5. "We praise You...Who causes Zion to rejoice in her children's happy return." Why does Zion enter the ceremony at this moment? Because redemption is when the Jews come home to Zion. Redemption is also when people come "home" to each other. Marriage is redemption from solitude.
6. "We praise You...Who causes bride and groom to rejoice. May these loving companions rejoice as have your creatures since the days of creation." At this moment, the bride and groom imagine themselves as Adam and Eve, standing in an updated version of the Garden of Eden, the land of potential joy open before them.

7. "We praise You...Creator of joy and gladness, bride and groom, love and kinship, peace and friendship. O God, may there always be heard in the cities of Israel and in the streets of Jerusalem: the sounds of joy and of happiness, the voice of the groom and the voice of the bride, the shouts of young people celebrating, and the songs of children at play. We praise You, our God, who causes the bride and groom to rejoice together." We hear the words of the prophet Jeremiah again. Jeremiah, who endured the first exile from Jerusalem, knew that we would come back. He prophesied that there would yet again be rejoicing in Judah and on the outskirts of Jerusalem.

THE PROMISE OF *TIKKUN* (HEALING): THE SHATTERING OF THE GLASS

The most famous aspect of the Jewish wedding is its final moment—the shattering of the glass. Here there are numerous interpretations.

There is the anthropological interpretation. Some scholars believe that shattering the glass will ward off the demons that tend to frequent celebrations.

There is the psychological interpretation. The *Talmud* (a body of texts of Jewish law) relates that a certain rabbi shattered a plate at his son's wedding in order to jar the revelers back to reality. So, too, we remember that life is not always *simcha* (celebration). There is work to do and tasks to perform and life to be lived on its own terms.

There is the historical interpretation. The shattering of the glass reminds us of the destructions of the Temples in Jerusalem. It reminds us of the pain of our people—a pain that is still fresh for us, living a half century away from the Holocaust.

In fact, shattering is the great metaphor of human existence. The Jewish mystics of sixteenth-century Safed believed that the world began with the shattering of divine vessels of light. The Jewish people began when Abraham, according to ancient legend, shattered his father's idols. Judaism began after the shattering of the Tablets of the Law, with the renewal of the covenant. At that moment, God and

Moses collaborated in creating a new set of tablets. The Diaspora began through the shattering of the Temples. The end of pre-Holocaust European Jewish rationalism and complacency was demonically heralded through the shattering of glass at *Kristallnacht*. Each of us has a piece of a shattered world. Our task, as Rabbi Lawrence Kushner once intimated, it is to find the connections between that piece and every other shattered piece in the world—to participate in *tikkun*, in cosmic and personal renewal.

So, the different aspects of *kedusha* all come together. Holiness in space: the Jewish home, the ancient Temple, and the rebuilt Jerusalem. Holiness in time: the wedding moment itself and the promise of the Messianic moment. And holiness in relationship: marriage itself.

The Jewish wedding ceremony is far more than a mere "celebration." It is Judaism in miniature—a cavalcade of Jewish meanings, images, theological notions, and historical memories.

2. Interfaith Relationships

Paula Brody, Ed.D., LICSW, is director of Outreach Programs and Training for the Northeast Council of the Union of American Hebrew Congregations (UAHC, the Reform Movement), where she develops and coordinates a wide range of programs and services to welcome interfaith families into Reform congregations. She is a consultant to, and the "Dear Dr. Paula" columnist for, InterfaithFamily.com.

Opening Up Communication in an Interfaith Relationship

PAULA BRODY

Interfaith couples often say that it is hard to know how to begin a conversation about the meaning of religion in one's life. Too often, discussions about religion end in a hurt silence or a nasty argument about how the children will be raised. How does an interfaith couple begin to open up communication about religion and strengthen communication in their relationship?

In truth, discussions about religion can be difficult. Individuals in interfaith relationships rarely talk about profound religious experiences or family holiday memories with each other because they fear it may be threatening to or rock the boat of their relationship. Couples often become so focused on the religious identity of future children that they never talk about their own religious needs.

Interfaith couples often find themselves unable to untangle the complicated threads by which religion ties each of us to our family of origin. Talking about parents and grandparents becomes fraught with anxiety because of fears that they may have hurt their families by falling in love with someone from another faith.

As director of Outreach Programs and Training for the Reform Movement in the Northeast, I develop and lead "Yours, Mine and Ours" support groups for interfaith couples. These groups are designed to strengthen communication for these couples. When couples call us to sign up for these groups, they often say that they "hit a roadblock" whenever they begin to discuss religion.

As I work with couples to overcome these roadblocks in their communication, I begin by encouraging them to put the "c" word— children—on a back shelf. I strongly urge them to make discussion of children and their children's religious identity off limits—taboo—until they have built a strong foundation of communication regarding religion in their lives. Only then should they begin to venture into discussions that involve children. This is often not an easy task for couples— especially pregnant couples or those who already have children. Postponing that discussion, however, is essential in order to address what religion means to each member of the couple. In other words, each person must fully understand his or her own religious inheritance in order to pass a religious inheritance along to future children.

Opening up communication in an interfaith relationship is a process that begins slowly. Each partner should listen with renewed care to the other while learning something new about his or her partner's religious inheritance.

Couples can try this simple exercise with each other. Remember—the goal is to learn something about each other that you did not know before.

1. Describe the religious behavior of your grandparents.
2. Describe the religious behavior of your parents.
3. Describe your own religious behavior and how it was transmitted to you from generation to generation.

In responding to these questions, don't just name the religion of your grandparents (for example, "He was Irish Catholic" or "She was Orthodox Jewish"). Avoid broad stereotypes and tell the full story of your emotional religious heritage. Describe behaviors you observed, and the meaning these behaviors may have had in your family background, such as "My mother said the rosary daily" or "My father was passionate about Israel."

Even if your grandparents (or parents) were not religious, the lack of religious behavior might have been significant in shaping your own identity. If there was a "break" in the transmission of religion in your family, through death or divorce, was it significant in shaping your feelings about your religion? For example, talk about what you remember after the death of your grandmother, who made every family holiday, or what occurred religiously in your home after your parents were divorced.

Listen carefully as your partner shares his or her family story. Ask questions or encourage your partner to tell you more about aspects of that religious heritage. Ask your partner to define terms with which you are unfamiliar.

For some couples, doing this exercise may be the first time you have really spoken in depth about your families' religious experiences. You may realize that you have learned more about your partner than you could have imagined. Listening is important because it validates your partner and your partner's religious experience. Validating the religious history of each partner is an essential ingredient in building strong, interfaith communication skills.

To further validate your partner's experience, tell your partner what you have learned about how his or her religious identity was passed from one generation to another. Tell your partner what you heard as to the significant events which may have shaped his or her religious identity. Check in with your partner regarding these perceptions. Are they accurate? Perhaps you can help your partner understand something about his or her feelings regarding religion that may not have been perceived before. But check it out with your partner, and make sure you have understood the essence of the story.

Usually at the end of this simple exercise, couples feel an intense closeness. You may be amazed that you have had such an in-depth, meaningful discussion about religion without conversational road-blocks or those old uncomfortable arguments! That is the optimal outcome, and if you experience success, enjoy it and keep the conversation flowing.

Here are two more discussion questions to continue the process of opening up your communication. Again, the goal is to learn something about your partner and his or her childhood that you did not know before.

1. Using the cycle of the calendar year, describe your memories of family holiday celebrations. Talk about any significant changes in these holiday celebrations as you grew up.
2. Using the cycle of life—birth ceremonies, marriages, death, and mourning—talk about how your family celebrated or marked these occasions. Discuss these life-cycle events, and the feelings they evoked, in the context of your family.

Again, as your partner shares his or her story, listen actively. Remember—these childhood experiences shaped the person you love. As you uncover these significant life-cycle and holiday events, you will help each other untangle the complex and sometimes twisted threads by which religion ties each of us to our family and family memories.

Remember, when doing the exercises provided above, keep the "c" word—the topic of your children's religious identity—taboo. These exercises are designed to open up communication about you— your religious differences and how your childhood experiences have shaped you as adults coming together to share your lives.

As you begin to understand what religion has meant in your own lives, you will understand what aspects of your religious heritage you want to pass on to your children. A strengthened foundation of communication will prove exceptionally worthwhile when you do take the "c" word off the shelf.

Bruce Kadden is rabbi of Temple Beth El in Salinas, California. He has taught interfaith Bible studies classes for more than ten years.

What Jews and Christians Should Know about Each Other

BRUCE KADDEN

One of the many challenges of intermarriage is learning about and understanding the religion of one's partner. Even if a couple has decided on a particular religion for the family, and even if one or both partners are non-religious, it is important for each to appreciate the religious background of the other, which often is the religion of in-laws and other family members.

Although Judaism and Christianity share common history, teachings, and values, they are two distinct religions, with different beliefs and rituals, particularly holiday and life-cycle observances. It is not unusual for both Jews and Christians to have misconceptions about each other's religion or to harbor stereotypes. Learning about each other's religion can help couples better understand each other and other family members. The following observations can help begin the learning process.

Neither Judaism nor Christianity is a monolithic religion. While to an outsider the differences among Jews or among Christians might seem small, they can be significant. Within both traditions there is a great deal of variation in belief, practice, and values.

Whereas Christianity is a religion, Judaism is—in many ways— more than a religion. Being a Christian means practicing the Christian religion. Many Jews, however, feel a strong connection to Israel and/or to the Jewish people, but do not attend synagogue or practice Jewish rituals. Non-Jews often mistakenly assume that because a Jew does not practice the Jewish religion, he or she does not have strong feelings about the Jewish people or Israel.

The primary theological difference between Judaism and Christianity centers on the interpretation of the life and death of a first-century Jew, Jesus of Nazareth. Christians believe that Jesus is the Christ, i.e., the Messiah who is spoken about in the Hebrew scriptures, that he died to atone for the sins of human beings, that he rose again and is present in the life of those who invite him in. For Christians, Jesus is the Son of God who represents all truth about God.

Jews do not believe that Jesus was the Messiah spoken about in the Hebrew scriptures because he did not free the first-century Jews from Roman oppression, nor did he bring about a world of peace and justice envisioned by the prophets. Some Jews are still waiting for the Messiah to come, while others believe that everyone has a role to play in perfecting the world and bringing about the Messianic Age.

Jews and Christians use wine and bread as part of their rituals, but in very different ways. In Judaism, wine is a symbol of joy. Blessings are said in the home and synagogue before drinking wine on the Sabbath, most Jewish holidays, and at life-cycle celebrations. A special braided egg bread called *challah* is eaten at the beginning of the Sabbath meal. For Christians, wine (some churches use grape juice) and bread or a wafer are used as part of the Communion ritual, which is a part of worship. Also called the sacrament of the Lord's Supper, the bread and wine symbolize (or in some interpretations actually become) the body and blood of Jesus. By eating the bread and drinking the wine, one is assured that God has forgiven one's sins.

Shabbat (the Jewish Sabbath) begins Friday at sunset and ends Saturday at sunset; most Christians observe the Sabbath on Sunday. Jews celebrate *Shabbat* with home rituals that include blessings for lighting candles, drinking wine, and eating *challah*, and may also attend synagogue. Christian Sabbath observance primarily consists of service attendance. Christians observe Sunday as the Sabbath because that is the day Christians believe that Jesus rose from the dead.

Major Jewish holidays commemorate important historical events and agricultural observances, whereas major Christian holidays reflect important times in Jesus' life. Passover, celebrating the rebirth of spring, commemorates the Exodus from Egypt; Shavuot (Pentecost, the festival of first fruits) recalls receiving the *Torah*, the first five books of the Hebrew Bible, at Mount Sinai; Sukkot (Tabernacles, the fall harvest festival) is a reminder of wandering in the wilderness. Other important Jewish holidays are Rosh Hashanah (Jewish New Year) and Yom Kippur (Day of Atonement). Hanukkah, the commemoration of the rededication of the Jerusalem Temple following the successful revolt of the Jews against the Syrian-Greek oppressors, and Purim, the celebration of delivery from destruction as recorded in the Book of Esther, are minor holidays in the Jewish calendar.

Christmas celebrates the birth of Jesus. Good Friday is the observance of his death on the cross and Easter the celebration of his resurrection. Ash Wednesday begins the forty-day period of Lent leading up to Easter. Pentecost, the seventh Sunday after Easter, commemorates the descent of the Holy Spirit. Although today many people have secularized the celebration of Christmas and Easter, at their core they remain religious observances.

In creating religious rituals for one's family, the integrity of these holidays should be respected. While it is often tempting to focus on secular aspects of the holidays or to attempt to combine celebrations, such approaches rob the holidays of their meaning and significance. It is usually easier for Christians to participate in the observance of Jewish holidays, which, after all, are also a part of Christian heritage, than for Jews to participate in Christian holidays, which are based upon theological beliefs Jews do not accept.

Life-cycle rituals reflect both the history and theology of each religious community. At birth, a Jewish child is entered into the covenant between God and the Jewish people with the ceremony of *brit milah* (covenant of circumcision) for boys and *brit banot* (covenant of the daughters) or similar ceremony for girls. Christian children, on the other hand, are usually baptized shortly after birth, a ritual that symbolizes the remission of sins and enters the child into the Christian community.

Parents who have selected a religion for their child should consult appropriate clergy about the ceremonies and any special preparations that might be necessary if the parents are of different religious traditions. Traditional Judaism, for example, recognizes the child of a Jewish mother and non-Jewish father as Jewish, but requires that the child of a Jewish father and non-Jewish mother undergo conversion. Reform and Reconstructionist Judaism, however, consider the child Jewish without conversion if the child is raised as a Jew. Christianity will generally accept a child into the community if either parent is Christian and the couple agrees to raise the child as a Christian.

Synagogues and churches often offer introductory educational classes for those interested in learning about the religion. In addition, many congregations and organizations offer programs or classes directed toward interfaith couples. Taking advantage of these opportunities can help a couple appreciate each other's religious traditions and promote greater understanding among family members.

Janice G. Fischel, wife of Bill and mother of Josh, is a native of Bethlehem, Pennsylvania. She has lived in Hanover, New Hampshire, since 1973, except for year-long visits to Davis, Santa Barbara, and Berkeley, California, and Seattle, Washington.

Approaching Our Twenty-seventh Anniversary

JANICE G. FISCHEL

I suppose that most of my family always assumed that I would marry someone Jewish. I think I was the one least surprised by the fact that I didn't.

Bethlehem, Pennsylvania, was my home. The Christmas City of the United States didn't ever sound like the hotbed of Jewish life to me. All through school I was part of a very small group of Jewish students. There were just seven of us who graduated in my high school class of more than 1,100. I was certainly aware that most of my friends celebrated Christmas.

In college, social life was not religiously centered. Sure, I dated men who were Jewish, but did not *not* date men who weren't. In fact, I had been engaged to someone who was "technically" Jewish. (His mother was Jewish, but he was not raised in the faith.) When that relationship broke up, I can clearly remember my grandfather's admonition that if I was going to marry someone who wasn't Jewish, he had, at least, better be "special."

Enter the man to whom I was married nearly twenty-seven years ago. Bill was gentle, kind, intelligent, thoughtful, romantic, and was not Jewish; but, in my grandfather's words, he was "special."

He grew up in the same area that I did, though, as he says, "we went to different high schools together." Bill was a graduate student at Princeton when we met. I was an investigator for the Pennsylvania Bureau of Consumer Protection, and living in Bethlehem, Pennsylvania. He, too, had once been engaged to someone else. We were twenty-five and twenty-eight years old. We knew what was important to us in terms of the kind of mate we wanted.

My family was probably typical of many second-generation American Jewish families. My grandparents had all been pretty Orthodox in their thinking. My parents raised my brother and sister and me in a Conservative home, and my feelings were far more Reform, though I liked the Conservative temple to which we belonged, and there was not a Reform temple in Bethlehem. My siblings were happy to know that I was marrying a good person, and did not make any reference to the fact that Bill was not Jewish. My brother, who is four years older than I am, was already married to a Jewish woman. Both he and my sister, who also married someone Jewish, are divorced.

My mother was concerned that Bill's family might not approve of his marrying someone Jewish. If his grandfather had still been alive, there might have been a comment made, but this was a moot point, and Bill's family had no negative reaction. They were accepting of me for who I was, and my mother and grandfather approved of my choice and our decision to marry. Unfortunately, my father had died five years earlier.

Our wedding, though a civil ceremony, contained a number of elements of a Jewish wedding, and none of a Christian one. Our life has been similar to our wedding. Adding some religious touches to our lives has enriched them immeasurably.

Bill had no concerns about marrying a Jewish woman. He and his family are not church-goers. When he was a child, he attended a Lutheran Sunday school, but since I have known them, he and his family have never attended church services except for weddings or funerals. Christmas is the one holiday observed by his family in which we participate. Bill's mother sees the holiday as a chance to get the entire family together, which includes five children, four spouses, eight grandchildren, and two great-grandchildren. Usually, most of the children and grandchildren make the "pilgrimage" back to Bethlehem in December. The tree at my in-laws' home is decorated, the packages are wrapped, and food is prepared in grand style. It is a family occasion, not a religious one.

Celebrating Christmas as a family event is one way we acknowledge and honor Bill's family's tradition. Over the years, we have had our own Christmas trees. On the other hand, we attend High Holiday services, light the Hanukkah *menorah* (candelabra) together, and make or attend Passover *seders* (ritual meals).

When our son Josh was born, it was an easy decision that he would be raised Jewish. Our feeling was that we were part of the Jewish community in our town, and that Bill had never chosen to participate in the Christian community here. We both felt strongly that Josh should have some kind of religious identity and that I was probably the one who would be responsible for that aspect of his education. Today, Josh identifies himself without hesitation as a Jew and is an active member of Hillel at his college.

Over the years, though Bill has not converted, he has been a willing participant in every aspect of our being a Jewish family. As Josh approached his *Bar Mitzvah* (the ceremony in which an individual chooses to assume the obligations and privileges of an adult member of the Jewish community), Bill encouraged him and found ways to participate in the service with the full approval and support of our rabbi. He and I were both asked to serve on a committee to help determine the rules for our new Jewish cemetery. He is acknowledged by people in our Jewish community as a full contributing member. He was the impetus behind our wonderful vacation to Israel. We have several friends who live there, and it was our chance to visit not only the country, but also many Israelis we have met along the way. Most of our trip was Jewish oriented, but we did take the tour of Old Jerusalem to see some of the Christian sites as well. Of course, having both grown up in Bethlehem, Pennsylvania, we had to see *Bet Lechem* (Bethlehem) in Israel.

Perhaps, if Bill had been a church-goer, we would have had more religious issues to deal with over the years. Perhaps, if we didn't live in an accepting, liberal environment, our life would have been more complicated. But we are fortunate to live in an academic community, where we are not the only interfaith couple. As a family, we are active members of just one religious group. Our loyalties are not divided by synagogue and church.

I value my identity as a Jew, though my ties are more cultural than spiritual, and I take pride in the fact that my husband respects that my Jewish identity is an important aspect of our life together. For us, having a marriage between people who come from two different religious traditions has not been a cause of tension, nor has it created problems.

Wendy Weltman Palmer, M.S.W., is the director of outreach for the Southwest Region of the Union of American Hebrew Congregations (UAHC, the Reform Movement) in Dallas, Texas. She is also a practicing clinical social worker.

Acknowledging a Dual Heritage While Choosing One Religion

WENDY WELTMAN PALMER

Years ago I was conducting an interfaith couples group in which the topic was deciding how to raise the children. One young man raised his hand with a comment. Paired with his decidedly Jewish wife, he had already identified himself as a "recovering Catholic." Now he had this to say: "I'm okay raising my future kids as Jews, but I'm afraid of being the only *goy* in my family." The group erupted in nervous laughter. Even those who didn't understand this young man's Yiddish reference (*goy* is a slang term for a non-Jewish male, sometimes referring to any gentile) immediately grasped his concern. He did not want to be the odd man out in his own family.

This young man had succinctly given voice to a tension felt by most interfaith couples. At its most superficial, it appears to be about winning and losing. And indeed, for some couples it's a bit like a pitched battle: If we choose to raise the children in your religion and not mine, you have won and I have lost. However, look beneath the battle and there emerges loss of a different kind.

What happens to my traditions, my rituals, and my special memories if we choose your religion as our family faith? How do I relate to my children if I can't refer to the religious values and beliefs with which I grew up? People fear a diminished connection, the possibility that their heritage, all that they stand for, will be diluted. They fear becoming invisible to their children in their own home.

When a parent consents to raise the children in a religion other than his or her own, that parent functionally becomes the "out-parent," a term coined by Petsonk and Remsen in their wonderfully comprehensive guide *The Intermarriage Handbook*. Petsonk and Remsen remind us that the out-parent has an obligation to be involved in the religious upbringing of the children *and* that the other parent has a responsibility to not exclude the parent who doesn't share in the family religion. They underscore the importance of sensitivity to the parent who seriously practices another religion. Helping this parent celebrate his or her rituals and accompanying this parent to worship services on occasion are ways the family can show support for the out-parent.

In the case of a Christian parent committed to raising Jewish children, what exactly is appropriate for this parent to teach the children about his or her own religion and background? In other words, how "visible" should this parent be?

The answer is, completely visible. To begin with, all parents exert influence on their children whether they intend to or not. Children absorb their parents' values, their perspective on life, and even their corny sense of humor along with the very air that they breathe. Without debating the question of nature versus nurture, we can all think of examples of how children develop certain facial expressions, take up a particular kind of hobby, or learn to cook food that "tastes just like Mom's," without having been explicitly instructed by their parents.

In the case of an interfaith family, it is incumbent upon the parents to teach their children explicitly that even though the family may practice one particular religion, the children enjoy a dual cultural heritage. To separate religious identity from cultural identity can be enormously helpful for kids in an interfaith family. In today's world, one may choose to be of a certain religion, but one's cultural identity is always a given, a birthright. There is no disputing, for example, that Dad's Catholic paternal grandparents came to America from Ireland to enjoy a better life. Dad's ruddy complexion and pioneer spirit are surely related to his ethnic and cultural background. Dad's kids deserve to hear stories about their Irish ancestors and their customs. They need to know that their grandparents faced religious persecution themselves and to hear about a renegade great-uncle who struck it rich out West. They need to know so that Dad and all that has made him who he is, including his predilection for Irish shortbread, will be more "visible."

Nor should the Christian parent refrain from discussing his or her religion and religious beliefs, especially if he or she is actively practicing. This parent should be prepared for hard theological questions—children do have a way of going right to the core of things. They sniff out inconsistency in a heartbeat and aren't reluctant to ask "Why?" Depending on their age and stage of life, children respond to clear, thoughtful answers, even on such weighty subjects as the nature of God.

The challenge for the religiously faithful out-parent is to be able to speak about the core concepts of his or her beliefs without glamorizing on the one hand or confusing the child on the other. The key is for this parent to be able to talk about why he or she holds true to this particular religious perspective without undermining the singular religious framework the family has chosen to put in place.

Ultimately, healthy interfaith families become good at talking about and honoring religious and cultural differences. Acknowledging a dual heritage allows both parents to feel represented and on equal ground in the developing personality of the family. No parent need fear becoming "invisible" because each parent is helping to create and shape the customs and memories of the family. Children are less troubled by problems of loyalty because they learn they stay connected to their parent and their parent's past even if Mom or Dad practices another religion. Openly discussing the contrasts between the family's religion and the out-parent's religion gives the children a context for understanding the decisions that the parents have made together. The family can then join together in a different, more conscious way. Some might even say it's a win-win situation.

3. Choosing a Religious Identity for Your Child

Andrea King is the author of *If I'm Jewish and You're Christian, What Are the Kids?* (UAHC Press) and supervises preschools for the Santa Monica School District.

"If I'm Jewish and You're Christian, What Are the Kids?"

ANDREA KING

Despite their parents' adamant claims to the contrary, children raised with both religions are often confused.

Sooner or later (usually sooner) every interfaith couple is asked, "What will the children be?" And sooner or later (often later) the couple finds an answer. Deciding which religion, if any, to pass on to the next generation can take many months of thoughtful, even painful, discussion.

Because I am both an intermarried parent and an early childhood educator, I was asked to write a book to help interfaith couples consider their options and make good decisions for their families. In *If I'm Jewish and You're Christian, What Are the Kids?* I recommend that interfaith couples decide on one religious identity for their children and observe just one set of holidays, rituals, and life-cycle events in the family.

Many interfaith couples bristle at this advice. They argue that they can blend Judaism and Christianity in their family celebrations, and that their children are genuinely "Jewish-Christian" or half-and-half. These parents often say they are giving their children the "best of both" religions.

In my twenty years' experience working with interfaith families, I have learned that when a couple says they are practicing "the best of both" religions, they mean that they follow the four-holiday calendar: they celebrate (in a mostly secular way) Christmas and Hanukkah, Passover and Easter. Their children usually do not attend any religious school, nor do they participate in the life-cycle events of either religion. The parents or grandparents may tell the children a little about each religion, but not enough to upset the delicate religious balance within the family.

There are myriad variations on the "best of both" theme. Some families celebrate Jewish and Christian holidays in alternate years. Others raise the boys in the father's religion and the girls in the mother's faith. A few couples choose to raise the first child in one religion, the next in the other, and so on. Still others introduce rituals, holidays, and customs from several faiths, giving the children a veritable course in comparative religions, rather than one of their own. Frankly, the "best of both" usually boils down to "not much of either."

Despite their parents' adamant claims to the contrary, children raised with both religions are often confused. They absorb very little about religion, tradition, heritage, or theology from the four-holiday calendar. One child, Jamie, age six, explained his interfaith family's celebrations this way: "Hanukkah is the Jewish Christmas, Easter is the Easter Bunny's birthday, and Passover, I don't know what that is."

In reality it is impossible to give a child the "best of both" religions. Christianity and Judaism share some values, but they are based on inherently contradictory belief systems. Children as young as five can accurately articulate the basic differences between the two religions. They understand, even if their parents don't, that they cannot be both Jewish and Christian.

The bottom line is that interfaith parents need to face the challenge and decide on one religion for their children, no matter how difficult the decision. And most likely it will be tough. One parent will

have to let go of the idea of recreating some favorite childhood memories with his or her own children, and learn a new set of customs.
The other parent will have to take on the major responsibility for not
only whatever religious traditions the family observes, but the children's religious training as well. Both partners have to adjust their
expectations.

But what starts out harder for the parents ends up easier for the
children. They grow up with one religious identification, one series of
holidays and traditions, one consistent set of ethics and values, one
answer to the most basic of all questions: Who am I?

Children with one religion look forward to holidays and life-
cycle ceremonies. They enjoy being part of a community, learning
about its history, continuing its customs, and putting its values into
practice. When he was six years old, Zeke (who is Jewish) and his
Christian mother donated some bread and vegetables left over from
a school function to the local soup kitchen. As they carried the food
into the building, Zeke's mom explained the work of the soup
kitchen, and the importance of their gift. They had completed the last
trip and were walking back to the car when Zeke stopped in his
tracks and exclaimed, "Mom! We did a *mitzvah* (commandment,
good deed)!" Even young children can feel important and special
when their religion relates to real life.

Most children want their parents to give them a religious identity. As seventeen-year-old Hannah said, "I think having a religion
should be like having a hometown. You know you belong there, you
know everyone and all the rules. You don't have to stay there, but you
always know where it is, and you can come back whenever you want."
It is this feeling of having a religious hometown that I would wish for
the children of intermarriage.

Annie Modesitt lives with her husband and two children in New Jersey, where she is a member of Temple Ner Tamid in Bloomfield. Formerly of *Martha Stewart Living TV*, she currently writes about crafts for children and is a hand knit designer. She has been a contributor to *Parents*, *Family Life*, and *Interweave Knits Magazine*.

Raising My Children as Jews

ANNIE MODESITT

Early in our interfaith marriage, before the advent of children, we were asked by friends, "What are your kids going to be?" My response was immediate—a knee-jerk reaction—"They'll be Jewish, naturally." My husband was surprised by my "snap" decision, but I had been pondering this issue for months.

Why would I decide to raise our not-yet-conceived children as Jews? The answer to this question is suitably complex and necessarily personal.

I am not Jewish. I was raised in a Protestant home. Our family church was a sect of Methodism known as Free Methodist. I am not a theologian, but my interpretation of the message of the New Testament—in very simple terms—is that each of us has a spark of divinity and that by working together in positive ways we can "see" the face of God. I do not believe in the divinity of Jesus—or rather, I should say that I believe in the possibility that divinity dwells in each of us. This belief is part of my own personal spiritual evolution.

My husband was raised in a nominally Conservative Jewish home and describes his Hebrew school education in disparaging terms. His post–*Bar Mitzvah* (the ceremony in which an individual chooses to assume the obligations and privileges of an adult member of the Jewish community), pre-marriage visits to a synagogue can be counted on one hand.

Soon after we were married, we heard of a very special Reform congregation near our home in Brooklyn which was holding High Holiday services. I was curious to attend, and what we discovered was an egalitarian, socially active spiritual home that encouraged lively debate on the weekly *Torah* (the first five books of the Hebrew Bible) portion. I had heard Reform Judaism dismissed as "Judaism Lite" but soon came to understand that this characterization was unfair and erroneous.

The Statement of Principles for Reform Judaism adopted at the 1999 Pittsburgh Convention reflect, in part, the reality of the Eternal, the sanctity of human life, the importance of *mitzvot* (sacred obligations), and the concept that "although God created us as finite beings, the spirit within us is eternal." I found that this dovetailed nicely with the lessons of my own religious heritage and provided a certain "comfort level" when I made the decision to raise our children as Jews.

My great respect for Judaism as a faith and as a culture also played a part in the decision to give our children a Jewish identity. I feel that I would be giving them a great gift by allowing them access to a religious education based in *Torah*. In our home we celebrate the holidays, we light candles on *Shabbat* (the Jewish Sabbath), and set the day aside as a break from more worldly activities. We practice *tikkun olam* (the commandment to repair the world) when we find the opportunity and pass on the importance of acts of loving kindness to our children. In this way I have been able to create a Jewish home that honors my own religious heritage of faith and works: faith in an Eternal spirit that guides the good (God) in all of us to work for justice, peace, and a healing of the world. The Methodist tradition has been, from the start, one of social responsibility and egalitarian worship, combined with a heavy dose of service to the community.

I feel that conversion is a blessing, a gift, and should not be accepted before the time is right. Thus far the time has not been right for me, but my growing love of Judaism encourages me to give my children the benefits of a Jewish upbringing. I don't want to put our children's Jewish education on hold while I work out my own path to Judaism.

In our family the role of spiritual educator is divided between my husband and myself, but many of the duties fall to me. There is a school of thought that only a Jewish "mama" can raise a Jewish child—obviously, I disagree. Not all great voice teachers are themselves great singers. One of the best ways to teach a subject is to learn along with your student. As I study Hebrew and Yiddish, learn Jewish songs and blessings, and round out my own Jewish education with *Torah* study, I pass all this on to my children with passion and excitement.

I am very aware of my inadequacy as a teacher of Jewish culture, so I seek out resources to help educate my children in a Jewish way: I utilize the Hebrew school of our temple, the Internet, books, and magazines. One of my favorite resources has been the music of Tanja Solnik—her two CDs of Hebrew, Yiddish, and Ladino music rotate as our "goodnight" music during the bedtime hour, and I often overhear my son and daughter singing little snatches of their favorite Yiddish songs.

We work on learning the *alef-bet* (Hebrew alphabet), and as my children grow we'll learn and perfect our Hebrew together. My children will always have the option of undergoing a Jewish conversion ceremony in the future if they choose—perhaps they'll want to incorporate it as part of another life-cycle event—but for the time being they are Jewish in my eyes, my husband's eyes, and in the eyes of our congregation.

I do not believe that the only path for an interfaith family is to adopt one religion. I have seen examples of families that merge two religions and impart to their children a sense of respect for both family faiths. For our family I feel a Jewish path is best. Sadly, I have seen families commit to a single religion—only to fall away from it through disinterest or because one parent eventually begins to regret the loss of his or her own traditions.

I have strong, positive memories of my own childhood Christmas celebrations, and I work each year to find a way to re-live these memories while maintaining a Jewish home. One route we've explored is to use the Christmas season as a time to teach our children about people who have used peaceful means to achieve their goals. We contrast this with Hanukkah, a holiday that stresses the importance of fighting to retain religious rights.

Our Jewish home is not a "typical" Jewish home, but I suspect that our practices reflect a growing movement in the Jewish community. The controversial "Who is a Jew?" question poses the query "What is a Jewish home?" To find my own answer to this, I must trust my intelligence and my ongoing education, and I constantly reevaluate my own place in Judaism.

To many, an interfaith family such as ours spells the end of Judaism; I disagree. Throughout history there has been a strong vein of diversity and disagreement within the Jewish community surrounding the different ways of fulfilling the commandments of the *Torah*. What many see as the challenge of intermarriage I see as an opportunity. I feel that, handled appropriately, interfaith families can enrich and enliven the Jewish community as a whole.

Our children will grow up knowing that what goes on in our home is part of *our* normal Jewish life.

HELPFUL BOOKS I'VE USED

Raising Your Jewish/Christian Child: How Interfaith Parents Can Give Children the Best of Both Their Heritages by Lee F. Gruzen, et al. (New York: Newmarket, 1991).

The Intermarriage Handbook: A Guide for Jews & Christians by Judy Petsonk, et al. New York: Morrow, 1991).

Jewish Literacy by Rabbi Joseph Telushkin (New York: William Morrow, 1991).

MUSIC RESOURCES

Tanja Solnik, *From Generation to Generation: A Legacy of Lullabies* (traditional Jewish lullabies sung in Ladino, Yiddish, and Hebrew) and *Lullabies and Love Songs* (Jewish lullabies and love songs sung in Ladino, Yiddish, and Hebrew). DreamSong Recordings, 615-383-3141, www.tanjasolnik.com.

WEBSITES

Beliefnet.com
uahc.org
jewishmusic.com
www.mich.com/~dovetail
JewishFamily.com

Christina Pertus-Hendelman; Aaron, her Texan husband; and their little
jewel Tess, born in June 2000, live in Palo Alto, California.

Intermarried and Pregnant: Thoughts about Our Child's Religious Future

CHRISTINA PERTUS-HENDELMAN

Six months ago, my husband Aaron and I discovered that I was pregnant. Along with pure joy and excitement, mixed with the common
apprehension of the road ahead, came another feeling: the fear of
opening old wounds. The carpet under which we had swept all religious issues and potential sources of conflict during the past two and
a half years was about to be lifted.

Aaron and I met in England five years ago, where we were both
studying. There started the unlikely love story of a Texan Jewish guy
and a French Catholic girl. Admittedly, religion was not a primary
topic of discussion during our first months of dating, but it became so
when we began to contemplate the possibility of a future together.
Were we to marry and have children, Aaron wanted me to convert.

Given my limited exposure to Judaism—primarily through movies
and Jewish delis—I didn't understand the need for me to convert, feel-

ing that we could accommodate two religions in our lives. However, I admired his strong beliefs and envied his sense of belonging. I myself had grown up as a Catholic, but my religion was only that, a religion. Aaron's transcended this concept: it was his childhood, his identity, his culture. I eventually told Aaron that I could not convert right away, but that in time, I would be able to consider his request seriously.

I followed Aaron back to his native Texas and began the search for my Jewish holy grail. Through months of study, reading, and discussion, I found in Judaism many beautiful traditions that I would eagerly pass on to my children. However, if Judaism was love and family, it was also often intolerance and rigidity. To convert, I needed a true call, deep enough to fully embrace Judaism, deep enough to turn me away from my own roots. The enormity of what had been asked of me became suddenly obvious. I could not convert for Aaron's sake only. Having already made Aaron the solemn promise to help him build a Jewish household, I believed that converting could not add to my Jewish commitment. Although disappointed, Aaron understood. We were married a year later, exchanging our vows through a civil ceremony in France and a Jewish ceremony in Texas. Both ceremonies preached tolerance and harmony; the prayers and symbols we chose reflected our spirituality and thoughtfulness.

The truth was, however, we had approached every possible issue hypothetically. Whether it be Christmas trees or Hebrew school and gefilte fish, we had not been able to commit to one single decision. We nonetheless naively thought we were sufficiently prepared for the day when a child would come.

Well, we were not. During our first two years of marriage, Aaron and I were so spiritually exhausted that we unconsciously decided to avoid any potential conflict, entering a long religious hibernation.

Expecting a baby re-awakened in Aaron the thought that our child would not grow up the way he did, fully immersed in a Jewish household. The burden of providing a Jewish education weighed mainly on his shoulders: as a man far from his family, where would he begin? Most importantly, the news resurrected certain feelings that he had managed to repress: the guilt of having married a non-Jew, as well as the fear of not being able to trust me again after what he perceived as a broken promise to convert.

I, in turn, was suddenly confronted with another solemn promise: my promise to raise our children as Jews. The month was December; Christmas was around the corner. I was looking sadly at my belly, remembering the joy this season always brought, and already blaming Aaron for depriving this child of a beautiful tradition.

Also, despite my desire not to know the sex of the baby, I realized with sorrow that I would have to find out, in order to prepare for the possibility of having a boy and, therefore, a *bris* (circumcision ceremony). Panic struck when I envisioned four hundred people in my house witnessing the mutilation of my child in front of my horrified parents.

Although a *bris* will apparently not be necessary this time, the prospect of a naming ceremony has already created tension. Aaron's wish to hold the ceremony back in Texas with his grandparents, both Holocaust survivors, led him to talk to his mother first, before even mentioning it to me. Needless to say, I was upset, feeling helpless and betrayed. Aaron apologized, admitting he only wanted her to inquire whether their Conservative synagogue would allow the naming there, as I had not converted.

The road towards religious harmony and balance in our life is long, filled with misunderstandings and anger. We were not prepared for the day a child would come; we still are not. With parenthood, Aaron and I will undoubtedly have to grow up. This pregnancy is for real, a baby is on her way, forcing us to face the crucial differences that divide us as a couple, but also giving us the opportunity to leave our stage of pure intellectual dilemmas to make concrete and correct decisions for her, and for us. We will need to reach out for support and wisdom; we will also have to learn to trust each other on our journey. The bottom line is that our child deserves a peaceful environment where confusion and frustration play no part, and so do we. Bonded by a love that transcends our differences, Aaron and I are deeply committed to this task.

Roberta Kesten Calderone has facilitated the "Times and Seasons Program" for Temple Emanuel-Beth-Shalom in Montreal, Canada, for the past twelve years. The program allows interfaith couples contemplating marriage to identify and discuss issues they are facing.

"But Josh Isn't Religious. Why Should We Raise Our Children as Jews?"

ROBERTA KESTEN CALDERONE

"But Josh isn't religious. Why should we raise our children as Jews?" Patricia asked this question during one of my premarital workshops for couples contemplating an interfaith marriage. Quite a few non-Jewish heads nodded in agreement.

Judaism is very difficult for the non-Jew to fully understand. There are many ideas that comprise the concept of "what is a Jew."

"Josh doesn't speak Hebrew, doesn't go to synagogue, and doesn't keep kosher! So why is he so insistent that we keep a Jewish home and raise our children as Jews?"

Explaining that a Jew isn't required to do any of these things to be identified as a Jew is a difficult task. I explain that being born a Jew or converting to Judaism makes a person part of the Jewish people. A Jew doesn't need to do any of the things Patricia mentioned in order to be considered Jewish.

Christianity requires that you do certain things, such as follow the teachings of Christ, go to church, and accept Christian doctrine to be considered a practicing Christian. Jews do not need to do any comparable things to be considered Jewish. In fact, some Jews are atheists but are still considered Jews.

Josh received very little Jewish education as he was growing up. He attended neither day nor afternoon Jewish school. He lived in a non-Jewish area, and most of his friends were not Jews. His parents didn't socialize with many Jewish people. A private teacher taught him his *Bar Mitzvah* (the ceremony in which an individual chooses to assume the obligations and privileges of an adult member of the Jewish community) lessons, and these lessons did not involve any more knowledge of the Hebrew language or religion than he needed for his portion. He rarely, if ever, attends a Sabbath or High Holiday service, and only enters a synagogue for a wedding or *Bar/Bat Mitzvah.*

Josh's parents' home was not kosher, although he liked to call it kosher style (no pork or shellfish products were served, but the meat was not necessarily bought from a kosher butcher). However, his parents celebrated many of the Jewish holidays and customs, such as lighting Hanukkah candles, eating *latkes* (potato pancakes), having *hamantashen* (fruit-filled pastries) for Purim (the celebration of delivery from destruction as recorded in the Book of Esther), having a Passover *seder* (ritual meal) and eating *matzah* (unleavened bread). To Josh and many like him, this is a Jewish way of life, a way of life with which he was very comfortable and through which he strongly identified with the Jewish people. No doubt he is an example of a secular Jew, but he nevertheless is still considered by others and by himself to be Jewish.

In anticipating a marriage to a non-Jew, Josh has no difficulty sharing his tradition with her and respecting her beliefs and traditions. But he is very anxious to maintain his Jewish heritage and to pass this heritage on to his children. He expects no less than that his future wife promise to bring the children up as Jews so that he can remain faithful to his tradition and fulfill his obligation to contribute to Jewish continuity.

Patricia and many in her position have trouble understanding why Josh is so anxious to pass on what seem to her to be meaningless traditions. She finds it difficult to understand his feelings as a Jew because of her own upbringing. In her mind, he never participated in what she would consider religious activity, and she wonders why he wants to start now. She doesn't recognize the Jewishness that Josh feels in his heart and soul.

How do we help her understand that many Jews feel their Judaism in a way that is foreign to a non-Jew? Josh has a large task in front of him. He has to become a teacher of his approach to Judaism. He has to recognize how difficult this is for Patricia. She is not letting go of her religion and has a difficult time understanding his concept of secular Judaism, yet she is expected to teach and nurture their children as Jews.

Josh's family can play a major role. They can help Patricia feel welcome in their home and life, and in the process they can help her learn their style of being Jewish. She can use their Jewish example in creating her own Jewish home. As well, Josh's family should try to understand that Patricia will still be connected to her own traditions and religion, and that these must be respected.

With patience, discussions, and hard work in setting an example and explaining his thoughts and feelings, Josh can help Patricia see why he wants his children to be brought up as Jews. In an atmosphere that allows Josh and Patricia to respect each other's beliefs, this family can grow more comfortable day by day.

Arlene Sarah Chernow is the regional outreach director for the Pacific Southwest Council of the Union of American Hebrew Congregations (UAHC, the Reform Movement). She has written and developed outreach programs for interfaith families, religious school teachers, and conversion mentoring.

Making Religious Choices for Our Children

ARLENE SARAH CHERNOW

It can be tempting for an interfaith couple to avoid making decisions about the religious identity of their family. Some couples avoid the subject, fearing that even a discussion could cause pain or stress to their relationship. It may appear that not making a choice is a path without consequences.

What happens when couples who have not addressed these issues become parents? How can an interfaith couple turn a possible conflict into a process that will help build a strong relationship and an even stronger interfaith family?

As Regional Outreach Director for the Reform Movement, I have met and worked with interfaith couples and parents as I visit congregations to lead discussion groups. Their stories and the unexpected consequences that they have experienced may be helpful to couples who are considering options and choices.

OPPORTUNITIES TO LEARN

A simple matter like picking a wedding date can bring a number of issues to the surface. In Jewish tradition, weddings are not performed on *Shabbat* (the Jewish Sabbath, from Friday at sunset until Saturday at sunset). Many Christian denominations do not have wedding ceremonies on their Sabbath, which is Sunday.

This difference can provide the couple with an opportunity to learn about each other's religion, and how holidays are sometimes different and other times not. It can become an even more significant opportunity if it is seen as a chance to share with each other feelings about religious practice, experiences related to childhood memories, and the role they each hope religion will play in the family they wish to create.

MAKING CHOICES

One temptation for new interfaith parents is to expose children to two religious experiences and let the children make a decision when they are older.

Children raised in this situation often report that they felt as if they were asked to make a choice between their mother and their father, not between their parents' religious traditions. They also report feeling as if they had no identity, that they did not belong to the religion of either their mother or their father. Adult children whose parents tried to be balanced often report a deep sense of confusion.

Parents taking a path of no choice face another dilemma: religious education. A formal religious education can provide a child with moral grounding, a sense of community, and a sense of spiritual identity. Enrollment in religious education and membership in a church or synagogue implies (and in many cases requires) embracing the belief system of the institution.

Many parents who did not choose a religious identity for their children prior to birth find themselves in a particular bind later. A decision made prior to marriage "to not decide" may later feel like a wedding vow. Also, parents sometimes realize once they have children that they want to give their children their own religious identity. Parents who have agreed to celebrate all holidays may find themselves trying to make their holiday bigger and brighter than their spouse's, thus inadvertently setting up tension and competition within the family. In these cases, a parent may not know how to approach a spouse to deal constructively with this issue.

It is important for the Jewish parent to be aware that raising a child with a Jewish identity takes some effort. American children who are not raised with parents who give them a sense of Jewish identity will make the assumption that they belong to the "general society." Almost inevitably, the children will become familiar with the calendar of Christian holidays and stories, and come to identify themselves as nominal Christians.

Young children tend to see the world in absolute terms. They would like their parents to give them concrete answers to questions when the world confuses them. Children who are taught two sets of beliefs about God and God's role in the world will often ask questions like "which one is right?"

A FAMILY'S RELIGIOUS IDENTITY

Many couples needlessly fear the consequences of choosing a single religion for their family. Choosing a single religious identity does not mean that holidays will not be celebrated with extended family. Nor does it mean that grandchildren will not have special relationships with all of their grandparents. Childhood memories and grandparents' recipes can easily be shared with children, regardless of the religious identity of the child.

Rather than seeing the choice of a religious identity as one where one side of the family wins and the other loses, the choice can be viewed as one of the family decisions that parents must make. Parents can then present the decision to the child, and help the child relate to and understand the diversity in their larger family. "We can all help Grandma celebrate her holidays, just as we celebrate her birthdays" is one way of approaching and honoring the interfaith extended family.

Interfaith families can raise children with a strong religious identity and a strong love for and bonding with all family members.

4. Telling Your Parents about Your Religious Decisions for Your Children

Paula Brody, Ed.D., LICSW, is director of Outreach Programs and Training for the Northeast Council of the Union of American Hebrew Congregations (UAHC, the Reform Movement), where she develops and coordinates a wide range of programs and services to welcome interfaith families into Reform congregations. She is a consultant to, and the "Dear Dr. Paula" columnist for, InterfaithFamily.com.

A Very Difficult Thing to Do: Telling Your Parents That You Are Raising Your Children in Your Partner's Faith

PAULA BRODY

Many interfaith couples delay telling their parents what decisions they have made regarding the religious identity of their children, or avoid making this critically important decision altogether, due to a fear of hurting one set of parents. The fear of disappointing parents or not knowing how parents may react to decisions keeps many couples from resolving the religious identity issue. Indeed, telling parents about the decision may be one of the hardest things a person has ever done. Yet, it is very important to make parents aware of the decisions made for their grandchildren.

In my professional role as the director of Outreach Programs and Training for the Reform Movement in the Northeast, I've been privileged to work with hundreds of interfaith couples, helping them to make these important life decisions. In my opinion, the partner who decides to raise his or her children in a partner's faith is giving that partner an enormous gift. This is a gift that must be given freely, lovingly, and for the right reasons.

Partners considering giving this tremendous gift—raising their children in their partner's faith—undoubtedly have many concerns: How do I tell my parents what I have decided? Will they feel I have betrayed them? Do they feel I made this choice for the right reasons? Will this distance me from my parents? Will my parents feel left out of our lives? Will I not be able to continue the family celebrations that were such a joyful part of my childhood? There are no easy answers to these questions. However, here are some suggestions that may be helpful when you have this conversation with your parents.

- If you are giving your partner the tremendous gift of raising children in his/her religious tradition, clarify and express what you need for yourself and your family in order to do this. Be sure that your partner understands these needs. This is essential to enable you to feel that you are giving this huge gift willingly, without giving too much of yourself away. You need to feel that this is a decision you have made out of love, a choice you made for the right reasons.

- If you are the partner receiving this beautiful and loving gift from your partner, listen carefully to what your partner needs to maintain his or her religious tradition. Make every effort to meet these needs.

- After you have made your decision, live with it for a while. For how long? Perhaps for several weeks, maybe even several months, until you are sure it feels right for both of you as a couple.

- When you have "lived with" your decision, when the decision feels comfortable and right, it is important that you tell both sets of your parents what you have decided. To not tell both sets of parents—or worse, to not tell the parents whose religion was not chosen—keeps them in the dark. If you do not tell your parents, you close down the opportunity for clear and honest communication about religious issues in the future. Not telling your parents keeps them guessing about your decisions and, possibly, imagining "the worst-case scenario" anyhow. Interestingly, no matter which religion you choose, both sets of parents will probably feel relieved that they now know what you will do.

- If you are the partner raising children in a faith other than your own, your parents will want to know that you came to this decision freely—that it feels right and comfortable for you. They will want to feel reassured that you have indeed made this choice for the right reasons and were not pressured by outside influences, most especially by your partner's parents. Reassure them. Continue to reassure them at appropriate moments in the future.

- Your parents need to know that they will not be "left out" of your life. Let them know that you will, in fact, go out of your way to include them in your family's religious celebrations. Invite them to your home and your in-laws' home, even knowing that they may choose not to accept these invitations. Be an ambassador for your parents and extended family into the traditions of the faith you have chosen. Provide information and encourage questions.

- Plan to be part of your parents' holiday celebrations and life-cycle ceremonies. Reassure your parents that they are not going to lose you and your children for these important family moments. Let them know that your partner and children will learn about their religious celebrations in order to honor and respect them.

- Choose to spend "extra" time with your parents on non-religious occasions such as July 4th weekend, Thanksgiving, your child's first dance recital or soccer awards ceremony, Mother's Day, or a fun family vacation. Remember that religion is just one aspect of your children's identity and that there are many ways to create cherished shared memories with your parents.

- Find meaningful ways to reinforce your parents' legacy in a non-religious way. Pass on a family name. Celebrate ethnic traditions.

Introduce your child to your parents' favorite hobbies, books, and music. Create non-religious special moments that will strengthen the bond between your children and your parents.

- When you do have children, you must discuss with your partner what you both feel comfortable with regarding your parents' role in teaching their grandchildren about their faith. Is it okay for Grandma to teach your child a holiday song? Can Nana give your child a gift for her holiday? Can Grandpa take your child with him when he goes to his worship setting? Can your parents talk to your children about their belief in God? It is important to set appropriate parameters with your parents before Grammy teaches your child her favorite bedtime prayer. As parents, you must set these guidelines for grandparents and communicate your wishes.

- Lastly, when I work with interfaith couples, I ask them to reflect on "the most valued aspect of their religious heritage" given to them by their parents. Think about your answer to this question. Share the answer with your partner. I always encourage interfaith couples to find ways to integrate this "most valued aspect of their religious heritage" into their marriage and family life. You may be able to pass on what you value most to your children, even in the context of another religion.

At the appropriate time, have a conversation with your parents and let them know what you value most from what they gave you. Assure your parents that this is a precious legacy. This will be a meaningful conversation. Your parents will realize that you value them and what they gave to you.

Always remember that honoring your father and mother is at the foundation of all religions. Continue to honor them and show respect for the legacy that they have given to you. This will help your parents begin to accept your choice of raising your children in your partner's faith. With time, your parents will come to realize that you have given this beautiful gift to your partner for the right reasons.

Cheryl Opper teaches childbirth education and senior fitness and is the youth group director at her church. She has been married for fifteen years and has one daughter, who celebrated her *Bat Mitzvah* in the spring of 2001.

Telling My Christian Parents I'm Raising My Children in the Jewish Faith

CHERYL OPPER

Neal and I met at the Jewish Community Center in Houston, Texas, in 1983. He was playing sports at the center, and I was teaching exercise classes. He participated in a few of my aerobic classes before he got up enough courage to ask me out. Our first date was the Sunday evening before Labor Day. That afternoon Neal called his mother in Boston to tell her he was going out with a really nice Jewish girl he had met at the JCC. Sunday evening Neal picked me up for our date, and on the way to the restaurant, he asked me, "What did you do today?" I said, "I went to church this morning, then I went out to the pool and had lunch with a friend." He didn't seem surprised I wasn't Jewish. A few days later Neal called his mother in Boston and said, "Mom, she is great. We had a wonderful time, and oh, by the way, she's not Jewish."

Neal made it clear while we were dating that he wanted to raise his children Jewish. I asked him to explain what that meant. I told him I needed more information before I could make a commitment to do that. I knew very little about Judaism at the time. We met with the rabbi from Neal's temple and the minister from my church in an attempt to seek counsel and gather information about this major decision in our lives. After many hours of serious thought and discussion, we decided to raise our future children in the Jewish faith. A few months later, we were engaged.

Neal's parents and family were thrilled about our marriage. They embraced our love for one another and trusted our wisdom. I never felt any pressure from them to convert to Judaism. They knew I had a strong Christian faith and they respected my religion.

When I told my Christian parents we were raising our children Jewish, there was a mixed reaction. My parents loved Neal very much. My father was excited about our interfaith marriage and our decision to raise our children Jewish. He had a deep love for Judaism, considering it to be part of ancient Christianity. He went to Israel two different times to visit the Holy Land with his church group. He loved learning how to speak Hebrew and sing Jewish songs and prayers, and at our wedding he sang "*Heveinu Shalom Aleichem*." My father felt that Judaism brought him closer to God. He even wanted a *mezuzah* (miniature parchment scroll containing the *Sh'ma* prayer that Jews put on the doorposts of their homes) for his house. One year for Christmas we gave him the book *Everything You Want to Know about Judaism and More*. After he finished the book, he asked if there was a second volume.

My mother, on the other hand, was more hesitant about our decision to raise our children Jewish. She was concerned that I wasn't going to teach my children about Jesus. She asked me, "How will your children go to heaven if they don't believe in Jesus?" I said, "Mom, our children will believe in God, and Jesus is a part of God. Christians believe this, but Jews do not." I told her that we planned to raise our children with a strong religious foundation. Although she still had concerns, she didn't make her concerns our problem.

After our daughter Lindsay was born in 1988, my mother flew out to Boston for two weeks to take care of her new Jewish grand-daughter. During the time she was with us, the rabbi from our temple led a beautiful baby-naming service at our home, and my mother had a chance to be a part of this special ceremony. It was her first Jewish experience, and I know it meant a lot to her. She participated in the Jewish prayers and felt a true sense of joy at being a part of this holy moment. She realized her granddaughter would never be baptized as an infant in church. Instead, she had the honor to be part of a beautiful religious ceremony welcoming her new granddaughter into the Jewish faith, into God's covenant. As my mother held Lindsay in her arms, Lindsay received her Hebrew name "Mira," which means "reflection of light."

Mira's naming service was a real reflection of acceptance and love from her Christian grandmother. Over the years my mother has learned to embrace the Jewish holidays and traditions with the same enthusiasm as my father. She makes a special effort to send Jewish holiday cards to my family and Jewish relatives. She is looking forward to my daughter's *Bat Mitzvah* (the ceremony in which an individual chooses to assume the obligations and privileges of an adult member of the Jewish community).

My parents' love and respect for me and my family has been a true gift. I am deeply grateful to them both for opening their hearts and accepting our decision to raise our daughter as a Jew.

Jim Keen is a freelance writer based in Ann Arbor, Michigan. He has fifteen years of experience in an interfaith relationship. He is married with two children.

"You're Raising Them What?" Telling Your Parents You Are Raising Jewish Kids

JIM KEEN

You never think of these things before you're married. I mean, c'mon, why wouldn't you raise your kids in the same fashion as your parents raised you? As a Protestant, I just assumed that one day I'd be taking my future kids to Sunday school. I also thought that I'd be teaching my future son to play baseball. But, as it turns out, I take my kids to *shul* (Yiddish word for synagogue) and my daughter to ballet! Life throws you unexpected curveballs, and you deal with it. Now that I actually have a family of my own, I feel blessed to have two wonderful girls. The decision to raise them in the Jewish faith, the faith of my wife, was not an easy one, but it's one I don't regret. What was equally hard was telling my parents.

Telling my in-laws was easy. After all, they're Jewish. Even though I did not convert, I think they felt fairly comfortable knowing that I would make every effort to help my wife teach the kids the Jewish faith and traditions. Telling my parents would be a different story. What on earth would I say? How would I broach the subject? What would their reaction be? Would they disapprove? Would they disown me?

Fortunately, my parents have always been loving and supportive, so I didn't think they would do anything rash. However, this was alien territory for them, as well as for me. I was aware that many interfaith families have faced strong disapproval from their parents. We've all heard the stories. We may even know someone who's had problems. Heck, that someone might now be me!

No matter how open your parents are, there are some talks you have to be well prepared for if you want to see them go right. My wife and I went over and over our reasons for raising the kids Jewish: we wanted to raise them in one faith so as not to confuse them. Also, because their mother is Jewish, and from a traditional Conservative background, they would be considered Jewish. However, we wanted to teach them about Christianity, my religion, to enrich their lives and give them an understanding of their heritage. They would still be allowed to "help" their Protestant grandparents and me celebrate Christmas and Easter. But, they would know that, bottom line, they are Jewish. Also, it would be really nice if my Protestant parents helped my children celebrate *Shabbat* (the Jewish Sabbath) and other Jewish holidays.

This was great in theory, but how would it work when we actually told my parents face to face? (I want to emphasize "face to face." This is not something I'd do over the phone.) If they gave us any argument or grief, we were prepared to tell them that it was important to us that they respect our decision. In addition, we'd planned to say that we had put a lot of thought into it, we feel it's best for the kids, and most of all, we want them to be included in the raising of our children.

I think that last part is the one that really helped us over the hump. Letting my parents know that we still wanted them to help raise our children was key. We want them to be every bit as active as they would have been if we had decided to raise the kids Protestant. This let them know that they are needed. Obviously, they won't know very much about the Jewish holidays and life-cycle events, but we can teach them. And in turn, they can participate. Actually, just their being there is important. The Protestant grandparents can come over for a *Shabbat* dinner. They can assist us in putting up the *sukkah* (wooden hut built for Sukkot, the fall harvest holiday). They can play *dreidel* (a Hanukkah spinning toy) for chocolate *gelt* (coins) or, in our family, Jelly Bellies.

As it turns out, we had "the talk" one evening over dinner at my parents' house. It was a little nerve-racking trying to find a way to bring it up, but somehow, we managed to find the courage. My mom was talking about Christmas stockings.

"Someday, when you two have kids, we have to remember to tell Aunt Ann to make them stockings," she said.

"Uh, well, Mom, Dad, we'd like to discuss that with you a little bit. You see, about Christmas..."

They didn't say too much while we explained our plan—they just let us talk. However, when we got to the part about how much we hoped they would help us, they finally spoke.

"We'd love to help," they said.

Huh? You mean, that's it? No arguments? No grief?

Of course, it wasn't that simple—it never is. They still had questions. For instance, they wanted to know what to do about Santa. And every once in a while, we have to tell them that "we prefer to do things such and such a way."

They may have had an inkling from our previous four years of dating and engagement that we'd choose this route. But, they hadn't been through the details of it like my wife and I had. My mom was very concerned that our children would go around telling their Protestant cousins that there's no such thing as Santa Claus. However, we explained how our kids would help them celebrate the Christian holidays. I also know that my mother, even today, feels a little uncertain when it comes to the religious issues. She has admitted to me that she is uncomfortable talking about baby Jesus in the manger. She doesn't quite know what we want her to say to our kids, or even if it's appropriate to talk about baby Jesus at all. And, I think she may be a little disappointed that she's in this position. I'm sure she's always had visions of teaching her grandkids the Bible stories that she taught me. My wife and I need to give my parents more guidance in this area.

My dad's biggest worry was that, in focusing on Judaism with my kids, somehow I would lose sight of my Protestant traditions and background. I'm sure that he will love me no matter what I do, but it's got to be hard on a parent to think that his child would turn his back on the past twenty-three years of upbringing. I reassured him that this upbringing was something that I would not and could not ever forget. As he watches us raise our kids today, I know he feels good about how we haven't neglected to teach our children about "Daddy's religion." This is evident in the fact that he and my mom really get into helping my family celebrate Jewish traditions. I think they would be less cooperative if they weren't comfortable with our parenting.

All in all, they were, and still are, supportive of our wish to raise our kids Jewish. I don't know if it was the part about including them, or the fact that they wouldn't have to share us with my in-laws on Christmas and Easter! But my wife and I are extremely lucky to have parents who are understanding and want to help.

5. Birth Ceremonies: Baptism, Baby Naming, and *Brit Milah*

Anita Diamant has written six guides to contemporary Jewish practice, including *The New Jewish Baby Book: Names, Ceremonies & Customs—A Guide for Today's Families* and *Bible Baby Names: Spiritual Choices from Judeo-Christian Tradition* (both Jewish Lights).

Welcoming Babies into Intermarried Families: Choosing Ceremonies

ANITA DIAMANT

Anyone who's ever been in a delivery room, or held an adopted child for the first time, knows that miracles do happen. Deciding what to name your own miracle can feel like an awesome choice, almost a second conception as you contemplate, who shall my baby be? A Deborah? A Benjamin? A Moses?

Filled with overwhelming feelings of gratitude and wonder, new parents often turn to their religious traditions to find a way to name their unspeakable happiness and to announce it to the world.

For intermarried couples, the arrival of a baby may become the moment to decide "how we're going to raise the kids." Or if you have already decided to raise children in one faith or the other, this may be the moment to make that choice concrete and public. In any event, you have many options open to you.

OPTIONS FOR WELCOMING BABIES

Parents who have settled on raising their child as a Christian are often affiliated with a church and can depend on the minister or priest for guidance in the christening and/or baptism, a ceremony that usually takes place in a church, though some families choose to have a less formal ritual at home.

For parents who have decided to raise children as Jews, the question of circumcision for sons is pressing, since the ritual is performed on the eighth day after birth—though it may be postponed if there is any question about the baby's health. Boys are traditionally named at a *brit milah* (covenant of circumcision ceremony), which is better known by its Yiddish name, *bris*. (If the baby's mother is not Jewish, there may also be a formal conversion of the child—a process that includes immersion in a ritual bath, or *mikvah*, as well as circumcision. The Reform and Reconstructionist movements consider a baby Jewish if either the mother or father is Jewish, and if the child is brought up as a Jew, but the Conservative and Orthodox movements only consider a baby Jewish if the mother is a Jew. Some parents choose to convert a baby whose father is Jewish and whose mother is not, so that there won't be any questions about whether or not the child is Jewish.)

Baby-naming ceremonies for daughters are a relatively new phenomenon for American Jews. They vary a lot both in content and timing; some take place seven days after birth, others aren't scheduled until the baby is a month or two old. Baby namings may be part of a synagogue service or held at home.

Announcing your decision about which religion your child will be raised in can stir powerful emotions in your extended families when their religion is not chosen. Grandparents in particular may see your choice as a personal rejection of them and all their values. Christian family members may voice genuine concern over a child's immortal soul if the parents forego baptism. Jewish parents may feel terribly guilty and ashamed.

While new parents should be unambiguous about this kind of

decision, it's important to be respectful and sensitive, too. Explain how and why you reached your decision. Reassure family members that your choice was not meant to hurt them, and that they will always be welcome in your home and will be beloved members of your baby's family. Welcome both sides of the family to any ritual and/or ensuing celebration. (My *The New Jewish Baby Book: Names, Ceremonies & Customs—A Guide for Today's Families* [Jewish Lights] contains many ritual options and chapters of special interest to intermarried families. Another helpful resource is Debra Nussbaum Cohen's *Celebrating Your New Jewish Daughter: Creating Jewish Ways to Welcome Baby Girls into the Covenant— New and Traditional Ceremonies* [Jewish Lights].)

INCLUDING NON-JEWISH RELATIVES IN JEWISH BABY-NAMING RITUALS

There are many ways to include non-Jewish family members in Jewish baby-naming rituals. Typically, both parents do readings about the choice of the child's name. Both sets of grandparents can be given ceremonial honors, such as carrying the baby into the room, and/or reading a poem or non-denominational prayer for the child.

Parents who have decided to raise their child as a Jew can find congregational and rabbinic support for their decisions and help in planning a welcoming ceremony. (Remember that there are major differences among denominations: the Reform and Reconstructionist movements are most open to interfaith families, but some Conservative rabbis can be equally gracious and welcoming. It's a good idea to do some advance "temple shopping" or even affiliate with a congregation if you're clear about raising Jewish children.)

If non-Jewish family members are uncomfortable participating in the ceremony, don't insist; perhaps they can make a toast at a meal that follows the baby naming.

NON-DENOMINATIONAL
BABY-NAMING CEREMONIES

Intermarried parents have the option of creating their own namings or ceremonies of welcome. These can be virtually secular, or they may invoke inclusive religious values and language by using readings from the Song of Songs or Psalms, for example.

It's a good idea to be clear about metaphors and symbols. Water rituals, in particular, can be confusing. For Christians, baptismal water is a sign of identification with the death and resurrection of Jesus, and a symbol of welcome to the Christian community. Jewish baby ceremonies that use water (sometimes the baby's hands and/or feet are washed—an echo of biblical scenes of welcome) signify the child's entry into the Jewish covenant *(brit)* with God.

A non-denominational welcoming or naming ceremony might look something like this:

A CEREMONY OF WELCOME

Guests gather in the living room with parents sitting in the front, or in the center of a circle.

Three candles can be set up on a central table. Each parent lights one candle and then, jointly, illuminates the third, explaining that this represents the new life in their family.

Both sets of grandparents carry the baby into the room and bring him or her to the parents, who announce the baby's name and tell the story of how they chose it. ("She is named in memory of my grandmother Sarah, who was a strong woman, and in memory of Tim's mother, Louise, a loving woman with a big heart.")

If the baby is not fussy, family members and friends can pass him or her from person to person for a blessing. ("May you always enjoy good health.")

Alternatively, parents can hold the baby up to each guest—making "formal" introductions: ("Myra, I would like you to meet my daughter, Sarah Louisa." "Sarah Louisa, this is my oldest friend in the world, and now your auntie.")

The friend might offer a "blessing." ("Sarah, may you grow up to be as good a friend as your mother, and as fine a musician as your father.")

Grandparents can be asked to do a reading.

Older siblings can participate in any age-appropriate way, which might include a reading or just giving the new baby a kiss.

After the ceremony, a festive meal brings everyone together to break bread and share the joy of the occasion.

According to an ancient Jewish saying, "With each baby, the world begins anew." The point of any ceremony or ritual is to give you, your family, and your community a chance to share this hope for a fresh start.

Fr. Walter H. Cuenin is pastor of Our Lady Help of Christians Church in Newton, Massachusetts. He has a doctorate in sacred theology from the Gregorian University in Rome and has been very active in the Newton Clergy Association and in interfaith work. The Jewish Community Day School is located at Our Lady's parish. In December 2000 Fr. Cuenin celebrated his thirtieth anniversary as a priest.

Is Heaven Denied to an Unbaptized Child? Advice and Perspective for Catholic Parents Who Are Raising Their Children within Judaism

WALTER H. CUENIN

As pastor of a Catholic church, I sometimes counsel Catholics in interfaith marriages who are struggling with the issue of baptism.

Many of them were brought up believing that if they did not baptize their children, the children would not go to heaven. Doctrine has changed dramatically since they were young, however, and we now teach that God saves all peoples, not only Christians. Everyone is welcome in the kingdom of heaven. The Church has also strongly affirmed its belief that the promises made to the Jewish people have never been revoked and that our faith in Jesus in no way diminishes the place of the Jewish people as God's chosen people.

Prior to the Second Vatican Council (1962–1965) of the Catholic Church, most Catholics were taught that unless you were baptized you could not go to heaven. The custom of baptizing infants as soon as possible after birth was predominant. Many times, in fact, mothers did not attend the baptism because it took place so soon after birth. People were encouraged not to bring their child out of the house until the child had been baptized.

This popular approach to the sacrament of baptism was based on a literal interpretation of a Christian Scripture from the Gospel of John, chapter 3, where it is written, "Unless a person is born again of water and the spirit, they can not enter the kingdom of heaven." Because of this it was customary, for example, for a Catholic nurse in a crisis situation to baptize babies in the hospital even without seeking parental permission. There was a strong focus on "saving" babies from dying without baptism. Today this is radically changed in the Catholic Church.

The Church today believes in the interpretation of Scripture—both the Hebrew and Christian texts. So, for example, when we read Genesis we do not take the stories of creation as described in chapters 1 and 2 as literal descriptions of the historical creation of the world. We see them as faith stories that have a message but use the myths and stories of ancient times. In other words, we interpret the text. This principle of interpretation is common to many Jewish and Christian traditions. Thus, the interpretation of Christian Scriptures and the words of Jesus allow us to understand the meaning of the text in a different manner. We do not see the aforementioned passage from John's

Gospel as physically requiring a baptism. It needs to be seen in the wider context of all of Jesus' teaching, in which he speaks of God's universal salvific will. This newer interpretation is a part of the common understanding of the Catholic Church today. We believe that God saves all peoples, not only Christians.

With this newer understanding, the meaning of baptism has also shifted. It is seen today primarily as an entrance ritual, for those entering the community of Christian faith. A person who is not baptized is equally loved by God, but is not a member of the Christian community. In fact, after the Second Vatican Council, a new ritual of infant baptism was developed that is almost exclusively focused on parents. The ritual stresses sharing the faith with the child and raising him or her in the Christian community. The washing in the water and anointing with oil are principally significant of becoming a member of the Christian faith community. This has resulted in a new look at baptism among Catholic parents. It no longer is something they rush to out of fear that their child might not go to heaven. Rather it is a ritual they plan and for which they often gather as many people as possible to celebrate the child's birth and new beginnings in the life of the Church. Baptisms are now sometimes celebrated in the context of a Sunday Mass—again to reflect this idea that baptism means entrance into the community.

The Jewish origins of baptism are better understood in light of this newer approach to baptism in the Church. The early Christians adopted the practice of Jewish baptism and used it as a ritual for new converts to Christianity. As a convert to Judaism would be asked to bathe in the *mikvah* (ritual bath) and perhaps be given a new name, so Christians entering the Church bathe in the waters of the baptism font and are named, usually after a Christian saint. Baptism, like the ritual bath in the *mikvah*, marks a return to the womb and rebirth into a new life of faith.

For interfaith couples who have chosen to raise their children within Judaism, problems with regard to not baptizing their children arise because traditions do not die easily. It would not be uncommon, for example, to have a relative, perhaps a grandmother or grandfather, who might be very upset that the baby is not baptized. Pressure can often be felt by interfaith couples to "at least have the child baptized secretly" so that if anything happened the baby would go to heaven. These notions remain long after the theology and practice of the Church has changed. Hopefully, if the couple understands today's approach of the Catholic Church, it will be easier for them to explain to "nervous" relatives that it is okay if their baby is not baptized.

More work needs to be done with interfaith couples so they can be secure, themselves, in the decisions they make about raising their children. Otherwise, ancient customs and traditions can rise like ghosts from some deep place to haunt and disturb a good marriage. If not attended to properly, these ancient traditions can erode even the best of marriages.

Roberta Kesten Calderone has facilitated the "Times and Seasons Program" for Temple Emanuel-Beth-Shalom in Montreal, Canada, for the past twelve years. The program allows interfaith couples contemplating marriage to identify and discuss issues they are facing.

Helping Couples Cope with the *Bris*/Baptism Question

ROBERTA KESTEN CALDERONE

Mary and Jed, married for one year and now pregnant with their first child, were having intense discussions about what to do after the child was born. Mary had agreed to raise the child Jewish, but now that she was pregnant, she began to fear that not having a baptism would mean that her child would not be able to go to heaven. Jed was now terrified. If Mary wanted to baptize their child, then how could they raise the child to be Jewish?

This couple is typical of many who have attended my workshops for interfaith couples considering marriage. For these couples, the issues of circumcision and baptism represent a major hurdle.

Often, when a non-Jewish partner makes a commitment to raise their future children as Jews, he or she doesn't realize at first that this means the child will not be baptized. To non-Jewish partners this is frequently a frightening prospect. Their religious upbringing has taught them that baptism is something they must do for the protection of their child. Many of the participants in my workshops express the belief that if they do not baptize their child, the child will not go to heaven. This weighs very heavily on their minds and consciences.

Communication must be open and sincere regarding this issue. A child cannot be both a Jew and a Christian. The baptism actually affirms the child's and parent's commitment to Christianity, while the *brit milah* (covenant of circumcision) confirms the parent's commitment to raising the child Jewishly.

How can this dilemma be worked out? For the sake of the child, a choice must be made and of course stuck with throughout the child's formative years. Often, in the process of discussing this decision, non-Jewish partners will express anxiety around losing a "connection" to the child. Their own baptism was frequently an important part of their background, and they would feel a discontinuity if the child were not baptized.

For those who choose to raise their children as Jews, I try to help the non-Jews understand that the circumcision or baby naming is a very meaningful religious life-cycle event. I encourage them to see that this connection to Judaism should give them peace of mind that the child does have a religious identity. The adjustment for the parent, of course, is that this religious connection, this personal identity, is one that the parent did not share as a child.

Their feeling of not having a connection to their child is troublesome. I encourage the parents to accept that they have a connection to the child just because the child is theirs. I point out that after a decision has been made to raise the child Jewish, and after actions are taken consistent with that decision—having a circumcision and/or baby naming, attending synagogue together, and sending the child to Hebrew school—then the new religious connection and the bond between parent and child will strengthen as this becomes a part of the lives of each member of the family.

I hope that couples realize how difficult these decisions are and that there must be a great deal of soul searching and understanding. I caution them to continue the dialogue.

Jim Keen is a freelance writer based in Ann Arbor, Michigan. He has fifteen years of experience in an interfaith relationship. He is married with two children.

Baby Namings in My Interfaith Family

JIM KEEN

Before we were married, my wife and I decided that we would raise our future children in her faith, Judaism. Being Protestant, I was accustomed to a whole different set of life-cycle events for kids. The world of baptisms and communions was all I knew. Now, I had to start learning about completely different ceremonies and their significance.

About the only event that Bonnie and I had in common was the annual birthday party, although I could argue that even these were very different. As a child, I took my friends sledding and to basketball games, while she went for pony rides. She probably even played house! Now, as an expectant dad, I had to become familiar with *Bar Mitzvahs* (the ceremonies in which individuals choose to assume the obligations and privileges of adult members of the Jewish community), *bris* ceremonies (circumcision ceremonies), and this thing called a baby naming. Hadn't we already named our daughter at the hospital? Why did we have to name her again?

When my wife got pregnant for the first time, we had no idea if we were having a boy or a girl. If we had a boy, we decided we'd have the circumcision ceremony known as a *bris*, or *brit milah*. If we had a girl, we'd have the ceremony known as a baby naming. The only thing I knew about either event was that there is lots of food, and the baby usually cries. What else would an infant do?

If we ended up having a baby boy, I wasn't sure how I'd react if we had to have a *bris*. Although I had been circumcised, it was by the doctor in the hospital—not in a room full of people trying to eat their bagels and lox. In the past few years, I had been to a friend's son's *bris* and survived. Fortunately, I don't get too squeamish about such things. But how would my family react? The ceremony would be a whole new experience for them, let alone one where the cutting of foreskin took place. Yikes! However, I reminded myself that this is what my wife and I had decided for our children, and that this was an important part of their Jewish identity. My family, thank goodness, is open-minded about our interfaith marriage, and probably would be excited for us anyway.

As it turns out, we had a girl and a baby naming. So why name her a second time? As my wife explained, this is to give our daughter her Hebrew name. Actually, she said, because baby namings are a relatively new ritual, there is a lot of flexibility in what we could do for a ceremony. Unlike the *bris*, which is commanded by the *Torah* (the first five books of the Hebrew Bible), we found that there are a few precedents out there, but no steadfast rules, for celebrating the birth of a daughter. We chose to have the baby naming in our home, rather than our temple, so that my family would feel more comfortable.

Before our daughter was born, we had decided what all her names were to be and after whom she would be named. We knew that we wanted to incorporate the names of our grandmothers, who had recently passed away. My wife told me that it is customary for Ashkenazic, or Eastern European, Jews to name their children after a deceased member of the family as a way of remembering them.

"Ah, that's why you don't see a lot of 'Juniors' in Jewish boys' names," I surmised. But wait a minute; we could have a problem. "What about when you want to name your child after someone with a name that's, let's just say, no longer in style—like your grandmother, Gertrude?" I asked. "Or your grandmother, Mildred?" she added. "Yeah, I don't want her to get beat up at school, or called 'Mildew.'" Bonnie explained that a lot of families use the first letter of the ancestor's Hebrew name. She said, "Gertrude's 'Hebrew' name was Gittel (which is actually Yiddish). So for our daughter, we can use Gittel and take the "G" to make Gabrielle for the English name." "Oh, so it's a loophole!" I replied.

For our second daughter, we used the "loophole" again and named her Molly, after my grandma Mildred. For the Hebrew name, we chose Chava. Now, I'm sure if my grandma had been Jewish, this would have been *her* Hebrew name. Actually, all joking aside, this was a nice opportunity to give Molly a Hebrew name belonging to another one of my wife's grandmothers. We felt it would be more appropriate to use this existing Hebrew name, rather than making one up for the name Molly. Bottom line, I learned that there are a lot of acceptable ways to come up with names in the Jewish tradition.

So for the baby namings of our two daughters, the order of events went something like this: Friends and family arrived at our home and began to mingle while waiting for the rabbi to begin. At noon, the rabbi was ready to start. But wait! Some of *my* family and friends weren't there yet. They were, as usual, sociably late! We had forgotten to tell them that this is one occasion where it is not fashionable to be tardy. Oops.

When the rabbi finally started, he introduced himself and welcomed everyone. After Bonnie lit the candles, we had my parents bring the baby into the room. The rabbi said a few blessings and then told everyone the significance of the baby naming. This was great for both Jews and Christians who had never witnessed one before. Later on in the ceremony, Bonnie's parents also participated by saying the blessings over the wine and *challah* (braided bread). As you can see, it was important to us to make sure both sides of the family were involved in a meaningful way and comfortable with their roles.

Looking back, I think that my wife and I were the only ones who were nervous. During our first daughter's ceremony, I remember not wanting to screw up. I could just hear my Jewish in-laws: "There he goes messing up one of our fine traditions." (For the record, though, I don't really believe anyone would have thought that.) After the rabbi gave our daughters their names, my wife and I wanted to say a few words about why we chose these names, the people after whom they were named, and what it all meant to us. We each had parts we wanted to say. But in both ceremonies, Bonnie was too emotional to speak. So it was up to me to do the talking. I began by telling everyone about the meanings these names had for us and how we hoped our daughters could emulate their loving great-grandmothers. I felt much more confident for my second daughter's naming three years later. You should have heard me pronounce "Chava." Of course, we ended the ceremonies by eating lots of great food. This, Bonnie explained, is an integral part of all Jewish rituals.

I'll never forget either ceremony, but the first one struck me as incredibly significant. Here I was, standing in my living room, the Protestant, in the middle of a Jewish ceremony, expounding on these Hebrew names. I looked out at the room full of loved ones. I looked down at my daughter's sweet face. I couldn't have felt more at home.

Anita Diamant has written six guides to contemporary Jewish practice. This article is excerpted from *The New Jewish Baby Book: Names, Ceremonies & Customs—A Guide for Today's Families* (Jewish Lights).

Planning a *Brit Bat* for Your Daughter

ANITA DIAMANT

Although there are precedents, there are no rules for *brit bat*, the ceremony that celebrates the birth of a daughter. There is no right or wrong here—only opportunities for creativity and holiness.

WHERE

Brit bat can take place at home or in the synagogue, and there are pros and cons associated with either. Some people use a sanctuary or social hall because they need the space and also because they want to make this a community celebration. It may be simpler for you to hire a caterer and keep the commotion out of the house.

But others feel that home is the only place for a family occasion like *brit bat*. Some people find it easier to care for the baby, reassure older siblings, and host a celebration in the comfort of their own home.

WHEN

Generally, parents schedule a *brit bat* on a day that is convenient for family and friends and when the mother feels well enough to enjoy the event. But some base their choice on Jewish criteria.

• *Eight days.* Having the ceremony on the eighth day taps into the ancient rite of *brit milah* (covenant of circumcision). The same traditional explanations apply, such as the sanctity associated with the number eight, and the spiritual strength the baby derives from her first contact with *Shabbat*. Holding the *brit bat* on the eighth day means that the miracle of birth is still very fresh in the parents' minds, and the ceremony will resound with the powerful emotions of labor and delivery. However, because many women often don't feel ready for a party so soon after giving birth, the eighth day is a relatively infrequent choice.

- *Fourteen days* has been advanced as another interval with traditional roots. In the Torah, after the birth of a daughter, a mother's ritual impurity ends after fourteen days. Two weeks allows for the mother's recovery and, according to some pediatricians, is a reasonable amount of time to keep a newborn away from crowds.

- *Thirty days* is a popular choice because it allows the family enough time to recover, plan, and invite. It too has a basis in tradition, because the early Rabbis believed a child was viable only after thirty days.

- *Rosh Chodesh.* Some parents schedule the ceremony on the first day of the next new moon. A day for new beginnings, *Rosh Chodesh* is a semi-holiday which traditionally was a day of rest for women.

- *Shabbat.* Whether days or weeks after the baby is born, most *brit bat* ceremonies are scheduled for the Sabbath. Because *Shabbat* is itself a covenant between God and Israel, it seems an appropriate time for a covenantal ceremony.

A *brit bat* on *Shabbat* can take place at different times in the day and in a number of contexts. In some congregations, the custom is to take the baby up to the *bimah* (the raised platform in the front of the synagogue) during services on Friday night or Saturday morning. There the rabbi generally conducts a brief ceremony. Blessings such as the traditional *mi shebeirach* are offered, and the name is announced. Additional readings may be incorporated as well. Afterward, the *oneg Shabbat* (literally means Sabbath joy and refers to the light refreshments served after the service) or *Shabbat kiddush* (the blessing sanctifying the Sabbath that is said over wine) is often sponsored by the new parents or in the family's honor.

Another option is to hold the *brit bat* immediately following the morning service, preceding *kiddush*. The celebration can coincide with the *Shabbat* midday meal, either in the synagogue or at home.

Brit bat is sometimes included in *havdalah,* the ceremony that marks the end of *Shabbat* and celebrates distinctions: *Shabbat* from the rest of the week, the mundane from the holy. A *havdalah brit bat* marks the separation between mother and baby, and the child's entrance into the community of Israel.

GUESTS AND PARTICIPANTS

Once you've settled on where and when, there is the question of whom to invite and involve in the ceremony. Jewish tradition encourages us to include as many people as possible. Although some parents do mail invitations to their daughter's *brit bat* ceremony, most invite guests by telephone.

Although there are many exceptions, when *brit bat* takes place at home, the baby's parents usually lead the ceremony. When it is held in a synagogue, the rabbi officiates, although sometimes with a great deal of parental participation. You do not need a rabbi to perform a *brit bat* ceremony. The parents or any honored guest can serve as the ceremonial leader.

In general, it is considered a *mitzvah*—a good and holy deed—to include as many people as possible in a ritual such as this. Grandparents are usually given the most important honors, especially the roles and titles associated with *brit milah*—*kvatterin, kvatter* (godmother and godfather, respectively) and *sandek* (sponsor). The *sandek* or *sandeket* (the feminine version of *sandek*) holds the baby during the naming. The *kvatter* and *kvatterin* bring the baby into the room, hold her during some part of the ceremony, or perform other ceremonial tasks such as candle-lighting.

NON-JEWS IN THE CEREMONY

Non-Jewish grandparents, aunts, uncles, cousins, and friends can participate in many ways—depending on their comfort level, of course. Unlike godparents in Christian ceremonies, the *kvatter* and *kvatterin* do not assume responsibility for the child's religious upbringing; their roles are strictly ceremonial. The same holds true for the *sandek,* a word that probably derives from the Greek for "patron."

Blessings, poems, readings, or prayers can be distributed to any and to as many guests as you choose. People can be honored with tasks like reciting the *motzi,* the blessing over bread (traditionally a braided challah) before the meal, or holding a prayer shawl over the *brit bat.*

The legend that the prophet Elijah attends all *brit milah* ceremonies has been attached to *brit bat.* The *kissei shel Eliyahu* (Elijah's chair) invokes the presence of the prophet, angel, protector, peripatetic guest, and harbinger of the days of the Messiah.

ELEMENTS OF THE *BRIT BAT* CEREMONY

Because *brit bat* ceremonies are still relatively new and because many guests—Jews and non-Jews alike—may not be familiar with the prayers and symbols, many parents prepare a printed guide to the proceedings. Samples of *brit bat* ceremonies can be found in *Celebrating Your New Jewish Daughter: Creating Jewish Ways to Welcome Baby Girls into the Covenant—New & Traditional Ceremonies* by Debra Nussbaum Cohen (Jewish Lights).

Of the hundreds of *brit bat* ceremonies in circulation, some are short and simple, others long and elaborate. Nevertheless, a few elements seem nearly universal.

Brit bat tends to have a four-part structure: introduction, covenant, naming and conclusion, and celebration. As you assemble your own ceremony, keep this general structure in mind.

Lillian R. G. Schapiro is a practicing obstetrician and gynecologist, who has been honored to fulfill the duties of *mohelet* in her community.

Through the Eyes of a *Mohelet:* An Interfaith *Bris*

LILLIAN R. G. SCHAPIRO

I am delighted that Chris and David decided to have a *bris* (circumcision ceremony). They are making an important commitment to each other, to the community, to their families, and for their son, Paul. Chris and David had many long discussions about the importance of religion to each of them. Initially, they wanted to let their child decide what religion he would be when he was older. "Can't we have a *bris* and a baptism?" they asked.

"No," I answered. "Your child can not have a baptism and be Jewish. If you baptize your child, your child is Christian. If you have a *bris*, you are entering your child into the Covenant between God and the Jewish people."

When Chris and David got married, they found a minister and a rabbi to co-officiate. They felt that they had a healthy respect for each other's customs. David celebrated Christmas with Chris' family, and Chris celebrated Passover with David's family. Chris prided herself on making a terrific *matzah brie* (unleavened bread and egg combination eaten during the week of Passover.)

When I arrive for the *bris*, Chris leads me through the guests to her son, Paul. I examine the baby. Jewish law puts health and safety above all. I confirm that the pediatrician gave the okay for a circumcision.

David shows me to the table where I will be doing the *brit milah*. On the table is a pillow, two *Kiddush* (blessing over wine) cups with kosher wine, A&D ointment, gauze, moist washcloths, and a clean diaper. Next to the table are two symbolic chairs, one for the prophet

Elijah and one for Moses' sister Miriam, to establish a connection with the messianic time.

I set up my equipment, put on my *yarmulke* (Jewish head covering worn as a sign of humility before God) and *tallit* (prayer shawl), and go to the kitchen to scrub my hands.

"Welcome," I begin. "We are here today to enter Paul into the Covenant. God commanded Abraham, the first Jew, to circumcise himself as a sign of the Covenant with God.

"Several people have positions of honor. Chris's sisters will be the *kvatterot* (people who carry the baby into the room). David's father, Saul, will be the *sandek* (traditionally a grandparent, who holds the baby for the *bris*)."

I chant in Hebrew and in English, "These are the chairs of Elijah and Miriam whose spirits are with us. May their remembrance be for good, bearing the promise of God's redemption. Blessed is he who comes here in God's name."

The *kvatterot*, Chris's sisters, enter with Paul.

I quote the passages from Genesis (Chapter 17) which command the circumcision.

David and Chris read a blessing, thanking God for the *Torah* (the first five books of the Hebrew Bible), for the warmth of family, and for the joy and privilege of parenthood.

After another blessing, I ask David for permission to perform the *bris* on his behalf. Not only is this a key time for comic relief, I am obligated to obtain his permission.

Chris asks if this is the point where she should leave if she doesn't want to see anything. I say yes and she slips away.

I place the baby gently on the pillow and instruct the *sandek* to place a wine-soaked gauze in the baby's mouth. When the baby sucks, I instruct Saul how to hold the legs. I swab with Betadine, then I place the first clamp. The baby screams. I continue, close the mogen clamp, and recite the blessing over circumcision.

David and Chris had to make a choice about which blessing I would say. One option is to simply bless the circumcision. The Reform Movement of the United States recognizes the child of any

Jewish parent, mother or father, to be a Jew as long as that child is raised as a Jew. Since Chris has not converted, they are also faced with a choice of doing a *bris* in the name of conversion. In that case, the *bris* would be followed by a visit to the ritual Jewish bath, witnessed by a jury of three rabbis. A *bris* with conversion would allow Paul to be recognized as a Jew by the world Reform and Conservative movements. After the blessing, I complete the circumcision.

David has a look of transformation. As a website designer, his daily life is far removed from this type of religious experience. He feels the power of the ceremony.

David calls Chris back into the room. Paul snuggles into his mother's embrace.

Chris and David read a prayer together. Then, everyone repeats after me, in Hebrew, a prayer for Paul. "As he has entered the covenant, so may he enter the blessings of *Torah, chuppah* (the Jewish wedding canopy), and a life of *maasim tovim* (good deeds)."

Avigail Lipman, a former dancer, lives in Berkeley, California, where she is the mother of two boys and is a Jewish educator.

Our Jewish Family: Two Sons, One Circumcised and One Not; a Scottish, Presbyterian, Circumcised Husband; and Me, the Jewish Mother

AVIGAIL LIPMAN

I hoped that I wouldn't have a boy. A girl would be so much easier—no *bris* (circumcision ceremony).

"But why circumcision?" asked my quiet, red-headed, polite,

of-Scottish-descent, not-Jewish, husband. As well he should, since we hadn't circumcised our first son when he was born.

Me: "But I wasn't involved in the Jewish community then. I'm in it now, we're raising our kids to be Jewish, they attend Jewish schools, we celebrate the Jewish holidays."

Him: "It's unnecessary, cruel, and barbaric. Judaism's supposed to be so ethical, moral, and civilized. Who's going to check, anyway?"

Me: "It's a way of welcoming a new male person into the tribe. It's a communal thing. Jews have done it for thousands of years. They're not any more violent or traumatized than anybody else."

Him: "This tribal stuff, that's the whole problem. It's the cause of so much violence, religious persecution, war, torture, suffering, inquisitions. My tribe's better than your tribe, so I'm going to kill you."

I remember this conversation and many more in the months of my pregnancy. Sometimes, in a haze of hormones and mother love, I could barely consider circumcision either. Other times, I felt that elemental pull of tradition impelling me to adopt more Jewish rituals in my life. The tug on the soul that led me down this path was leading me into the primeval heart of my people. I asked every Jewish mother I met about her experience with circumcision. Even the most unobservant circumcised their sons. It seemed unthinkable to them not to circumcise, even though they would never consider keeping kosher or going to a *mikvah* (ritual bath) or observing the other 613 *mitzvot* (commandments).

This is one *mitzvah* (commandment) that most of us seem to have remembered with great clarity from that moment standing at Mt. Sinai.

"We wanted him to look like his father, of course," one friend said.

"It has to do with cleanliness," said another.

"My parents insisted," another friend explained.

But our older son never once mentioned that he looked different from his Dad. After all, the obvious difference was size, not foreskin. He never once had a urinary tract infection. And my parents would never insist; they were simply happy that I was returning to Judaism;

after my years of New Age searching, they didn't really care what form my Judaism took. They, too, accepted circumcision unquestioningly, even though they were totally secular in every other way. What was it about circumcision that forced us beyond science, beyond reason, to embrace this elemental, blood ritual that seemed to define us as a people throughout our history? It became hard for me to defend this aspect of my religion to my husband. As a woman, how could I know what he would or wouldn't experience?

The complexities of Jewish law and communal practice were not what my husband bargained for sixteen years ago when we were first married. I became observant fairly suddenly about a year after our first son was born, and changed all the rules on him after the game had already started. Not easy, but he could see how wonderful Judaism was for our older son; the holidays, the *shul* (synagogue) we belong to, the schools. But circumcision just seemed to be too much, too final, too Jewish.

Would I still be a good Jew if I didn't circumcise my son? The circumcision of the infant is the father's obligation. If there is no father or the father is unwilling, it is the obligation of the *beit din* (rabbinic court). And what if there is no *beit din*, but only a very tense, hysterical mother? I comforted myself with the idea that if I didn't observe all of the *mitzvot*, I shouldn't be discouraged. If I can't do this one, there are 612 others.

My internal dialogue became saturated with thinking about *brit milah* (covenant of circumcision). Do we observe without questioning? Can we pick and choose which commandments we want to observe, take the easy ones, and toss out the politically incorrect or difficult ones? What about *kavannah* (intention)? Some people choose to observe the ritual of circumcision without the actual cutting. But to me that felt like cheating.

There was something about Jewish ritual that commanded that you actually do it, not sanitize it or spiritualize it. Certainly one can think about commandments and study and pray and question, but the thing itself has to be done, whether it's *tzedakah* (giving charity), lighting *Shabbat* (the Jewish Sabbath) candles, or *brit milah*. In fact, *brit milah* really symbolized a quality that I craved in my spiritual searches—the bridging of the bitter and the sweet, heaven and earth, being and doing. It's the *charoset* (sweet Passover dish of apples and honey) and the *maror* (Passover bitters), the sweetness of birth and the pain of the *milah*.

I began to realize how Jewish my life had become. Even married to a non-Jew, I felt I was living as rich and full a Jewish life as I could. I was managing this incredible balancing act. Part of what helped was belonging to a wonderful, modern Orthodox *shul*. What also helped was that we did not live near my husband's family (they were involved only peripherally in our lives), and they knew nothing of our dilemma.

"Everyone's circumcised now; it's not a symbol of being Jewish anymore," my husband added in amazement and perplexity as it seemed that I would not compromise on this one.

"We're living Jewish lives; this will make it easier for him as he grows up. I want this for him," I answered.

As it turned out, the decision seemed to be made, somewhat mysteriously, through God's grace, or our love for one another, or through sheer exhaustion. My husband acquiesced, not totally understanding, not knowing why, but I would have to attribute his decision to the strength of his love for me and our children and this sometimes strange entity that is our family.

So we have two sons, one circumcised, one not; a father who is not Jewish but is circumcised; and we are a Jewish family. Sometimes I relish this experiment that is our Jewish family; sometimes I wish it could be easier.

Rabbi Kenneth S. Weiss is the executive director of the Hillel Foundation of Greater Houston, and serves as the co-chair of the Berit Milah Board of Reform Judaism. He is married to Rabbi Ami Weiss, and they enjoy spending time with their sons, Eli and Joshua.

Welcoming a Son into an Interfaith Family: What Is a *Mohel* and How Do You Find One?

KENNETH S. WEISS

A child's birth brings with it all the hopes, dreams, and promises we have for that child. As with any life-cycle event, the birth can also bring a bit of uncertainty regarding how to appropriately celebrate such an important family occasion in a Jewish context. Especially for boys, whom we welcome into the covenant with God through *brit milah* (covenant of circumcision ceremony) on the eighth day after birth, the brief time we have to prepare for the ceremony adds a bit of anxiety. (A similar covenant ceremony for girls, called a *brit bat*, also can be held on the eighth day.)

Traditionally, the father is responsible for arranging his son's *brit milah*. Fortunately, with just a few phone calls, you can arrange for a *mohel* (person trained to perform ritual circumcision), who will take care of everything from calming nervous parents to helping arrange for a celebration after the *brit milah*.

A *mohel* (*mohelet*, if a woman) is a person—sometimes a rabbi, cantor, or physician—who has specialized training in the rituals, laws, and procedures surrounding ritual circumcision. Many *mohelim* and *mohelot* train through apprenticeships, while others are medical doctors who enroll in specific programs, such as the one offered by the Reform Movement. A circumcision performed without a *mohel* and the associated Jewish rituals is just a circumcision; it is not a *brit milah* and does not welcome the child into the Jewish covenant with God.

The best way to find a *mohel* is through a personal reference, whether a rabbi or a friend. Do not hesitate to call the local synagogue for the name of a *mohel*, even if you are not a member. If you choose a *mohel* through an ad, perhaps in a Jewish newspaper, be sure to get a few references. Reform Movement–trained *mohelim* and *mohelot* can be found through the *Berit Milah* Board of Reform Judaism website at www.rj.org/beritmila. If you live in a remote area in which a *mohel* is not available, then you can use a doctor and a knowledgeable Jew who can help you with the appropriate prayers.

The *mohel* is capable of conducting the entire *brit milah* ceremony, although often the parents will ask their rabbi or cantor to co-officiate with the *mohel*. If you have the desire, in addition to the time and energy, to personalize the *brit milah* service with special readings or participation from family members, be sure to ask the *mohel* if he or she will accommodate you. Some Orthodox *mohelim* will not co-officiate with liberal rabbis or perform a *brit milah* for a child of an intermarriage, although many will. Again, references can help you determine who is the most appropriate *mohel* for your son, and will save a lot of heartache on the day of the circumcision.

When looking for a *mohel*, you might want to keep the following in mind:

- Availability—Will the *mohel* be available around the anticipated date?
- Experience—Where did the *mohel* train and for how long?
- Type of restraint—Will someone need to physically hold the baby, or does the *mohel* use a restraining board?
- Anesthetic—Some *mohelim* will use an anesthetic, if desired by the family.
- Circumcision instrument—The circumcision may take more or less time depending on the surgical instrument the *mohel* prefers.
- Post-circumcision care—Is the *mohel* available for a follow-up visit, if necessary?

- Fee—This may range from $250 to $550, and may be covered by medical insurance.

Welcoming a son into Judaism is just the first of many opportunities a family has to raise a child as a Jew. Take care when selecting a *mohel*, but remember that a wealth of Jewish tradition waits for your family in the future. After the *brit milah*, help your son become involved in the life of a synagogue and the Jewish community.

Rabbi Bradley Shavit Artson serves as the dean of the Conservative Movement's Ziegler School of Rabbinic Studies at the University of Judaism, and is the author of *It's a Mitzvah! Step-by-Step to Jewish Living* (Behrman House and the Rabbinical Assembly).

On the Eighth Day, in Every Generation: A Guide to *Brit Milah*

BRADLEY SHAVIT ARTSON

At the age of eight days, every male among you shall be circumcised throughout your generations.

—Genesis 17:12

The *mitzvah* (commandment) of *brit milah* (ritual circumcision) is the oldest continually practiced ritual in the world. For almost four thousand years, beginning with our Patriarch Abraham, Jewish males have entered the covenant between God and the Jewish people through the *mitzvah* of *brit milah*. Even today, we link ourselves and our children to our Jewish heritage through this important *mitzvah*. *Am Yisrael Chai* (the Jewish people still thrives)!

In giving this gift to your son, you provide membership in an eternal people, bestow the blessings of holiness and sanctity, respond to the will of God, and affirm your family's commitment to the lofty moral standards of the *Torah* (the first five books of the Hebrew Bible) and our Jewish traditions. You publicly assert that the repeated attempts to destroy our people will not succeed, that your family provides an ongoing link to our sacred past and our messianic future.

Because *brit milah* is such an important commandment, it is also an occasion of great joy. We celebrate the arrival of a new Jewish baby through blessings, song, and a festive kosher meal after the ritual is complete.

FESTIVE OCCASION OR SURGERY?

Some Jewish parents feel tempted to have a hospital circumcision rather than a ritual one at home. Some even consider abandoning circumcision altogether. Often their motive—however ill-advised—is the health and well-being of the child.

Circumcision is safe. The American Academy of Pediatrics declared in 1989 that there are "potential medical benefits to circumcision." The California Medical Association overwhelmingly endorsed newborn circumcision.

A *mohel* (person trained to perform ritual circumcision) should do the circumcision. When a pediatrician does a circumcision in the hospital, it actually takes longer than when a *mohel* does it at home! It also loses the warmth and religious significance of *brit milah*.

To address both medical and religious concerns, the *mohelim* (plural of mohel) trained by Conservative Judaism are pediatricians who have received additional training in the religious laws of *brit milah*. They are able to assure the safety of your son while also making the ceremony—strictly in accordance with *halakha* (Jewish law)—one you will remember for the rest of your life.

Brit milah is not just a medical procedure. It is a sacred occasion, a moment of holiness for the Jewish people, and a peak event in your family's life. Only a *mohel* can make this moment both safe and sacred.

THE CEREMONY

The ceremony takes place on the eighth day following birth, during daylight. It is generally held in the home, unless the eighth day falls on the Sabbath or a holy day, in which case our communal practice is to transfer the ritual to the synagogue. In either case, a *minyan* (ten adult Jews) should be present to symbolically represent the entire Jewish people.

A special chair is designated as the "Chair of Elijah," the prophet who announces the coming of the Messiah. Since any Jewish baby just might be the Messiah, every *brit milah* becomes a messianic event, which we mark by inviting Elijah to join us.

Parents designate three honored participants: the *sandek* (traditionally one of the grandfathers, who sits with the baby during the *brit milah)*, and the *Kvatter* and *Kvatterin* (Godparents, who escort the baby into the room).

The obligation and privilege of circumcising the baby belongs to the parents, who recite a blessing before and after the actual circumcision. Since the responsibility is theirs, the parents also have the option of performing the final cut after the *mohel* has prepared and positioned the baby. Of course, the parents can decline this honor, choosing instead to let the *mohel* act as their agent. After the *brit milah* is complete, either the rabbi or the *mohel* blesses the child and bestows his name.

The event concludes with a festive meal. Since the meal itself is part of a religious celebration, it should be in accordance with *kashrut* (Jewish dietary laws). This is easily accomplished by serving only dairy foods (no meat or poultry), fish (except for shellfish), and breads and baked goods (that use only vegetable shortening).

THE MEANINGS OF *BRIT MILAH*

The birth of a child is one of the most exhilarating experiences in the world: the most God-like act a couple can perform. The birth of a child is also one of the most terrifying experiences: a weighty, lifelong responsibility for the welfare of another person, the recognition that we are mortal, the end of our youth. Blood is a powerfully ambivalent symbol, a symbol of life and of death. What more appropriate medium can there be to dramatize the ambivalence of childbirth than by requiring the ritualized shedding of blood to express the parents' hopes, fears, joy, and panic?

Ours is an age that no longer hears the divine voice in standards of sexual morality. We no longer know how to sanctify our sexuality, and many dispute whether we should even try. Is our sexuality a mere drive, or is it a gift of God, to be used to enhance the divine image in our loving partner? *Brit milah* represents the Jewish conviction that sexuality can be, must be, sacred. Sex can strengthen responsibility and commitment, or it can destroy trust and self-worth. By cutting away the foreskin, we pledge to harness sexuality to sanctify, to enjoy the gift of sex in an affirmative, life-supporting way.

Ours is an age of shattered male identity and friendship. *Brit milah* establishes a powerful, non-verbal bond between fathers and sons that constitutes an eloquent reminder to look to Judaism for a new/old vision of what is truly masculine: men who are profoundly spiritual; who value life-long learning; who are not ashamed to dance, to cry, or to sing; men who love their families and their faith; men who can nurture other people.

We still need *brit milah*.

6. Parenting in Interfaith Relationships

Andrea King is the author of *If I'm Jewish and You're Christian, What Are the Kids?* (UAHC Press) and supervises preschools for the Santa Monica School District.

"Why Isn't Daddy Jewish?" Questions Children of Intermarriage Ask

ANDREA KING

Ready or not, here they come—questions you've been waiting for, such as "Where do babies come from?" and "Why do we have toenails?" And some you may not be prepared for, such as "Why isn't Daddy Jewish?"

Children of intermarriage ask all the regular questions, along with others that reflect their special concerns. Every interfaith couple will have to find its own "right" answers, but you'll want to think about, discuss, and have answers ready for the questions that are most likely to come up.

If you have decided to raise your child with one religious identity, his questions will focus on why and how he is different from other people—family, friends, and even strangers: "I'm Jewish and you're Jewish, why isn't Daddy Jewish?" "We are a Jewish family; so why are Grandpa Joe and Grandma Eva Christian?" "Do you think the ice cream man is Jewish?"

These questions are part of a young child's efforts to make sense of the world; don't interpret them as budding bias or prejudice.

Answer them as simply as you can. Something like "Grandpa Joe is Christian because he grew up in a Christian family" will often suffice.

A child may have questions about her relationships with people of different religions: "Leslie is Jewish like me, and Tina is Christian. So how come Tina is my friend and Leslie isn't?" "Can I invite Jessie to my birthday party even though he's Christian?"

With these questions, your child is asking for your reassurance that it is okay to have friends of different religions.

At some point, usually between the ages of four and seven, children start asking specific questions about religious practices and beliefs. You may hear questions like these: "Richard says that Jews don't go to Heaven. Is that true?" "Why do (or don't) we have a Christmas tree?" "Why do I have go to church/synagogue?" "Do I/you/we believe in Jesus?"

By asking these questions, your child is collecting new information and integrating what other people believe.

Around fifth or sixth grade, you can expect your child to begin to challenge everyone and everything, including religion. Your child may ask, "If you chose this religion for me, why didn't you choose it for yourself?" Or conversely, "If your religion is good enough for you, why didn't you choose it for me?" "Why didn't you make me half-and-half?" "I'm really both religions, since you and Dad are different religions. Why can't we celebrate all the holidays?" "Do I have to be this religion forever? What if I want to change?"

Challenging your beliefs and practices is your child's way of finding out what is really important to you. It's his or her way of asking, "How much do you value my religious identity?" Interfaith couples should discuss in advance how to answer these questions. You might say something like "We chose this religion for you because we both agreed that it will give you good ideas about how to live your life." "I'm Christian because when I was a kid my mom and dad raised me as a Christian." "Mom and I believe that it would be too hard for one person to be two religions, so we talked about it and chose one for you." "Most people stay the same religion all their life, but everyone can choose what religion to be when they grow up."

The older child's questions about religious belief get stickier: "Will you and Mom go to the same place when you die?" "Do Christians and Jews have the same God?" "Why do they usually show only Christian things on TV?"

As always, direct, honest answers are best. And sometimes "I don't know" is the best answer.

If you decided to raise your child to be "bi-religious," you are likely to face a somewhat more complex set of questions: "If Jesus is the Messiah, how can I be Jewish? But if he's not, how can I be Christian?" "If I'm half-Christian, does that mean I half-believe in Jesus?" "How can I be Jewish and celebrate Christmas?"

The decision to raise a child with "the best of both religions" is usually based on the parents' need to continue certain celebrations, and ignores the child's need for a clear religious identity. Few young children are able to understand the ambiguity inherent in a bi-religious upbringing, no matter how inclusive and democratic it may seem.

Advice for parents: talk early, talk often, and agree on your answers in advance.

Jim Keen is a freelance writer based in Ann Arbor, Michigan. He has fifteen years of experience in an interfaith relationship. He is married with two children.

Raising My Kids Jewish, When I'm Protestant

JIM KEEN

When I was younger, I never even dreamed about the complications that I would have celebrating Christmas with my wife and kids. I naturally assumed that the holiday would be experienced exactly the way I grew up celebrating it—writing Santa a letter, maybe seeing him at the mall, learning about the story of Baby Jesus, Mary, Joseph— the whole nine yards.

Then in college I met a wonderful woman and married her. One thing I had never considered as a young daydreamer was that my future wife might be Jewish, but Bonnie was. Fortunately, she was also a smart woman who made sure that she and I had a game plan for when we had kids. We worked hard on an agreement for at least a couple of years and made sure it made sense to both of us before we got married. We knew it was very likely that details would change when our bundles of joy arrived, but at least we had a framework.

Today, Bonnie and I have two girls—a three-and-a-half-year-old and a newborn. We felt it was important to raise them in one faith, while making sure they learn about the other (faith). We talked about these decisions a lot, and for a variety of reasons decided to raise our children within the Jewish faith. During Jewish holidays I "help" them celebrate their festivities. I go along to temple, build the *sukkah* (wooden hut that Jews celebrate in during Sukkot, the fall harvest holiday), and help teach them the blessings on *Shabbat* (the Jewish Sabbath).

In return, they help me celebrate my Christian holidays. For instance, they assist me in decorating "Daddy's tree," and go to church with me on Christmas Eve. It may just seem like semantics, but it's important that our kids grow up thinking in these terms. They are taught that they are Jewish, but that it's okay for them to learn about and have fun with my holidays.

The first Christmases with my oldest daughter went just fine. She wasn't old enough yet to comprehend what was going on. However, during her third holiday season, my wife and I quickly learned that things would be different. It started one day in November when, out of the blue, she began asking members of our family, both nuclear and extended, "Are you Jewish?" Okay, so she was starting to categorize things. It's cool; she does this with her stuffed animals: "These three are bears, these two are froggies" etc. In early December, however, she realized that my parents (to whose house we travel to celebrate Christmas) were Protestant. She started putting two and two together in an appropriate three-year-old way, and realized that...it's the Christians—not the Jews—who celebrate this holiday with the tree and Santa. Well, this led to one big anxiety attack that she wasn't going to get *any* presents at Christmas this year. We calmed her anxiety by reminding her of all the nice Hanukkah presents she had just received, and how, in both holidays, it's much more important to give than to receive. Bonnie and I also explained to her that, as always, she will still get a few small presents on Christmas day.

Santa has probably been the greatest challenge that Bonnie and I have had in our parental game plan. Our strategy about Santa certainly has been the most revised. Each member of our family gives and receives some sort of present on Hanukkah and Christmas, no matter whose holiday it is. This is mainly to prevent someone from feeling left out. In addition, it's one more time we can teach the kids about the importance of giving, as well as receiving. Imagine being eight years old and watching your cousin of another religion amass great quantities of loot while you don't get diddly.

We also ask my parents to reinforce our philosophy. We want them to follow in step when we tell our children that "Yes, Santa brings you a couple of presents, but they are late Hanukkah presents because he knows you're Jewish." We have our children believing in Santa, for now, so they don't ruin the fun for their Protestant cousins. This may seem awkward for some interfaith couples, and it's certainly not for everyone. But, believe it or not, I think our family has made it through this holiday season relatively unscathed, with our bi-religious family backgrounds still intact. Fortunately for us, all of our parents have been extremely understanding and supportive. The most important thing in parenting is not what plan you put forward, but your consistency in implementing it. Besides, as my wife's stepmom pointed out, we won't make or break our children's Jewish education at Christmas. What matters most is how we reinforce their Jewish identity and teach them to be a good person every day of the year.

Rabbi Barbara Rosman Penzner serves Temple Hillel B'nai Torah in West Roxbury, Massachusetts. A graduate of the Reconstructionist Rabbinical College, Rabbi Penzner is married to Brian Rosman and is the mother of Aviva and Yonah.

So You Want to Be a Jewish Mother, but You're Not Jewish?

BARBARA ROSMAN PENZNER

So you want to be a Jewish mother, but you're not Jewish?

Welcome, fellow-traveler! You join a long line of venerated women, including Tzipporah, the wife of Moses, and Asenat, the wife of Joseph and mother of Manasseh and Ephraim, whose names are invoked in the blessing for our sons in the *Shabbat* (the Jewish Sabbath) evening ritual. These women receive little attention in our tradition, certainly less than Ruth, who is known for her choice to join the Jewish people. Yet, they raised up leaders for the Jewish people, as you yourself dream of giving your child a strong grounding in the Jewish people, Jewish values, and Jewish living.

You may be a lapsed Catholic, or a non-church-goer, or an active member of your church. You may know a little about Judaism, or have come to accept certain *Shabbat* and holiday rituals as a part of your life. You may be thinking conversion as a possibility, or you may be firm in your decision not to become Jewish yourself. Whoever you are, I want you to think about the following three principles:

- Every marriage is an inter-marriage. That is, every couple comes to understand that they bring to the marriage differences in religious and cultural background, differences in family style, differences in educational philosophy. Most of us are not even aware of or attuned to these differences. When a Jew marries someone who is not Jewish, the differences in religion become a focal point, even when you think you agree. When a Jew who was raised Reform marries a Jew raised in a traditional household, often similar issues arise: what synagogue (if any) should we join; which (or whose) rituals should we observe at home; whose parents host the holiday celebrations; who can help with Hebrew school homework; what foods do we serve on festivals? Consider yourself lucky that you are consciously addressing these questions, and they are not lurking in the background, waiting to blow up like a time bomb.

• You are not alone. Help is on the way. Ideally, you can find this help among like-minded people with whom you come into personal contact at work, in your neighborhood, in a synagogue or Jewish community group. Judaism cannot be lived in isolation. It literally requires a community, a quorum of Jews who look out for each other, who teach and model for each other. Don't be ashamed to talk to a rabbi—most of us meet people like you every day, and are open to listening, talking, and referring you to others. Take a class. If your synagogue or Jewish community provides an Introduction to Judaism class, that's a great place to start. These introductory classes do not usually demand an up-front commitment to conversion, and are often filled with born Jews who are still learning how to walk, or even crawl, as Jews. Consider delving into this rich tradition from whatever perspective most interests you: history, philosophy, ritual practice, *Torah* (the first five books of the Hebrew Bible) study. You prepared for childbirth, didn't you? You read books on child development, on caring for sick children, on choosing schools. Visit a Jewish bookstore or website and pick up a Jewish parenting book, or cassette tape, or video.

What if you are not a reader, or you just can't find time for a class? Even if you can, it helps to find a friend, a relative, someone who can be a mentor, who can show you how to make *latkes* (potato pancakes) and *matzah* (unleavened bread) balls, talk about how other families handle gifts during Hanukkah, share family bedtime and mealtime rituals. Find other couples or families to share your celebrations, including potluck *Shabbat* dinners.

Most people love sharing their stories and their traditions. Consider this a learning experience on behalf of your children, and for yourself as an engaged parent.

• You are not the only source for your child's Jewish life, but you are an important one. Whatever your child's Hebrew school may teach, while it can provide skills and introduce values and ideas, the lessons will not take root without your home support, enthusiasm, and willingness to experiment. Unfortunately, the statistics do not bode well for children whose formal religious training is their sole educational source of Judaism. On the other hand, you know more than you give yourself credit for. You can teach your child a lot about what you believe, and do not believe, about the importance of family, about belonging to a community. By taking classes yourself, you demonstrate to your child that Jewish education is not just for kids. The choices you make, about what to do and what *not* to do, teach by example.

You can create a Jewish home even if you yourself do not participate in Jewish rituals or groups. Look around your house. What makes a Jewish home? Ritual objects, art, a *mezuzah* (parchment scroll containing the *Sh'ma* prayer that is posted on doorposts of Jewish homes), Jewish books. Does your child have Jewish books, games, art? Does your dinner table discussion include what is happening at Hebrew school, what is happening in the Jewish world? Do you discuss your choices for giving *tzedakah* (philanthropy) with your children, and do these choices include Jewish organizations or causes? Judaism belongs in the home, and you can bring it there.

Remember, you are not alone. All of the above advice could just as easily work for someone who was born Jewish. We as a people believe in learning. That includes life-long personal growth. Treat this as one of your parenting paths. To learn to be a better parent, you want to model physical health and emotional wholeness. You also want to inspire your child to respect the culture that is his or her heritage, to love and connect to the people of the Jewish community, and to seek refuge in the spiritual treasures of Jewish life.

One caveat: you will likely find out that, hard as you try to create a Jewish home and provide a Jewish education for your children, many rabbis will hold to the definition that the child of a non-Jewish (non-converted) mother is not officially Jewish. In this case, the ritual of immersion in a *mikvah* (Jewish ritual pool) is a requirement for affirming your child's Jewish identity (usually called a conversion). Immersion of infants at six months is routine for many rabbis. Older children, ages eight and up, can have a positive experience as long as they are comfortable putting their heads under water. For boys, the question of circumcision will undoubtedly arise. Reform rabbis will most likely accept your child as a Jew without conversion rituals, as will many Reconstructionist rabbis. Be prepared to have this conversation with a rabbi, particularly if you are enrolling your children in a Jewish school, to prevent any misunderstanding.

Patricia Lombard works part-time as a writer and public relations consultant in Los Angeles. She was raised Catholic, but she and her husband are raising their two daughters Jewish. They are members of Temple Israel of Hollywood, where they have been active in creating the temple's outreach efforts to interfaith families.

A Catholic Mother of Jewish Children

PATRICIA LOMBARD

Sitting in a small Catholic church on a warm summer Saturday afternoon for the wedding of some friends, I am reminded that I haven't been here in a long time. It's a nice little church with simple wooden benches and lovely stained-glass windows. It's the windows that fascinate my youngest daughter. My husband teases that of course she'll like the church, and that after our careful decision to raise her and her sister Jewish, she'll marry a Catholic! Maybe, who knows, after all, she's only two. Right now our biggest concern is getting through the wedding without her screaming.

Still, in the quiet peace of this space I wonder how I will feel when my daughters get married in a temple, not a church. Who knows for sure, but ultimately, if my experience with our interfaith family is any indication, I will be happy for them if they are happy with their spouses and really love them, regardless of their religion.

Whenever there's a holiday or a reason to go to temple, or church for that matter, I always think about how complicated our life is in this arena. I look around at our friends and wonder if they've got it easier. One decided to convert, one doesn't practice any other religion, one doesn't have kids, one doesn't do anything...the inventory list goes on. Ultimately, after running through my mental Rolodex, I usually decide that while it's a bit messy, ours is the only path we could have chosen. I could not convert, and my husband needed to raise his children Jewish.

Soon summer will be over and it will be fall. Within a matter of weeks, Rosh Hashanah (Jewish New Year), Yom Kippur (Jewish Day of Atonement), and my oldest daughter's first days of first grade will be upon us. Our life is busy and full with all the Jewish holidays that are celebrated at her Jewish day school. In fact, it reminds me of my Catholic grade school. There was always some holiday or saint's day for which we would practice songs that we would sing for our parents as we marched into the church. Ironically, that's what I like about my daughter's school—the similarity to my Catholic experiences in which the church and the school were connected, and holidays were special and fun times because everyone came together to celebrate.

At my daughter's Jewish day school, they connect life and spirituality in everything they do. It's more intense than I think things were when I was growing up. Hopefully my children will feel grounded and won't be wandering around the world looking for a place to belong.

The rabbis who teach my two daughters, Emily and Alexandra, are more spiritual than the priests and nuns who taught us. My daughters' teachers inspire all of us to push the limits of our holiday experiences and really make them special times. Even though it's not my religion, the message resonates because our time as a family is special and all too limited.

Perhaps my greatest frustration around the Jewish holidays is that my husband doesn't make enough time, in my opinion, to really enjoy the days with the children. And to complicate matters, his parents and immediate family don't seem to celebrate in a spiritual way. This is especially poignant to me on Rosh Hashanah and Yom Kippur, since the message of forgiveness and rejuvenation is so central to these days. I find it painful that holidays are sometimes used to express disapproval of our marriage and choices when his parents won't come to our home for holiday celebrations. On the other hand, I suppose one benefit of not having observant in-laws is they can't tell you what to do. Still, it seems sad because they are missing this annual opportunity to start over and try to get it right next year.

While I often feel that I am the only one who is contemplating and "celebrating" these Jewish holidays and I am the least qualified to do so, I must say that each year I get more and more confident that I will give my girls the sense of belonging and joy that can come from these special days. This sense of belonging and joy is a gift that my parents gave me, in a different faith. I have learned to adapt my spirituality to these occasions, to find a middle ground for all of us to stand on while filling the void my husband's family leaves.

Instead of relying on my husband's family traditions, I have chosen to find ways to celebrate and enjoy these holidays without feeling left out. I am becoming an expert at creating our own holiday traditions. With the help of both my Jewish and interfaith friends, we enrich our holiday experiences from year to year by sharing the traditions of others, doing more ourselves and getting better at it, and learning more each year as our children learn more in school. We all struggle together to balance our expectations for each holiday with the reality of spending time with our less-than-perfect families. I think this struggle is the same no matter what your religion.

Ultimately as parents, each of us reviews what we bring to the table—religion, life skills, coping strategies, family traditions—and we try to pick only the best parts to share with our children. Being in an interfaith family means that we must examine the things on the table more often, and sometimes we have to find ways to celebrate someone else's ideas as our own. Occasionally, it's very hard, but the most difficult part is that it's never over. There's always another holiday or a wedding, something to remind us that we have to keep working on it.

Debra B. Darvick is a freelance writer based in Michigan. Her book *This Jewish Life: Stories of Discovery, Connection and Joy* will be published by the CCAR (Central Conference of American Rabbis) Press, Fall 2002.

How to Talk to Your Kids about Jesus

DEBRA B. DARVICK

It's not easy for Jewish parents to talk about Jesus Christ. Many of us possess sketchy knowledge of Christianity and know even less about the very real theological differences between our two religions. We want our children to be respectful of other faiths, but what we Jews do know about Christianity is often shadowed by historic anti-Semitic experiences. It can get quite complicated to explain to a young child who Jesus was and why Jews don't believe in him.

"We're nervous about talking about Jesus," says Rabbi David Wolpe, "because we live in a Christian society and we're afraid that we'll lose our kids to Christianity. It's hard talking about Jesus Christ because throughout history, relations have been so charged and difficult. It doesn't evoke the same reaction to have your child ask, 'Who was Buddha?' But it's not fair to put our nervousness onto our kids."

Wolpe advises parents to give as simple an explanation as possible. "For parents of real young kids, it's enough to say, 'Jesus was a Jewish man who lived 2,000 years ago and taught a number of things about Judaism and faith. Some we agree with and some we don't. After his death some of his followers created a religion around his personality, Christianity.'"

Particularly in families in which one parent is not Jewish and the decision has been made to raise the children as Jews, parents may want to explain that, while some other people have different beliefs, Jews believe that Jesus was a truly great, wise, and kind human being, yet still a man with faults and virtues. The discussion can get knotty when children try to sort out the issue of Jesus, the person, and Jesus, the Messiah. Christians believe that Jesus was the Messiah. Jews do not. As Rabbi Wolpe phrased it, "The difference is that Jews believe that when the Messiah comes the world will be different. We believe that if the Messiah had come, the world wouldn't be as messed up as it in fact is. That is the central difference."

Rabbi Barry Diamond, educator at Temple Emanuel in Dallas, Texas, advises parents to listen closely to make sure they understand what their children are asking. "A Jewish parent can say that from what we know, Jesus was a teacher who sometimes agreed with the rabbis and sometimes argued with the rabbis. He may have thought he was the Messiah, but in Judaism, the Messiah is not the son of God, but is more like a king or ruler."

Professor Paula Fredricksen, Aurelio Professor of the Appreciation of Scripture at Boston University, explains that "Even though Christians believe Jesus was the Messiah," she says, "and has come once, it's clear that the age of peace didn't come. They believe that the second time will be the time of peace."

Another confusing aspect is some Christians' belief that Jesus is a child of God. But as Professor Fredricksen notes, "There is incredible variety in Christian churches on this point. The Roman Catholic

Church believes that Christ is a second divine entity. But there are other Christian churches who believe that Jesus is an exceptional person and because of that was granted extra divinity."

For parent Don Cohen, his daughters' questions about Jesus surface around Christmas time and even, he says, "when they see someone wearing a cross or when we drive by a house with a Madonna on the front lawn." Cohen approaches the issue from two directions. First, he tells his daughters that "Just as some Jews use the phrase *HaShem* for God's name, Christians use the name Jesus for God. I also explain that for Christians, God came in a human form and had a name, but that this is not a Jewish belief."

"I am loath to say one religion is superior to the other," Cohen adds. "I do say that Christianity needs to be respected, but it is not our belief. It gets tricky when my daughters want to know which one is right. I say that one is right for Christians and one is right for us."

Rabbi Diamond sometimes takes the discussion in another direction by making this distinction: "Christians believe that God lives in Heaven and people live on earth, and that God gave Jesus to the world to save it. Jews also believe that God is in heaven and people are on earth, but for us, *Torah* (the first five books of the Hebrew Bible) is our main connection to God, and it's for instruction, not salvation."

And how might a parent handle the Jews-killed-Jesus issue, should this age-old accusation rear its head? Even though the Catholic Church has finally recanted that belief, it is a lie that perseveres. Professor Fredricksen, a Jew-by-Choice, offers a clear-cut reply should your children bring this home from school or the playground one day: "Jesus died on a cross, and when he died, only Romans were killing people like that." It might help to explain to children, she adds, that sometimes when we're mad at someone we say bad things about them: "A lot of Christians blamed Jews for Jesus' death because the Jews didn't want to be Christian."

The very name Jesus Christ can make some moms and dads very nervous, but it might help to keep in mind that talking about Jesus does give parents the opportunity to talk about Jewish values and

Jewish identity. In that light, questions about Jesus Christ become not a threat but the door to greater Jewish awareness. And every Jewish parent can use more of that.

Wendy Case has been a clinical social worker for over twenty-five years. She works with individuals, couples, and families in a private psychotherapy practice.

Parenting My Jewish Children in Our Interfaith Family: A Non-Jewish Parent's Point of View

WENDY CASE

I am the mother of two young adults. My husband was the president of our temple. Both of our children became *B'nai Mitzvah* (assumed the obligations and privileges of adult members of the Jewish community). We regularly have a *Shabbat* (the Jewish Sabbath) dinner and attend *Shabbat* evening services. I have served as the co-chair of our temple's social action committee for many years.

Many people would say that I lead a very Jewish life. However, when the random form inquiring about my religious affiliation presents itself, I am stumped. I am a non-Jew who does live a Jewish life, a major part of which includes parenting Jewish children. When I chose this life, my sole concern about this situation was that I would feel different from my children in a very fundamental way, as my father had during my own childhood.

As a family therapist, I believe that the past provides clues for understanding the present. I was raised in a less pronounced variation of an interfaith family. My mother was Episcopalian, my father

Congregationalist—two different branches of Protestantism. My mother, sister, and I attended the Episcopal church. I recall being a regular churchgoer, especially as a child; singing in the choir; going to Sunday school and church events. I remember at least one year that I went to church every Tuesday morning during Lent before going on to school. Church was a very comforting place for me. I loved the structure and predictability of the service in the prayers and hymns that were familiar to me. I also distinctly remember how palpably uncomfortable my father was when he occasionally, for special events, came to church with us. As a sensitive child, I felt uncomfortable for him.

As I passed into my adolescence and young adulthood, I became less actively connected to the church. I started dating my husband in my late adolescence. Our relationship was characterized by some of the typical dilemmas of interfaith dating at the time. We were acutely aware that my husband's parents would not approve. Indeed, when we announced our intention to marry after six years of dating, they were not particularly happy about the development. As eager-to-please second children, we tried hard to accommodate everyone's sensitivities in the wedding ceremony. A judge officiated, and the ceremony took place in a lovely, non-religious room in my husband's college with the reception in an adjoining courtyard. The setting was neutral but had a special meaning for my husband and myself. Both sets of parents seemed comfortable with this arrangement.

I was always completely aware of how important my husband's Judaism was to him. From the beginning, it was clear that we would raise our children as Jews. Actually, this was not a serious problem. For me, it was just important that my children have a faith. Despite the heartaches of our interfaith relationship, which primarily entailed finding ways to include the special rituals and traditions of our two religions without over-compromising or offending the other, we were a good match: I brought the spiritual component of religion and my husband brought the peoplehood of Judaism.

In my own parenting, I wanted to spare my children the experience of a parent uncomfortable with the other parent's religion and the designated religion for the family. Therefore, over the more than twenty-five years since my husband and I announced our intention to marry, I have had an on-going commitment to learn about Judaism and consequently become more comfortable with it. Before marrying, I took conversion classes, although with the explicit goal of education, not conversion. Shortly thereafter, I took a class to learn how to read Hebrew.

We initially joined a temple in which the worship service was almost excruciatingly foreign to me, and I felt very self-conscious and out of place. For several years, we worshipped in a local university, but I missed the sense of community and rootedness of a more established congregation. After some searching, we joined a Reform temple located in our neighborhood, across the street from our children's elementary school. In this temple, I began to experience the peacefulness I recalled from my childhood experience of worship. Each year I become more familiar with the prayers and songs, and notice my ability to read and sing along expand. I now feel a comfort reminiscent of my childhood, is the structure and predictability of the service. I have even found a home for my spirituality. In fact, I have begun to realize that my children were not the only beneficiaries of my on-going efforts.

Why have I chosen to emphasize my own spiritual journey in these musings about parenting in an interfaith family? I believe that our sense of ourselves as people strongly infuses our parenting. Our thoughts and feelings precede our action (as well as at times inaction). Interfaith parenting, which encompasses issues of identity, is complex and fraught with confusing thoughts and emotions, some originating from our earlier experiences of religion. I believe that it is important to honestly wrestle with these issues. We owe this to ourselves as well as to our children. Sometimes this involves taking different paths and maintaining the flexibility to change direction until the fit feels right.

After more than twenty-five years of searching, I do not feel that I have reached all my destinations. However, I know that I have provided not only my children but also myself with the foundation for an evolving role that religion can play throughout the inevitable vicissitudes of our lives.

Edmund Case is the publisher of InterfaithFamily.com. He is intermarried and is the husband of Wendy and father of Emily and Adam Case.

Parenting My Jewish Children in Our Interfaith Family: A Jewish Parent's Point of View

EDMUND CASE

When my daughter Emily was sixteen, she started to date an observant Conservative Jew. One night she was invited for *Shabbat* (the Jewish Sabbath) dinner. By that point she knew all about our Reform Movement's policy on patrilineal descent, under which she is recognized as a Jew. However, I thought I should remind her that in the eyes of some other Jews, because her mother is not Jewish she would not be considered Jewish at all. When I did point that out, Emily defiantly stated, "No one is going to tell me that I'm not Jewish!" This was a bittersweet moment for me. I was happy and proud of how strongly she felt. But I was, and still am, pained about this—why would any Jew want to reject, to exclude from the Jewish people, my caring, intelligent, beautiful, and very Jewishly committed daughter?

I've talked quite a bit with Emily, who is now in her twenties, about how her Jewish identity was formed. She remembers feeling, when she was little, that she was "half and half." She also remembers that while she and I were walking hand in hand one day, I told her that she wasn't half and half, that her Mom and I had decided that she was all Jewish. She says that from that point on, that's what she felt. It's hard to believe that it was that simple, but I guess that our children do pay attention to what we say, and at least some of the time it has a real impact.

I do think it's important for parents to make sure to communicate their thoughts on religious identity to their children. When Emily's *Bat Mitzvah* (the ceremony in which an individual chooses to assume the obligations and privileges of an adult member of the Jewish community) approached, she asked, "Why is it so important to you, anyway?" (By then she had stopped accepting everything I said.) I remember being really taken aback, because I assumed that she knew why it was so important to me. But I hadn't told her. So I ended up writing a long letter to her, about how I loved my immigrant grandparents, how I experienced some anti-Semitism growing up, how I was one of the rare people who enjoyed Hebrew school and Jewish learning, how I felt about Israel, and more. I learned that we can't expect our children to know what's in our heads if we don't express it to them explicitly.

I'm pretty confident that both Emily and my son Adam have strong Jewish identities. Emily was the co-leader of the Yale Hillel Reform Chavurah one year. Adam has read most of the novels of Leon Uris and Herman Wouk, and every once in a while, when he hears a positive story in the media about Jews, he says, "There's another one for *us*." He loved Israel when we went as a family, and he returned on a NFTY (National Federation of Temple Youth) trip.

I'm very fortunate in that my wife does not practice another religious faith and fully participates in our family's Jewish experiences, even though she has not converted to Judaism. We are as close to my wife's parents as we are to mine, and our children clearly know that their mother and her parents come from a different tradition. They're certainly reminded of this every Christmas, which we have always spent at my in-laws. Yet, they aren't confused about being Jewish themselves.

If you had looked at our behavior early in our marriage, you might have wondered whether our children would have a Jewish identity. I always had in the back of my mind that I wanted the children to be Jewish, but in their earliest years I didn't do much about it. For example, when my daughter was born, I didn't even think about giving her a Hebrew name, and my parents didn't raise the subject either. She got her Hebrew name one day at the Boston Children's Museum, which was having a "multicultural" festival. One of the activities involved learning the Hebrew name that had the same meaning as your English name. The person at the booth looked up the meaning of the name "Emily," found that it means "industrious," then looked up the Hebrew name that means industrious, and found "Tirzah." She then calligraphied "Tirzah" in Hebrew, and we still have the paper that Emily was handed that day. (When she was ten, we had our rabbi over and he did a somewhat more official naming ceremony for her and Adam.)

I was never comfortable with the idea of having a Christmas tree in our house, but when the kids were pre-school age, we did have a Norfolk pine all year long, and at Christmas time we did put a few ornaments on it. By the time the children started school, though, they also started at Jewish religious school. By then, I think all of us were uncomfortable even with that degree of "decorating" a tree, and we stopped. Looking back now, our Norfolk pine with ornaments seems a little foolish. But the point is that our attitudes and our practices evolved. When our children were younger, my wife and I were still negotiating how we would adjust our individual traditions, and that takes time. I think that my agreeing to put some ornaments on the Norfolk pine showed my wife that I respected her tradition and helped to enable us to reach a mutual decision later on.

Although my children have strong Jewish identities now, one can never know what the future will bring, and I suppose the real test of their Jewish identity will be whether they choose to raise their own children as Jews. But our experience to date shows that it is very possible, and extremely rewarding, to raise Jewish children in a Jewish interfaith family.

Wendy Case has been a clinical social worker for over twenty-five years. She works with individuals, couples, and families in a private psychotherapy practice.

Musings about Raising Children of a Different Religion

WENDY CASE

When I was invited to write an article about giving my children "permission" to be a different religion than myself, it occurred to me that I had never conceptualized the issue of our interfaith family in that way. More accurately, I think that I gave my husband "permission" to raise our children in a religion different than mine. This was done long before we considered having our children. Although at the time I had some qualms that I would feel different from the rest of my family, that feeling never materialized. Recently, however, I learned that the difference in our religious identities was a factor for my daughter.

I experience myself as a non-Jew who leads a very Jewish life, regularly having *Shabbat* (the Jewish Sabbath) dinner and attending services, actively participating in my temple's Social Action committee, and celebrating Jewish holidays in the same fashion as my Jewish husband. I do not actively practice another religion. In fact, I might go as far as to say that Judaism is my religion. But because I do not experience the ethnicity of being a Jew, it is not my identity, and therefore I have not chosen to convert to Judaism.

We chose to live in a town with a significantly large Jewish population. My children count many Jews among their friends. We chose our temple in part because it is in our neighborhood. For many years, Emily and Adam and numerous friends crossed the street from their elementary school to go to Hebrew school. Both children have become *Bat* and *Bar Mitzvah* (taken on the obligations and privileges of adult members of the Jewish community), as well as confirmed. We have traveled to Israel as a family.

I would summarize our approach as commitment to a Jewish lifestyle. I believe that in general, actions rather than words are more powerful in conveying values to children. I believe that my non-verbal message has been that Judaism is a religion worth practicing, that it is enriching to one's life, and that I have chosen to enrich my life as well as my family's life with it, despite the fact that I am a non-Jew. I did not focus on being a different religion from my children, and therefore I did not think about talking explicitly to them about it.

Given my attitude and philosophy, I was surprised to read Emily's responses last year to questions regarding her religious identity. My husband was writing a paper on the development of identity, and he interviewed her via e-mail. Her responses were interestingly inconsistent. On the one hand, she was adamant about her Jewishness. She says, somewhat defiantly, that "my religion really comes from within me and it really doesn't matter what others think." She goes on to say that she "is insulted when people look down on her or do not recognize her as a legitimate Jew." On the other hand, Emily writes to her father, "I don't think my identity as a Jew is as enormous a part of my personal identity as it is for some people. I feel more connected to (Mom) when I don't see myself as a Jew first and foremost. Maybe it's that I need to compromise in a way because I am not the product of two Jews, so I can't see myself entirely as a Jew in some respects. Although I don't know if I really feel that way, because I do think of myself as fully being a Jew, I just think this is not the basis of my identity."

I believe, as do some important researchers on the subject, that children identify with their same-gender parent. This religious difference creates a dilemma for both Emily and me in terms of the integrity of our identity. Although we both practice Judaism, I am a non-Jew and she is a Jew. This is a reality that is not easily bridged.

Moreover, I am concerned that Emily's confusion regarding her religious identity gets played out in dating situations. While it certainly would be hypocritical to suggest that she or her brother date only Jews, my husband and I have consistently taken the position with our children that if it is important to them to have a Jewish life and family, then marrying another Jew would maximize that possibility. Of the young men Emily has dated seriously, only one (the first) was Jewish.

As I write this article, it occurs to me that perhaps my husband and I make intermarriage look simple. My children are unaware of the early years of our marriage and the adaptations, compromises, uncertainty, and awkwardness that we went through. I certainly want to give my children permission to give important consideration to their relationship with their Judaism in connection with their prospective partner's religious identity.

As I close these "musings," I grapple with the reality that my daughter does not feel she has complete "permission" to be Jewish despite all of my non-verbal messages that Judaism is a religion worth practicing. With the benefit of hindsight, I wish that I had talked more explicitly with her.

7. *Bar* and *Bat Mitzvah* in an Interfaith Family

Rabbi Daniel Siegel is the rabbinic director of ALEPH: Alliance for Jewish Renewal and, with his life-partner Hanna Tiferet, co-spiritual leader of B'nai Or of Boston.

Of *Bar* and *Bat Mitzvahs* and Non-Jewish Parents

DANIEL SIEGEL

Can you raise a Jewish child in a home with only one Jewish parent? Could that child become *Bar* or *Bat Mitzvah* (assume the obligations and privileges of an adult member of the Jewish community)? If I officiated as the rabbi, would I be giving approval to mixed marriages, eliminating the last remaining arguments for marriages between Jews? Not long ago, my answers were those that you would expect from a rabbi. No, you can't raise a Jewish child in a home where one key person does not participate actively in the rhythms of Jewish life, can't make *Kiddush* (the sanctification of the Sabbath or holiday over a cup of wine), or recite the blessings when called to the *Torah*. The *Bar* or *Bat Mitzvah* of the child would be spiritually empty, the shell of a ceremony without content. Maybe if the non-Jewish parent had decided to become Jewish, even if after the child was born, then it might be possible. But otherwise, it just won't work.

Working as a rabbi in a small town with only one congregation is a great way to have your beliefs and preconceptions challenged.

J. moved up from Florida between the *Bar Mitzvah* of her son and the *Bat Mitzvah* of her daughter. J. is their non-Jewish mother, divorced from their father just after the *Bar Mitzvah*. Both parents moved to the same town to share the parenting of their children.

For a while, it didn't even occur to me that J. wasn't Jewish. She was the one who took out the family membership in our community and made sure that her daughter was enrolled in our religious school. She came to services and volunteered for committees. As the date for her daughter's *Bat Mitzvah* neared, she shared the tape of her son's *Bar Mitzvah* with me. The rabbi at their previous synagogue had treated her as though she were Jewish, calling her to the *Torah* (scroll containing the first five books of the Hebrew Bible) with a Hebrew name, having her recite the blessings, and speaking of their family as a unit even as the divorce was already pending. Something didn't feel right.

It was J. much more than the father who guided her daughter through the *Bat Mitzvah* process. Though she had chosen not to become Jewish herself, she supported both her family and our community in a way that made that decision totally understandable and nearly irrelevant. Long after the *Bat Mitzvah*, she remained an active and contributing member of our community.

B.'s situation was different. His wife is strongly conscious of her Jewishness. There was never any question that their home was a Jewish one, that their son would attend religious school, that he would become *Bar Mitzvah* in a public ceremony.

What was extraordinary about B. was revealed during one of the classes I gave for the *Bar* and *Bat Mitzvah* families of his son's year. I don't remember exactly what we were discussing, but I guess he thought people were being ambivalent and giving me a hard time. All of a sudden he stood up and addressed the group, saying something like: "My son is Jewish. I am not. The fact that he is Jewish fills me with pride. I think the Jewish people are very special, with a belief system that results in wonderful families, deeply ethical behavior, and a meaningful religious practice. While I don't want to become Jewish myself, I deeply admire the Jewish people and am proud to be part of raising a Jewish child. And you should feel that way yourselves, since it is your people and heritage." And he sat down.

B. went on to give the parents' talk to his son at his *Bar Mitzvah*, reminding his son of the wonderfulness of his Jewish heritage. And, several years later, he again spoke up when our steering committee invited couples in mixed marriages to share their thoughts about our community. He reviewed his feelings of pride in his son's Jewishness and then voiced his concern that after all the effort and expense to which they had gone to instill a strong sense of Jewishness in him, he hoped he would find someone Jewish to marry!

There was a time, just before Christianity became the alternative to Judaism, when many non-Jews hung out with Jews, particularly at synagogues. They liked the intellectual honesty and excitement of Judaism, appreciated our rituals, understood the profound beauty and significance of the Sabbath, and honored the love we showed in our families. But they didn't want to become Jews. Most likely, they didn't want to be circumcised (if they were men); and perhaps learning Hebrew was too much for them; or cutting themselves off from their own families was more than they could bear. In turn, we acknowledged their presence and called them *gerei toshav* (something like resident aliens in the United States or landed immigrants in Canada). While they weren't fully initiated into Judaism and adopted into our tribe, we felt close to them, trusted them, and learned from them.

I see J. and B. and others I have had the privilege to meet in my lifetime as modern day *gerei toshav*. Unlike many of my colleagues, I don't give them Hebrew names and call them to the *Torah* as though they were Jews. And unlike many other of my colleagues, I do call them to the *Torah* together with the Jews they love, by their English names, and honor them as the supportive parents they are, lending their energies and influence to our own Jewish renewal in this generation. I confess that, at times, I wish they would join us completely and simplify things. At the same time, I appreciate how they help me stretch, become more accepting, and practice trust in a loving God who helped us get this far and will help us take the next steps as well.

One last anecdote. B. was a part of our cemetery committee as we struggled to decide what it meant for our little Jewish community to have its own burial land. He wanted to know where we would bury him. Could he and his wife be together in the main part of the cemetery or would we have to either bury them separately or in a special corner? I thought deeply about his question and realized that he had become such an important teacher in my life that I would be happy to be buried next to him myself. So we decided that the main part of the cemetery would belong to the members of our community, recognizing that some of our members were not themselves Jews.

Martha Little is a psychotherapist in Moab, Utah, and runs a women's wilderness adventure company called Soultreks.net. She spends her free time writing and adventuring in the deserts of the Southwest.

Attending My Niece's *Bat Mitzvah:* A Non-Jewish Perspective

MARTHA LITTLE

I am part of an interfaith family.

Writing this is strange, because it makes me define my own spiritual life and label a tradition that is by nature interfaith. I practice Buddhist meditation at a Catholic altar, and celebrate Passover with friends each year. Yet, in writing this essay I became aware that I don't know the distinctly Jewish language surrounding the *Bar Mitzvah* (the ceremony in which an individual chooses to assume the obligations and privileges of an adult member of the Jewish community). I wondered what the verb is: is it "to be *mitzvahed?*" Is the place of the ceremony called a chapel or a synagogue? I feel a kind of closet shame that I don't know more about my relatives' religion. It is shame that makes me not ask simple yet obvious questions. Shame that prevents me from knowing more about my closest relations.

I feel the double bind of being in an interfaith family—that those I love deeply have another life, another language as foreign to me as Chinese, beliefs and ceremonies that have never been explained to me. The shame of not understanding keeps me isolated and silent.

Going to my niece's *Bat Mitzvah* meant going to an unknown. Growing up with a splattering of Presbyterianism and Catholicism, I associated organized religious ceremonies with dread and loathing— having to wear poorly fitting clothes, having to sit still for inordinate amounts of time, having to listen to boring and pedantic "preaching." I associated such ceremonies with hearing only "blah blah blah" and waiting for the rush to the door at the end.

As I entered the small chapel that would host my niece's *Bat Mitzvah*, I felt the familiar dread of religious scrutiny. Am I doing the right thing, wearing the right outfit, saying the right words, showing the right degree of sacred deference? My self-conscious scrutiny melted away as I looked up to see the radiant face of my woman/child niece. It was then I realized she was no longer a child. This person I had cradled as a baby, taken through woods as a toddler, and swum rivers with was now standing in front of a host of people with the grace of an exceptional adult. I felt a torrent of feelings—outrage that her childhood had gotten away from me, sad that I had missed so much of her growing up, proud that she had become such a charmed individual.

As I settled back into the stiff bench of the pews, I started to actually listen to the "blah blah blah" of the rabbi, and as the words came into focus I realized that he was celebrating this very thing. He was putting words of honor to this blossoming orchid and offering condolences to those of us who felt so sharply the loss of her childhood.

Her parents stood up with tears in their eyes and voiced their loving permission for her to grow up and blossom. At that moment I felt a solidarity of family that I had never before felt quite so acutely. As I looked around to my Catholic father, Presbyterian mother, atheist brother, agnostic sisters, Jewish sister-in-law and nephew, I felt a unity of spirit. We were honoring one of our own in a passage that both frightened and thrilled us. The pomp and circumstance of the ceremony both mattered and didn't—without it we would not have gathered from all over the country. The very nature of celebration lends itself to worship. The nature of faith lends itself to understanding diversity in the context of love. I did not feel that there was more than one kind of faith in that room at that moment.

As I left the chapel, I didn't rush for the exit with a sense of claustrophobic urgency. In fact, I wanted to linger and take something from that ceremony back to my life. I left with the exhilarating knowledge that I had been part of a ceremony celebrating the difficult journey into adulthood, and that I was not alone in my conflicted feelings about my niece growing up. The shared sense of beliefs far outweighed any feelings of separation. The very word "interfaith" connotes a dialectic of belief that I didn't experience on this day. I held my niece in an embrace, feeling for the first time resolved to let her grow into the person she had become, with all her fresh multifaceted faith in this world as a hopeful place to be.

Rabbi Barbara Rosman Penzner serves Temple Hillel B'nai Torah in West Roxbury, Massachusetts. A graduate of the Reconstructionist Rabbinical College, Rabbi Penzner is married to Brian Rosman and is the mother of Aviva and Yonah.

Creating a Comfortable *Bar* or *Bat Mitzvah* for Intermarried Families

BARBARA ROSMAN PENZNER

When it comes to Jewish celebrations, every family is an intermarried family. That is, every family combines different backgrounds, expectations, memories, and baggage. Sometimes the gap between the two families is narrow and hardly noticeable; other times it looms and threatens to become another family member to be placated.

Bar and *Bat Mitzvah* (the ceremonies in which an individual chooses to assume the obligations and privileges of an adult member of the Jewish community) are the kinds of celebrations that appear to feature the child first and the family second. Whether preparing for the service or the party, the child ought to be at the center—but at the center of what? The center of a synagogue community, ideally, in which she or he suddenly receives recognition as a member who "counts"—counts in the *minyan* (the ten people needed to read from the *Torah*, the scroll containing the first five books of the Hebrew Bible), counts as a skilled reader of *Torah* or service leader, counts as a voice in the congregation, an individual with needs beyond child care. From a rabbi's perspective, that is the "achievement" of the *Bar* or *Bat Mitzvah* ceremony, not a performance or a show, but a welcome to a new young adult who is ready to take on more Jewish responsibility as a caring and contributing member of the community.

But we also know that the *Bar* or *Bat Mitzvah* event brings families into focus, highlighting joys and sorrows, those who attend and those who are absent, those who feel "comfortable" with the service and those who don't. Attending to family needs, from hotel rooms to place cards, can enter the foreground, often overshadowing the message and the meaning of the *simcha* (celebration).

There are two sets of people to consider, the immediate family and the guests (everyone else). The immediate family, including parents of the *Bar* or *Bat Mitzvah*, should, wherever possible, have special roles in the service. Find out what parts non-Jews can play in your synagogue. Remember, every synagogue is different, even within a particular Jewish movement or stream (Reform, Conservative, Reconstructionist, Orthodox, Humanistic). For example, in many Reconstructionist congregations, non-Jews can take non-speaking parts, like opening the ark or wrapping the *Torah*, or can lead English readings, but may not lead the congregation in the *Torah* blessings or other prayers that assume a formal commitment to Judaism.

The key is what is appropriate, both from the synagogue's point of view and that of someone who has not declared membership in the Jewish people. Sometimes, a parent is simply a proud parent and doesn't need to play a religious part, just a family part. In many synagogues, a non-Jewish parent will join the family group on the *bimah* (podium) for the rabbis' blessing. In other cases, one parent participates in the ceremony while the other takes the limelight at the reception.

Ask the rabbi how the family can be treated as an organic unit—how much the synagogue will allow, and how much the non-Jew is willing to do! For example, often parents are offered an opportunity to speak to the child, and one does not necessarily have to be Jewish to do this. In some synagogues, both parents can come up to the *bimah* for an *aliyah* (recite the blessing over the *Torah* reading). The Jewish parent may recite the blessing, which is an affirmation of Jewish commitment, while the non-Jewish parent may stand by.

Most *Bar* or *Bat Mitzvah* services today will have non-Jews as guests. In an intermarried family, many of the non-Jewish guests will undoubtedly be close family. Here are a few ideas for trying to help them—with the understanding that different people will respond to your efforts in different ways.

1. Give out as much information as you can to non-Jews who attend. You can explain the service, the *Shabbat* (the Jewish Sabbath) and prayer customs, including the *kippah* or *yarmulke* (head covering) and *tallit* (prayer shawl), standing and sitting. Find out the customs of your synagogue that might not be obvious to someone who is not Jewish, such as not taking photographs or not writing in the synagogue. Ask the rabbi if the synagogue has a booklet with explanations. Jeffrey Salkin's bestseller, *Putting God on the Guest List,* contains an explanation of the *Bar/Bat Mitzvah* service specifically for non-Jews, with permission to photocopy and distribute.

2. Some synagogues allow families to create a supplement that includes English readings, the *Torah* portion, and explanations. You might also consider asking friends to serve as greeters at the door if the synagogue does not have this custom already, to hand out the prayer book and supplement, *kippah* and *tallit* where necessary, and to point out where they are in the service.

3. Let the rabbi know who's coming and whom you want to involve, if possible. Perhaps he or she can add explanations during the service, or help individuals fulfill their tasks without embarrassment.

4. If non-Jews can't take leading parts in the service, find ways to acknowledge them appropriately and authentically—at the party, at home, by mentioning them in a speech.

5. Don't feel you need to change the service to accommodate non-Jews (or even Jews) who don't know what's going on. Have respect for the choices you and your family have made—the synagogue, the rabbi, the kind of service—and help your family and guests appreciate what you have found meaningful in your Jewish community.

Deborah Freeman is on the board of directors of The City Congregation for Humanistic Judaism. She lives in Brooklyn Heights, New York, with her husband and daughter.

Our Jewish-Italian Family's Celebration of Our Daughter's *Bat Mitzvah*

DEBORAH FREEMAN

My daughter's *Bat Mitzvah* (the ceremony in which an individual chooses to assume the obligations and privileges of an adult member of the Jewish community) was approaching. I am Jewish, my husband is Catholic. We had chosen to raise our daughter as a member of one religion, Judaism, as we feared that she would have no religion if we tried to do both. But for this important life-cycle ceremony, we did not want my husband and his family to feel or to be excluded.

The reality of our life is that we are not a Jewish family. We're a family with some Jewish members and some Catholics. Our daughter has a dual heritage. We were lucky to have found a congregation, The City Congregation for Humanistic Judaism in New York, that offers an individualized *Bar/Bat Mitzvah* program to enable each child to come to terms with her specific situation. In addition, our congregation enables non-Jewish family members to participate in ways that most other congregations would not allow.

Like all students in our congregation, our daughter Irene did a lot of work to prepare for her *Bat Mitzvah*. She attended *B'nai Mitzvah* classes, chose and researched a major topic to present at her ceremony—why Albert Einstein never became *Bar Mitzvah*—and prepared essays about Jewish values, heroes, and social action programs. In addition, she had an assignment designed just for her—to write about the similarities and differences between Judaism and Catholicism.

I had always glossed over differences in holidays and services by saying that Catholics do things differently than we do. This explanation was adequate for a child, but not for a young adult being welcomed as a member of the Jewish community. As Irene began doing research, I realized that her need to learn more about Catholicism could also be an opportunity to include non-Jewish family members in the *Bat Mitzvah* preparation.

Irene and I met with my husband's son Joseph, who was raised, like his mother, as a Catholic. Joseph had received a wonderful Jesuit education and is a recent graduate of Fordham University. He and I explained to Irene that although Jews and Catholics share the early books of the Bible, these same books are interpreted very differently. For example, Catholics believe that people need Christ in their lives because everyone is born in sin, and that this original sin started with Adam and Eve. Humanistic Jews understand the story of Adam and Eve as our creation myth, analogous to other cultural myths. We see it as an example of our fundamental belief that each person has free will and individual responsibility. Other branches of Judaism interpret this somewhat differently.

By discussing differing interpretations of the same story, including a Catholic one, Irene gained insight into Judaism. We compared Joseph's Confirmation ceremony and how it differed in purpose and intent from Irene's *Bat Mitzvah* ceremony. Through our conversations, Joseph began to feel part of his sister's religious education in a meaningful way, consistent with his beliefs. If these conversations had never taken place, our family would have missed an opportunity to really understand each other's beliefs and backgrounds.

My husband gave a lot of thought to his role in this process. He acknowledged that there are few opportunities for a parent to publicly articulate his feelings about his child, and he wanted to take advantage of the opportunity to speak at her service. Besides expressing pride in his daughter, he thanked the congregation for including him. He closed his speech by saying: "I was raised a Catholic, and I don't expect to ever change. However, this hasn't stopped me from accepting what The City Congregation has offered—a way to embrace the spirituality and sense of community, without the theology. Maybe this gift is the best part of all religion."

My husband's parents chose to participate by preparing enough of their very delicious lasagna to serve to the entire congregation after Irene's ceremony. They were able to share their Italian heritage in a way that everyone enjoyed!

In case you're wondering, Einstein started studying physics when he was thirteen years old and decided on his own not to become a *Bar Mitzvah* because it made no sense to him. According to his biographers, his parents were secular Jews who raised no real objection to his decision. Although he did not become a *Bar Mitzvah*, Einstein always took pride in being a Jew and gave generously to many Jewish causes throughout his life.

8. Talking to Your Kids about Interfaith Dating

Edmund Case is the publisher of InterfaithFamily.com. He is intermarried and is the husband of Wendy and father of Emily and Adam Case.

How to Talk to Your Kids about Interfaith Dating

EDMUND CASE

There's a book written by a leading Conservative rabbi, Alan Silverstein, titled *It All Begins with a Date*. The goal of the book, as I understood it, is to promote an approach to preventing intermarriage. I don't think that intermarriage can be prevented, and I think that trying to do so can be very counter-productive. If the message communicated is that intermarriage is wrong, you shouldn't intermarry, though if you do we'll welcome you—then the last part of the message is likely not to be heard.

If intermarriage can't be prevented, then being totally inclusive and welcoming of intermarrieds from the outset is a much wiser approach for the Jewish community, in my opinion. But there certainly is an element of truth to the book's title, because it—intermarriage—usually does all begin with a date. So how do we talk to kids about interdating?

In theory, it shouldn't be all that complicated if the parents have raised their children as Jews and conveyed to them through their own actions the value that they place on living Jewishly. The message then seems pretty clear to me, and it goes like this:

We, your parents, would like to see you live a Jewish life because we have found it to be a source of meaning and purpose in our own lives, although we recognize that you will have to decide for yourself whether you want to live Jewishly.

If you want to have a Jewish family and a Jewish life, we want you to know that your chances of doing so are far greater if you marry someone who is Jewish. You may know and see intermarried parents who are living Jewishly and think that you could do the same, if you intermarry, but the statistics clearly show, for example, that a relatively small percentage of intermarried parents raise their children as Jews. If you ask intermarried parents about it, they'll tell you that although it is possible, it isn't so easy to have a Jewish family and to raise Jewish children in an intermarriage.

If you want to marry someone who is Jewish, your chances of doing so are far greater if you only date Jews. You may think that dating is only dating, but we don't think you can control whom you fall in love with, and if you think about it, your first experience with the person you end up marrying is highly likely to be—a date.

I've tried this approach with my own children. My daughter, who's now in her twenties, has had several serious boyfriends. She met the first one on a bicycle trip on the West Coast, and he happened to be Jewish. The second was a classmate in high school, the third a classmate in college, and neither was Jewish. My son, who is eighteen, is involved with a Jewish girl he met on a trip to Israel. To be honest, I haven't talked about this with my daughter recently. I suspect that her primary value would be finding someone to love, and whether he was Jewish or not would be of only secondary concern.

When I look at the approach I've outlined, it occurs to me that although I would very much like my children to marry Jews, it's not my primary value either: it's more important to me that they find a good mate than that they find a Jewish mate. After all, while it may be difficult, and statistically unlikely, to raise Jewish children in an intermarriage, it's still possible. I'm intermarried myself, and my children know that they were raised with strong Jewish identities in an intermarriage.

But I don't think the way to talk about interfaith dating should be very different whether the parents are both Jewish, or if they are intermarried. If the parents are intermarried, the statement that it isn't easy for intermarried parents to raise Jewish children will probably be more credible, although the children may also be more likely to think that if their parents did it, they could, too.

One difference between intermarried parents and two Jewish parents is that it would be pretty hypocritical for intermarried parents to tell their children that it would be wrong for them to intermarry. But I don't think it's effective for any parents to tell teenagers and young adults that interfaith dating is wrong—that message won't take hold in the vast majority of young American Jews who are living in a very open society, mixing constantly with others who are not Jewish, and who are likely to find the message exclusive or discriminatory. I also don't think it's effective to tell teenagers and young adults that they should do something because it's important to you as their parents—they have to make their own decisions.

What do *you* think?

Charles B. McMillan sells real estate in Newton, Massachusetts, and is active in civic affairs.

Feelings about My Sons' Interfaith Dating

CHARLES B. MCMILLAN

My Jewish wife married a non-Jew twenty-eight years ago. I was the first non-Jew she had ever dated. We've had a good marriage and are most fortunate to have three sons—all healthy, handsome, and intel-ligent; all *B'nai Mitzvah* (assumed the obligations and privileges of adult members of the Jewish community); ages seventeen, twenty, and twenty-three.

Many of our interfaith friends at Temple Shalom in Newton, Massachusetts, also have children who are in their late teens or early twenties. We have been active in an interfaith group there and have spent many years bemoaning the fact that most Reform rabbis refuse to marry interfaith couples. Now many of us are beginning to won-der whether our interfaith experiment in raising our children Jewish will amount to nothing—if our children will marry non-Jews and our grandchildren will lose any attachment to Judaism—or whether our interfaith marriages will contribute to a continuation of Judaism, through marriage to another Jew.

Though I have not converted, I am committed to the values of Judaism. I am not a very religious person, nor is my wife, but I think our children have adopted and understand their identity as Jews. Unfortunately, none of them make any distinctions in dating patterns between Jews and non-Jews. My wife and I have said to them, "We hope you marry Jews," but they are unresponsive. Only the oldest, who is twenty-three, is even remotely interested in the subject of marriage.

My oldest boy had a three-year relationship with an Orthodox Jewish girl. She was charming and intelligent. If they had become engaged, we would have been thrilled. But she broke it off last year, saying to my son, "You're not Jewish enough." It has taken him a while to recover from his heartache. Now he says he's not looking particularly for a Jewish girl to date or marry; he is looking for some-one who is not "married" to her religion. An "Orthodox" Catholic or an "Orthodox" Protestant would be as difficult a person to love as an Orthodox Jew.

But the funny part of his story is this: he doesn't make any dis-tinctions by religion. It's a non-issue for him. If I told him he's more likely to be happy with a Jewish girl because her thinking patterns and ways of relating would be closer to his own, he would think I was nuts. He would think I was categorizing and stereotyping and simplifying in a foolish way. My wife might say the same thing. And this is precisely where I am confused about this issue: What exactly does one say to one's twenty-three-year-old Jewish offspring, especially if one is not Jewish himself, to make that person understand that it is important that he or she marry a Jew?

Maybe the answer is: nothing. Maybe if you have to ask the question, you have already failed in your obligation to inculcate a particular set of values. That may explain why so many Jewish parents are uneasy in today's world.

My answer, as a non-Jew, is startlingly naive and simplistic. Jews as a people, despite adversity, have an extraordinary history of intelligence, compassion, achievement, and leadership in the world. If you're in the club, stay there and make sure your children do, too.

But talk like this makes my wife, and probably most Jews, nervous. I know exactly why. I know that any sentence that begins "Jews are..." can only lead to trouble. I know that intelligence, compassion, achievement, and leadership have to be transferred from generation to generation, carefully and painstakingly, in a thousand-thousand interactions between parent and child, in the study of *Torah* (the first five books of the Hebrew Bible), in the ways that adult Jews live their lives.

I asked my second son, who is a junior in college and who went out all last year with an Asian girl, whether he was aware of any differences between Jewish girls and non-Jewish girls. He looked at me quizzically: "What are you talking about?" he said. I said, "Let's broaden the question: Do you think that Jews are different from non-Jews?" He said he didn't know.

Then, later, I asked my wife that same question. She hesitated, looked around, thought about what to say for a second, and then said, "Yes." And then she made a joke. And I smiled at her, because her answer was so totally Jewish. She wouldn't ever think of saying anything out loud about how good or different Jews are. We gentiles have to thank Max Dimont, who wrote *Jews, God, and History*, if we want to hear a Jew tell us how great the Jews are.

Yet there has to be an answer to the questions that our children inevitably ask us: "Why should it make any difference if I marry a Jew or a non-Jew if I love that person?" "Who are you trying to please when you ask me to marry a Jew?" "Did God say only marry Jews? Didn't Moses marry a non-Jew? What is the big deal?"

These are tough questions, coming from our wise children. Besides, with interfaith couples, they have the final rejoinder: "You married out of your faith, how can you say it's wrong for me?"

But my wife and I would still like to see our boys marry Jewish girls.

Ronnie Caplane is a freelance writer based in Piedmont, California.

My Quandary: A Happily Intermarried Mom Talks to Her Daughter about Potential Problems in Interfaith Marriages

RONNIE CAPLANE

"I was very lucky with Daddy," I said to Morgan as we drove into San Francisco for a day of shopping. Car time is quality time, and I thought I'd use the opportunity for a serious discussion. It was a rare occasion. With Morgan in college and my son a high school senior, any time with them was hard to come by.

"Yeah, I know," Morgan said. I waited for her to say something more, or at least ask me why.

"I mean the way things worked out," I continued. "That even though Daddy isn't Jewish, it hasn't been a problem raising you and Sammy Jewish."

Joe and I come from completely different backgrounds—ethnically, economically, and religiously. His family is Catholic, but Joe claims he broke with the Church when he was seven, only thirty minutes after his First Communion. It was over graham crackers and milk, the mid-morning snack for which he paid a quarter a week. When Joe returned from his Communion to the classroom, he asked the nun for his crackers and milk. The nun said it was too late, that everything had been given out. So Joe asked for his quarter back, and the nun rapped his knuckles for being insolent. That was it for Joe and the Church.

Although I attended religious school through high school and was active in our temple youth group, I considered Judaism a cultural thing having more to do with corned beef and weekend retreats than religion. I always considered myself Jewish, but for many years after I left home I wasn't observant.

When Joe and I got married, "who" would marry us seemed more important than what kind of marriage we would have. We didn't discuss religion or how we'd raise children. Even when the children were born I didn't bother with a naming ceremony or *bris* (circumcision ceremony). It didn't occur to me. It wasn't until Morgan was in third grade that we even joined a temple.

"If you marry someone who's not Jewish, it's important to settle things before you get married," I said, not wanting Morgan to stumble into a situation that may not work out as well for her as it did for me. Although I don't expect her to get married anytime soon, I wanted to get Morgan thinking along the right lines early. "Negotiating religious differences is hard work."

I had been to interfaith workshops at Temple Sinai in Oakland, where we belong, and at Lehrhaus Judaica in Berkeley, and had heard horror stories. I told Morgan stories of non-Jewish spouses refusing to participate in their own child's *Bar* or *Bat Mitzvah* (the ceremony in which an individual chooses to assume the obligations and privileges of an adult member of the Jewish community), of failed attempts to raise children as both Jews and Christians, of marital discord over the question of religion, and of families that opted for no religion at all. I told her about one new mother who cried through an entire workshop describing how her husband changed his mind about raising their child Jewish when their baby turned out to be a boy.

I had also heard Bruce Phillips, a sociologist, say that children from interfaith families were more likely to marry non-Jews than those from Jewish families, and that the interfaith marriages that were most likely to survive were like mine—where one spouse had a strong religious identity and the other had none. There's no guarantee Morgan would get that if she married a non-Jew.

"It's easier if you marry someone who's Jewish. Someone who shares the same traditions, who knows the rituals, who goes to services with you," I said. "It can be very lonely going to services by yourself."

"But sometimes Daddy goes with you, and besides, you know a lot of people at temple and always have someone to sit with," Morgan said. It's true. Being the Jewish partner, the one who is responsible for my children's religious education, has made me more Jewish, more involved in the temple, and I have put more effort into my own Jewish education than I probably would have had I married a Jewish man.

"I know," I said. "But it's still nice to have someone to share that part of your life with."

"You have Sammy and me," Morgan said. "If you could it to do all over again, would you still marry Daddy?"

"Of course I would," I said. "But I would have talked some of this stuff out first."

"Look Mom. I know who I am. I'm very Jewish and I couldn't raise my children anything but Jewish," Morgan said, sounding exasperated. "I wouldn't marry anyone who wouldn't agree to that. I know it can be hard marrying a non-Jew, but it would also be hard if I married someone who was Orthodox. Besides, we've had this discussion a thousand times."

"We have?" I said. "Well you know what they say in Yiddish: Anything worth saying is worth repeating."

9. Relationships with the Extended Family

Eleanor W. Jaffe, M.S.W., M.Ed., has been a teacher, counselor, and psycho-
therapist. She is the mother of two children; both are in interfaith marriages.

Him, Her, or Us: The Family Loyalty Knot

ELEANOR W. JAFFE

Parents: Have you ever wished to be a fly on the wall at a support
group for young people in interfaith relationships? You might hear
your child and his sweetheart who is not Jewish discuss their difficulties with their families.

Couples: Have you ever wished you also could be a fly on the
wall at a parents' support group? You might hear your parents discuss the effects your interfaith relationship is having on them. What
would you hear? What would you learn about your families?

As a social worker facilitating interfaith workshops for young
couples twelve to fifteen years ago, I heard myriad reactions and emotions as the young people sought ways of presenting their non-Jewish
sweethearts to their families. And, as a recent participant in support
groups for parents, I heard similar emotions echoed in the voices of
their parents as they struggled with this challenging situation. From
each side, I heard confusion, anxiety, anger, bitterness, love, grief,
defiance, and acceptance.

Let me share with you the range of comments I heard at a meeting of young adults in interfaith relationships:

- We don't need religion in our lives.
- I don't have the right to ask my sweetheart to convert to my religion.
- I respect and like his family, but that doesn't mean I have to be Jewish, does it?
- I don't want my sweetheart to convert; I love him just the way he is.
- My father adores my sweetheart, even if he isn't Jewish. He is the son my dad never had.
- I look forward to being part of a Jewish family. Will my mother-in-law teach me what I need to know about being a Jewish wife and mother?

Now let me share with you the range of comments I heard at a parents' meeting:

- How can Judaism mean so much to me and so little to my son?
- I feel like a failure. I feel betrayed.
- I'm glad my parents are dead. This would have killed them.
- My son-in-law lied to me. He said they would bring up the children Jewish, and now he says he has changed his mind.
- How can I talk to them about religion without offending them?
- She is the girl I would have picked for my son, but she's not Jewish.

What seems to be one cause of so much of the pain and misunderstanding between the generations is a heightened and intense form of family loyalty. This loyalty asks the person in the interfaith relationship to consider putting his or her family's needs for religious continuity before his or her own need to marry the person (of another religion) whom he or she loves.

The typical Jewish family is strong, holding its members close. In fact, this is one of the qualities that is attractive to non-Jews. Relationships exist not only between the parent and child generation, but easily encompass three or more generations of the living and the dead within a family. In the case of the contemporary Jewish family, strong ties of memory and love reach back three or four generations to the *shtetls* (small villages where Jews lived) of Eastern Europe at the turn of the century. Jewish guilt has considerable force in influencing thought and behavior. This feeling of guilt, combined with loyalty to one's parents and grandparents, exerts strong pulls and can create intense conflict for the family when the young person chooses a mate from another religion.

Who are the people in both generations who are most likely to feel torn by this crossfire of intergenerational loyalty conflicts? Is it the parents whose memories of their *bubba*s (grandmothers) and *zaidas* (grandfathers) pull on their hearts as their children choose non-Jewish mates? Is it the young people, torn between love and loyalty to parents and love and loyalty to a mate, who feel pressured to choose only one? Which one will it be: him, her, or us?

In general, the family that experiences the most pain in these interfaith situations is one that has rigid boundaries and rigid defenses protecting it from outside influences. Strong barriers exist between "them" and "us," between the Jew and the "other," with the "other" frequently seen as an enemy. The Jewish people, after all, have experienced religious warfare from the "other" throughout history and particularly during the twentieth century. It is commonplace, therefore, for many older Jews to distrust non-Jews. This vulnerable family is also one where relationships are often "enmeshed," that is, boundaries between family members are more porous and ill defined.

Among the parents who have the deepest conflicts about their child's choice are those with intense relationships to their own parents, whether living or dead. This elderly generation of grandparents may be the most rigid of all, since they easily recall people sitting *shiva* (in mourning) when a child married out of the religion. The middle generation of parents—sandwiched between grandparents' memories of religious practices, their own living memories of the Holocaust and the painful political birth of Israel, and the multicultural potpourri of the 1990s in the United States—shuttles back and forth between the two generations, trying to create some elasticity and acceptance. Ironically, they feel betrayed by their child and, simultaneously, like the betrayer of their parents.

The young Jews who have fallen in love with someone of another religion and who belong to more rigid family systems feel sorely challenged as well. They want to please their parents, but not at the cost of their relationships. Oftentimes parents may push for a pre-marital conversion, but the non-Jew feels bewildered because her Jewish sweetheart cannot articulate his own Jewish beliefs, nor does he even attend religious services. Why, then, is conversion so important to him? In these instances, the young Jew has not yet developed his own personal religious belief system. In its absence, however, he still does not want to disappoint his parents, so he pushes his sweetheart toward conversion. At this point in his maturation, the young adult may feel and express his religious feelings only through his bond with his family.

One of the best ways to reconcile this dilemma and loosen this loyalty knot is for the young people to evaluate the role of religion in their own lives for themselves, to become "individuated," religiously speaking—that is, to develop adult, independent religious views based on information, discussion, and evaluations. Both the Reform and Conservative Movements offer introductory courses to Judaism and other workshops to help interfaith couples unscramble their diverse religious backgrounds and preferences. Other workshops are available through secular institutions. Once the adult child has a stronger sense of his own adult needs, as well as the needs of his sweetheart, he will be on a more level playing field for an adult-child to an adult-parent dialogue.

One of life's pivotal decisions is the choice of a mate. While parents hope to influence this choice, ultimately and appropriately the choice must be made freely by the young couple. No one should feel coerced to choose—him, her, or us—among the people he or she loves. Such a choice will be resented and regretted forever. Instead, let conflicted families work toward the unraveling of the family loyalty knot. As the tensions are worked out, the newest family member can be embraced with affection and acceptance into a strengthened Jewish family.

Rabbi Reena G. W. Judd skates between her obligations as a Jewish mother, wife, daughter, and rabbi.

Honor Thy Father and Thy Mother: Reflections on Being Part of an Interfaith Family

REENA G. W. JUDD

Hanging in my dining room, above the cabinet holding my tea cup collection, is a picture of my father-in-law, William Henry Judd, as a young man, proudly wearing his new sailor suit. He had left high school prior to graduating in order to serve in the United States Navy during World War II. To the right of this cabinet hangs a small photo of my father at age five, with his two-year-old brother, his mother, and his father. The photo was taken in Berlin, Germany, in 1938, a few weeks before my grandfather left Germany for Baltimore, Maryland, where he would work for the next sixty years as a furrier. My father, along with his brother and mother, followed by ship the next Christmas. How ironic that these two pictures hang side by side so many years later, functioning as pictorial brackets for the family my husband, Jim, and I have created together. In between the photos are two individual pictures of our daughters, Lilly, now four and a half, and Emma Michal, eighteen months.

I met my husband, James Edward Judd, in the laundry room of our condo building in the beginning of February 1992. I was in my third year of rabbinical school at the Reform Movement's Hebrew Union College–Jewish Institute of Religion. Jim was born a Catholic and received his elementary education in parochial school. When we met we said little, but about three weeks later I walked into the garden shop where he worked, and although I didn't recognize him, he recognized me, saying, "You're the lady from the laundry room, right?" I stuttered through those few first awkward moments. I needed seeds and soil for a religious school project for Tu B'Shevat, Judaism's Arbor Day. Buying what was needed, I asked him if he could please bring the soil back to our building, as it was too heavy for me to carry. He said, "Sure, yeah, whatever."

That evening I stopped by to get my dirt, and sort of never left. For the next six weeks we sat and talked nearly every night. During those weeks *Pesach* (Passover) came and went. Jim was there when I *shlepped* (dragged) down my *Pesach* foods—*matzah* (unleavened bread), and gefilte fish with horseradish. Our friendship needed to change direction—either move towards romance, or end. After so much talking during those weeks, we were aware of many differences in our lives that could present a challenge to a developing relationship.

By observing the intensity of my religious feelings and the nature of my educational and professional pursuits (to be a rabbi), Jim knew I could share my life and raise a family only with a Jewish man. When romance cornered us, Jim was not surprised when I told him I could not marry someone who was not Jewish. He asked how I would feel if he converted, and six weeks later we were engaged. During the upcoming year Jim became better acquainted and more comfortable with Judaism and Jewish life. He began an "Introduction to Judaism" class at one of the local synagogues. Two weeks before our wedding, Jim underwent conversion, choosing as his Hebrew name Adam Tzadok—a Man of Righteousness.

Most people I talk with, be it as a rabbi or a wife, express the thought that if a person chooses Judaism and marries a fellow Jew, the family is not an interfaith family. But on both a personal as well as professional level, I challenge this understanding of what makes an interfaith family precisely that—interfaith.

While the home Jim and I have worked hard to make for our family practices only Judaism, Jim's entire family of origin, as well as all his extended family, worship according to various denominations of Christianity. Yet, these people are very much a part of our family and our lives.

I am an only child, as is my mother. My father's brother never married, so I have no extended family with which to gather at celebrations or holidays. It is with Jim's family, during secular holiday celebrations, that our family creates the memories of family life. It is these family occasions, adorned with children's laughter and family antics, where memories will be made and cherished forever.

Jim's family has been completely supportive of our Jewish life. They send appropriate holiday cards not only to Jim and me, but to our girls as well. It is more than just Jim's siblings and mother who have enhanced our family's observance of Judaism. His Aunt Peggy and her family and his Uncle John in France remember us with holiday cards and gave us our treasured recording of *Fiddler on the Roof*. Throughout the years my in-laws have added to our Lenox china collection with a *Kiddush* (blessing over wine) cup for the sanctification of Sabbath wine, and a *challah* (braided bread) plate for the special bread eaten during the Sabbath meal. And when, during vacations, we have been able to break bread together and relish the joy of the Sabbath, we have all appreciated these ritual objects, embracing the enormous love and support they represent. When our daughters were born, both received a special charm, a *chai* (the Hebrew word and symbol for life).

As I write these words, our daughters are four and a half and one and a half, and their own Judaism is still being formed and solidified within the context of who they are. Both Jim and I believe that to share in the Christmas experience right now would present more confusion than our girls could handle. We have enough to explain with classrooms and malls, television and neighborhood decorations. And so we have chosen for the time being to abstain from participating in the extended family experiences of Christmas. We feel wholehearted gratitude toward Jim's family for their understanding of our religious dilemma. Jim and I are confident that the time will come, when our children are older, that we will come together to share in his family's Holy Day celebrations. For now, we enjoy shopping for their holiday tree and decorations. Each year I order my mother-in-law an ornament with a picture of the girls, and our family sends religiously neutral holiday cards.

For many years now, I have been grateful to my father-in-law for putting his life on the line for Europe's Jews, people he didn't know and would never meet. I have often thought about the irony of marrying a man whose father fought to save families like my own, and about how indebted I feel to this man, whom I will never be able to thank in person. Before beginning to write this essay, I discussed it with my mother-in-law, sharing with her how honored and excited I was to write about my appreciation of her unadulterated support of our home and our family. She said, "Why shouldn't I be supportive? You raise your children to be capable, thinking adults, able to make wise choices they can live with. I am only happy for you both."

Being part of an interfaith family has added enormously to my depth as a rabbi. It has enabled me to understand from a visceral perspective what so many contemporary Jewish families experience. It has allowed me to better serve contemporary Judaism at a more universal level while addressing the needs of individual Jews at a more particular level. It has enabled me to connect with people whom my title has, through no fault of my own, kept at bay. But most importantly, being part of an interfaith family has enriched my life—teaching me through personal encounter that God is alive and flourishing within each and every person! This truth motivates my every action and helps form my every thought.

Jeri Zeder is a freelance writer.

How I Prepared My Kids for Their First Mass and Their Aunt's Catholic Wedding

JERI ZEDER

My guys, Isaac and Dylan, eight and four respectively, had never been inside a Catholic church when my sister-in-law Ana asked them to be ring bearers at her wedding. The ceremony was to occur complete with a public celebration of the Eucharist, otherwise known as Holy Communion.

Okay. I'd read parenting books ad nauseam. I knew that to raise the odds my kids would behave like perfect gentlemen, I needed to prepare them. What I didn't know, but quickly discovered, was that I had to prepare myself first.

Lurking just below my American melting pot values are fears directly traceable to the *shtetl* (small villages where Jews in Eastern Europe used to live). When I encounter crucifixes, statues of Mary, and celibate priests, not to mention centuries of anti-Jewish doctrine the Church has only recently begun to address, I feel my Jewish sensibilities resisting all things Catholic. Obviously, if I was going to help my kids, the first thing I had to do was to acknowledge these feelings, shake hands with them, and then see them to the door, determined not to let them direct my actions.

I looked for a principle to guide me when I got stuck making decisions about specifics. One challenge for interfaith families like mine who are raising our children exclusively as Jews is how to teach them to embrace Judaism while being loving and respectful toward the faith, customs, and heritage of their non-Jewish relatives, especially their non-Jewish parent. Religious politics are one thing, family relationships another. I decided that Ana was lovely to honor my children with a role in her wedding, and that they would reciprocate by participating. However, they would not partake in Communion or any other Catholic rituals, because that would be disrespectful of both Judaism and Catholicism.

Pleased with this mature, reasonable attitude, I began preparing my kids. Ana's church was too far away, so I took them to the Church of the Sacred Heart around the corner to meet the priest, Father Coletti, see the inside of the sanctuary, and ask questions about what would happen at Mass and during the wedding. I had the impression that no one had ever asked Father Coletti to get Jewish children ready for a Catholic Mass, but he gamely agreed to see us.

When we arrived on the designated afternoon, we found that everyone expected us and helped shepherd us to the sanctuary. Dylan initially clung to me with a plaintive, "Mommy, I'm scared," but he warmed up gradually as Father Coletti gently and patiently explained the symbols around the church, the process of Communion, and the order of the wedding ceremony. Dylan and Isaac asked about the bas-relief pictorials on the walls, and Father Coletti explained the story they told of the crucifixion and resurrection of Jesus. I beat back the *shtetl* and reminded myself of all my mature and reasonable intentions.

Wedding weekend finally came. As we traveled to upstate New York, I imagined that child experts Leach, Brazelton, and Spock were smiling down upon my skillful mothering. It was when we brought the boys to church that I got knocked off balance. As the procession-al reached the end of the aisle, the priest was requiring each person to bow or curtsy before the cross.

Hello? Open-mindedness and exceptional parenting skills? I was totally unprepared for this detail. My mind raced over the significance of the gesture. Did bowing to the cross belong in the permissible column of the ledger sheet? I didn't know what to do, but I had to do it fast. I considered Ana, so happy and beautiful in her wedding dress next to her groom, and my mother-in-law, who had informed the priest in advance that her Jewish grandsons would have a place in the ceremony right beside their Catholic cousins. I decided that bow-ing in front of the cross was not the same as kneeling or taking

Communion, but more like a non-Jew wearing a *kippah* (head covering) in synagogue: a sign of respect only. I let my boys bow.

I hope my children absorbed two lessons from that day: that religious differences can make people closer, and that their Judaism is compassionate enough, warm enough, and strong enough to withstand intimate exposure to another religion.

Oh, yes, and the reception was a blast.

10. Grandparenting

Paula Lee Hellman has been active in Jewish education for the past twelve years, working with adults, senior adults, and children. She and her Jewish husband have a blended family that includes children and stepchildren, grandchildren, and a stepgrandchild from their previous interfaith marriages.

On Being the Jewish Grandmother of a Christian Grandchild

PAULA LEE HELLMAN

When my daughter called to tell me that she was getting married to the young man she had been dating for over a year—the son of a Baptist minister—my heart sank. The announcement and the reality were so different from my fantasy of what should happen: my daughter and I together in her girlish bedroom, her announcement eliciting mutual whoops of delight, then my gathering her in my arms as we happily planned her Jewish wedding. In contrast to the fantasy, my reaction was somber silence and internal tears.

After a brief moment, I recovered my composure. "I don't know what to say," I admitted. "Say you are happy for me," she replied. I did my best to acknowledge her happiness. I knew she loved this man and that her wedding was not about my happiness, but hers.

My daughter reminded me that her own father wasn't Jewish. "Yes," I said. "But your father did not practice any religion, while your boyfriend is very connected to his Christian faith. Besides, for the past eleven years you have lived in a Jewish home with two Jewish parents." "Mom," she told me gently, "I find it comforting to know that Jesus loves me." At that moment, I faced the probability that any future grandchild from this marriage would not be Jewish.

What I knew about being the grandparent of a Christian grandchild had been learned working with Elderhostel students who attended classes I led during the eight years I coordinated and taught at Eisner Camp Elderhostels in the Berkshires. Those classes often offered a first opportunity for many senior adults to discuss, within a Jewish context, their emotional responses to their children's interfaith marriages. Universally, they expressed ambivalence about being grandparents to Jewish grandchildren whose other grandparents are Christian. And those whose adult children were raising children in a Christian tradition were especially confused. Most of them loved their Christian sons- or daughters-in-law, and they loved their grandchildren, yet they struggled with their feelings.

"I feel like I'm walking on eggshells," was an often-used expression. And many held themselves back, not giving their grandchildren books of Jewish stories in case the "other grandparents" would bring them Christian books. The hurt and heartache I had felt from them as they told their stories were now resonating in me.

My experience with the Elderhostelers taught me that what we want most as grandparents is to be freely ourselves. We want to tell our stories, to transmit our culture and heritage to our own grandchildren. But in this new world of interfaith marriage, we need to seek permission from our children to fully express ourselves and to assure them that what we want to do is to be relaxed grandparents, not proselytize for Judaism.

Many of the couples I met in Elderhostel workshops began to explore Judaism only after their children intermarried. Many responded to their children's interfaith marriages by starting to light candles on *Shabbat* (the Jewish Sabbath). Their grown children didn't always like it. I heard about the discomfort of grown children when they came "home" for Friday night dinner and saw a white cloth on their parents' dining table, a covered *challah* next to shiny candle holders. Adult children challenged this new ritual behavior by saying, "We never did that when we grew up."

Over and over, parents told me that they had to convince their adult children that their new relationship to Judaism was real, not a charade put on for the grandchildren. The Elderhostelers attended our workshops in order to learn what they hadn't had time to learn when they were younger. Most were immigrants or children of immigrants. If a job required working on *Shabbat*, they worked on Saturdays. They grew up in families that emphasized living freely in America, and ethical more than religious lives. Now, they wonder if they had missed something by assimilating so thoroughly into American society. Now, they wonder how to be authentically themselves and still honor their children's choice of religion for their grandchildren.

Since interfaith marriage on a large scale is relatively new, we are the ones creating the new etiquette for grandparenting children in interfaith families. There are questions about holidays and ritual objects: questions about whether to give gifts at Hanukkah or Christmas and whether it is appropriate to give Jewish books or tapes. I think that the new etiquette means openly talking about your children's choices and being willing to hear the answers. I try not to ask a question if I am not willing to hear the response. When I am openly looking for information, then I am willing to hear any answer. Sometimes the answer hurts. But the flip side is that you can ask your children to listen to you.

Open communication helps establish boundaries and gives all participants permission to be themselves. It's important not to invite the interfaith family to dinner on a Christian holiday. But it's great to bring them home for Passover or *Shabbat* or Hanukkah. Ask if they would like to receive a *menorah* (candelabra) for Hanukkah, if they would like tapes of Jewish songs. And be clear about what your own needs are. If it would be hard to see a cross or a crucifix around your young grandchild's neck, say so: It is possible that the child can practice their religion without such an overt sign. (By the time your grandchild is a teenager, communication can be directly with the teen.)

My daughter now has a one-year-old son. He is a smiling delight. When they are with me, she and her son come to family

Shabbat services at our temple, and my daughter chants the appropriate responses. She says the *Motzi* (blessing over bread) at our dinner table. I often wonder what will happen when my grandson is older, how he will make the distinction between Christianity in one place and Judaism at Grandma and Grandpa's house.

Through our open communication, I know that I have permission to be myself, to tell Bible stories, to light *Shabbat* candles and give Hanukkah gifts rather than Christmas presents. Knowing the boundaries of what I can and can't do has helped. And for now, I am happy. I don't walk on eggshells.

Nan Meyer, a retired newspaper woman, is the author of the user-friendly *hagaddah*, *The Inter-Faith Family Seder Book: How to Celebrate a Jewish Passover Supper with Christian In-laws and Non-Jewish Friends* (Heritage).

On Learning That My Jewish Son Would Raise His Daughter Catholic

NAN MEYER

"Wait, I'll walk you to your car," our son had said. It had been a lovely visit with him and his Christian wife. She was struggling to get into her coat, not easy since she was eight months pregnant. "Don't think this is a rejection of you," our son continued. "But we have decided not to raise the baby Jewish." The world stopped.

Oh, we managed to put a good face on, saying good-bye in our usual manner, but once we were driving down the road.... There would be no child to name for my father. There would not be Jewish descendants named in memory of us. What of my grandfather's piety and sacrifices? Who would make the Passover *seder* (ritual meal) after I was gone? What would keep the family together? And who was to blame?

Was it because he hadn't lived in a Jewish neighborhood? Not easy when you're the only Jewish family in town. Or when the nearest synagogue's youth group has nine boys and one girl. (Try organizing a dance with those demographics.) We had a Jewish home, observed the holidays, have always been temple members, sent our children on every possible Jewish outing, and even researched colleges for religious breakdowns. Yet, each of our children had married "out."

Or was it us? Both my husband and I are products of three generations of interfaith marriages. He's a convert. Was it, as my younger son said, "You betrayed Judaism first when you married Dad. What did you expect?" Three years later, that son would himself be engaged to a Christian girl.

The family joke was that Mom's first question is always: "Is she Jewish?" But my opposition stopped once each declared his intention to marry. I never wanted anyone else to experience the rejection I was subjected to as a fiancée, when the only one who welcomed me was my husband's Jewish grandmother. She had grasped my hands and whispered in amazement, "You're Jewish?"

Was it the fault of rabbis? When our oldest son and his fiancée were planning their wedding, they talked with our rabbi. He agreed to participate in their marriage ceremony along with the bride's uncle, a priest. But two months before the wedding, the poor man died. When we tried to replace him, we hit cruel refusals, including "A Christian and a Jew, that's water and dirt; and I don't do mud." We finally found a rabbi to perform the Jewish part of the wedding, but the damage was done. Our son never entered a synagogue again.

Still, we hadn't expected his children to be baptized.

I try to see the positive. So my daughter-in-law wasn't Jewish; less chance for Tay Sachs. She certainly treats my son well. Since the holidays are different, we won't be competing with her family for their attendance.

But the most important incident came as I hugged my daughter-in-law good-bye that evening. As usual, I dropped a hand to her stomach and felt a fluttering, my first contact with my grandchild.

Later, I remembered my husband's Jewish grandmother. When she married out, her family declared her dead and recited *Kaddish* (the prayer said when a person dies) for her. Yet, she only had one grandchild, my husband. He was dating Jewish girls when I met him. In his Irish-Catholic world, his wanting to teach school wasn't considered manly. Because teaching children is an acceptable profession for a Jewish male, he had discovered he had nothing to prove to a Jewish date. He spoke of converting and, of course, agreed that our children would be Jewish. So why had his grandmother gone through such anguish? All of her great grandchildren were Jewish.

Maybe I should concentrate on what was truly important. I wanted a normal, healthy grandchild, who would grow up to be a decent person. Perhaps I had to trust what the child would have within her. If she had a Jewish heart, she could be drawn back like my husband was. Or her children would be.

This is not to say I didn't feel anguish when I saw her being baptized. My husband might still have scars where my nails dug into his arm as I saw my grandchild under a cross. But I suddenly felt a strange kinship with my Catholic mother-in-law. She smiled at my son's *Bar Mitzvah* (the ceremony in which an individual chooses to assume the obligations and privileges of an adult member of the Jewish community). I owed it to her memory to be as gracious as she had been.

And I would have to be the best Jew I could because I had now become a living example of this religion I so love. Besides, one day my granddaughter would choose a husband. Her standards would be her Jewish father. And her mother had shown her that marrying a Jew was a good thing.

We are all in God's hands. I would leave it so.

Bobbie Friedman is a middle-aged American wife, mother, and grandmother who is trying to balance the demands of work, home, and aging gracefully. She lives with her husband in Needham, Massachusetts, where she is active in the Jewish community.

How Joining a "Parents of Children with Interfaith Relationships" Group Helped Me

BOBBIE FRIEDMAN

My husband and I are hardworking people, the parents of a son and daughter, temple members, and givers of our time and energy to Jewish and non-sectarian causes.

Our daughter Judy is our older child. Six years ago she met and started dating a young man who comes from a fine, observant Catholic family. At the time we didn't think too much about it, because she was young and would meet and date other boys, or so we expected. As you know, things don't always work out the way parents expect them to.

Time went by, and Judy and Sean grew closer. After several years it became apparent that they were, indeed, a couple with no interest in going their separate ways. After another year or so, we were just waiting for their engagement announcement and an official declaration of their feelings and plans. We knew they would be getting married. My husband and I were happy, but we also had doubts and unsettled feelings about this relationship. I was more uncomfortable than my husband.

My daughter's happiness created an odyssey for me. I experienced a wide range of emotions, from true happiness to the depths of despair. There were nights when I could not sleep. I worried about what I had done wrong to cause my child to find happiness with someone who wasn't Jewish. I worried about losing my adult child to forces I could not control. I knew my future son-in-law probably had no interest in converting. What would happen when they had children? The thought that they might raise children outside of the Jewish faith was enough to make me sick.

Rifat Sonsino, the rabbi of our temple, had already begun to address the growth of interfaith relationships. He asked Paula Brody, who was then the director of outreach of the Reform Movement's local office, to run a series of meetings at our temple for parents of children in interfaith relationships. I decided that my husband and I should join the Parents of Children with Interfaith Relationships group. This was a support group rather than a therapy group. This group became my salvation. Through our discussions I realized that I was not alone, that my worries and feelings of loss were not unique. In the privacy of our group, we were free to share and bare our worries and fears, as well as our joys and successes, in dealing with difficult issues related to holidays and rituals.

As the year went by I came to terms with my concerns. The most important things to me were our daughter's happiness and the fact that her future husband was such a wonderful person. Now that they are married, he has become a very valued member of our family, and we are comfortable with him and his family.

Because of my opportunity to be a member of our group, I realized the value of having a support like this as an ongoing resource for others, and I attended a training program for lay leaders to become facilitators of parent groups like ours. Through discussion and analysis of Jewish thought and literature, we worked on issues that would help parents understand their feelings of loss when their children interdate and intermarry. We learned how to strengthen communication between parents and their children on complex religious identity issues. We learned how to help clarify Jewish values and encourage positive Jewish parenting and grandparenting.

Through my association with Paula Brody and with the leaders and members of our group, I have come to see that we and the families of those our children love are tied together by many common bonds. We can all take comfort from knowing that we are not alone.

All group members are able to share their experiences. We realize that our children are still our children. We have shared memories—of good times and bad times. Our group discusses the origins of our interfaith situations and what continues to hold our children to us and to our faith. We talk about new traditions and how to approach them. As the year progresses, people begin to relax and to enjoy the new experiences and interactions. We learn that we and our children who are sharing interfaith experiences deserve happiness and respect. This brings a great feeling of satisfaction.

Through membership in my group, I have come to terms with my feelings. I am comfortable now facing whatever will come with my children. I will try to be sensitive to their needs and will always try to communicate openly. A few years ago I did not feel this way. I have grown as a person as a result of this group opportunity, as a member and then a lay leader of my Parents of Children with Interfaith Relationships group.

11. Divorce and Stepfamily Issues for Interfaith Families

Jeffrey A. Marx is rabbi of Sha'arei Am in Santa Monica, California, and is a founding partner of Pulling Together Mediation Center.

Divorce and the Interfaith Family

JEFFREY A. MARX

Let's face it: relationships are hard work. In all marriages and commitments, two individuals enter into their relationship loaded with plenty of baggage—habits, values, opinions, likes, and dislikes—all of which must be negotiated with the other. Many marriages fail precisely because the partners are not able to compromise and trade off with one another.

Interfaith couples add yet an additional component to the compromise list: religious observance. For some couples, especially those whose religious attachments are not strong, their differences are easy to work out. Other couples, however, to reduce conflict in their lives, negotiate complex agreements concerning respect for one another's religious backgrounds, the raising of their children with one religious identity, home observance, holiday celebrations with in-laws, displays of ritual objects, and the like. Still others, rather than highlight their religious differences, develop unique, syncretistic home rituals—Hanukkah bushes, Easter eggs at the Passover *seder* (ritual meal). Though these rituals wreak havoc with traditional religious symbols, they also arise from a desire not to rock the couple's "relational boat."

When separation and/or divorce occur, these negotiated compromises and creative solutions are often the first to break down. In the midst of the anger and pain that often are part of separation and divorce, some couples immediately go to their respective "corners." With their relationship no longer intact, they feel that the religious compromises they have made are no longer necessary.

A common initial reaction is for one partner to declare: "I agreed to help raise our kids as Catholic/Jewish/Christian Scientist, but I'm done with that, now. You want your kids to be X, Y, or Z, then you take them to services and religious school!" Or, knowing how it will hurt and anger the other, one partner declares: "Okay, now I'm going to raise them in my religion. I know we agreed to raise them in your religion, but that was then. Now, I'll do as I please!"

Of course, the ones who suffer here are the children. Especially at a time when their accustomed structure has been suddenly ripped apart, a time often filled with uncertainties and fears, children need as much of the structured and usual as we can give them. For children who have been raised with a particular set of beliefs and rituals, it does them no service, especially at this time of uncertainty, to remove yet another familiar set of structures. And, of course, asking children to now choose between two religions—in effect saying to them: choose one or the other parent—is to place them in an intolerable and unfair position.

For parents to make decisions which are truly in the best interest of their children, it is important to address a number of issues at the time of separation or when creating the divorce agreement. First of all, there needs to be a written affirmation that regardless of what will transpire between the parents, the child will be raised in a specified religion. Second, questions need to be settled as to how the children will spend holidays and festivals and with whom, in terms of parents and grandparents—Rosh Hashanah (Jewish New Year) and Passover with one, Christmas and Easter with the other, for example.

The issues of who will pay for religious instruction, church or synagogue dues, whether the children will attend religious school, and how they will be transported need to be addressed. If the Jewish partner keeps kosher (observes Jewish dietary laws) or is *shomer shabbos* (Sabbath observant), compromises must be reached. For example, some couples make a commitment that while each partner is free to make his or her own food choices, *treif* (unkosher) foods will not be sent back and forth with the children. Often, separating or divorcing interfaith couples need to decide whether the other parent will have the freedom to attend their child's religious life-cycle moments: Baptism, Confirmation, *Bar/Bat Mitzvah* (the ceremony in which an individual chooses to assume the obligations and privileges of an adult member of the Jewish community).

It is important to remember that the courts are loath to decide between the competing claims of parents concerning the religious instruction and upbringing of their children. As long as a particular religious upbringing is not harmful to the children, the court will usually simply allow the children to be brought up in two different religions, rather than decide in favor of one parent over another.

The interfaith couple with the best interests of their children in mind will keep them out of a religious tug-of-war. Rather, just as they made conscious decisions about how to rear their children religiously, now they must work together to make new decisions about raising them in an interfaith divorce.

Daniel Little is a professor and administrator in Michigan. He is the author of several books on the philosophy of social science.

Divorced, Not Jewish, but My Kids Are

DANIEL LITTLE

I'm divorced, and my kids are Jewish. That's not so exceptional, I suppose, though it's the outcome of a long itinerary. So let me explain.

We married in 1976. I was raised Presbyterian in the Midwest, but developed a slightly ironic distance from what I, as an adolescent, saw as a lot of hypocrisy in the church membership around me. I became non-practicing, so I wasn't much inclined towards religious experience in my life or in those of the people I cared about. Mine was a very secular, rational, pragmatic approach.

My former wife was raised as a suburban Jew, sharing some of the distaste for hypocrisy that she saw around her in her own religious community. She, too, had a very limited level of religiosity and was probably somewhat alienated from the affluent, socially conscious slice of the Jewish world of northern New Jersey.

When we married and chose to have children, we each felt that we would prefer for our children to have a greater sense of spiritual or religious place in the world than we had experienced. And we each preferred that their religious identities should be Jewish. Not, perhaps, a highly religious version of Judaism, but a sense of the moral commitments, the interpersonal empathy, the concern for others and sympathy for the oppressed, which I attribute to the most admirable form of Jewish religious and cultural life. As a parenthesis, it is sometimes interesting to me to wonder why it is that I find myself most comfortable with Jewish people. Not, of course, universally, but often enough to be predictive.

So we joined an informal Reconstructionist group in our town in the Boston area. It was a group created ten years earlier by couples of mixed religious backgrounds, Christian and Jewish, who wanted a Jewish identity for their children and a welcoming place for both parents. We joined, in some part, for the occasional services and the sense of an adult and caring community; but in greater part, we joined in order to provide a context in which Josh and Rebecca could have a Sunday school experience and move toward *Bar* and *Bat Mitzvah* (the ceremony in which an individual chooses to assume the obligations and privileges of an adult member of the Jewish community). They learned a little bit of Hebrew and got a bit more acquainted with Jewish traditions and biblical stories. And, imperceptibly, they developed a sense of Jewishness that greatly pleased me.

I overheard an interesting snippet of conversation between Josh and my mother as Josh was explaining his upcoming Reconstructionist *Bar Mitzvah* service. I had explained to my mother that our service would be a "counter-cultural extreme of contemporary Judaism." Josh then interjected, "My mom's form of Judaism may be counter-cultural, but I'm a little more traditional." I am happy that our children have somehow developed a more spiritual worldview than I have, and I am moved that they seem to have a strong sense of their place in a community of caring people.

Josh's *Bar Mitzvah* was in 1991, and Rebecca had her *Bat Mitzvah* in 1995. They were both highly moving occasions for me and for our families. As was the custom in our Jewish Sunday school, the services were designed by our family, and the poetry, stories, readings, and prayers had a personal resonance for me that no Presbyterian service in my adolescence ever had.

The *Bar* and *Bat Mitzvah* were signal, important events in the history of our family. They were occasions that all our sisters, brothers, mothers, and fathers remember and savor.

So let's bring the story forward. A few days before Rebecca's *Bat Mitzvah*, my former wife and I stood before a judge in Massachusetts. In our own ways we still loved and respected one another, but we had decided that there were reasons enough to dissolve our marriage. And so we divorced, only a few days before Rebecca's journey into the quiet, peaceful chapel at Brandeis University.

Our family has endured, in its own way. My former wife and I still communicate easily and caringly. Rebecca and Josh and I have retained the strongest possible family relationship. I don't think we could be closer under any alternative fork in the road. I speak to Rebecca daily (as I did with Josh before he went to college). We see each other frequently—every other week in Rebecca's case, and as often as the college calendar permits, in Josh's case. We camp and hike in the summers, and love being "on the road again, going places we've never been," as soon as we hit the Denver airport each August. I love being a father, and feel that my children know this. And they know that they have two parents who love and support them.

They also know, however, that they are part of a larger world. And I think, though you'd have to ask them, that the spiritual and moral resources that they have gained from their Jewish identities, and the sense of connectedness with others that this identity gives them, is an important part of their strength as a young man and woman. So I am delighted that being Jewish is a part of their identity, and I will do everything possible to nourish it.

Ronnie Caplane is a freelance writer based in Piedmont, California.

When Her Christian Mother and Her Jewish Stepfather Divorced, She Kept Her Judaism

RONNIE CAPLANE

When Carolyn Housman's mother and stepfather divorced, she lost her Jewish father. But she didn't lose her Judaism.

"I have considered myself Jewish since I was five," says Housman, now eighteen. "I'm more Jewish than a lot of my friends who are Jewish by blood."

Carolyn comes from one of those modern California families with step-siblings, half-siblings, and an assortment of stepparents with almost as many religions as there are in Jerusalem. There's a Christian Scientist, a Buddhist, several Protestants, and a Jewish stepfather.

Although neither of Carolyn's birth parents are Jewish, when her mother, Katherine Endicott, married Steven Mendelson, they decided to raise Carolyn and Laurel, Mendelson's daughter by his first marriage, Jewish.

"Steven and I decided it would be good to raise the children with a religious background because it would give them a moral grounding. They don't teach that at school," says Endicott. "My personal reason was that I felt it would be an honor to bring Jews into the world after the Holocaust."

For the girls it was like something out of the movies. Only six months apart, they had been friends at a Montessori pre-school in Oakland, California, which is how their parents met. Laurel had almost no contact with her birth mother, and the girls were raised as sisters.

For Endicott, who had no Jewish training, it meant learning how to keep a Jewish home. She studied with their rabbi, took classes at the Jewish Community Center, and read. She became active in their synagogue and oversaw the celebration of all the Jewish holidays. Ultimately she was the parent in charge of the girls' Jewish education and of making them feel Jewish.

"We did a big *Shabbat* (the Jewish Sabbath) thing all though their childhood," said Endicott. "It was the best part of the week."

But Housman always felt that it was her decision whether or not to be Jewish. "One of the things that really made me appreciate Judaism and stick with it is that my mother and stepfather gave me the choice of being Jewish and going to Hebrew school," she says. One year she attended a Christian Sunday school as well as religious school at her synagogue. But that, she says, was more out of intellectual curiosity and for the social aspect. "Judaism has the right feel for me. I can say that because I have seen and learned about other religions."

And just like many kids, she only wavered once.

"Around the time of my *Bat Mitzvah* (the ceremony in which an individual chooses to assume the obligations and privileges of an adult member of the Jewish community) I thought, is this what I want to do? It's really a lot of work," remembers Carolyn. But she went through with it and continued her Jewish education, getting confirmed and later graduating from a Jewish high school.

At the end of her sophomore year in high school, Carolyn decided to convert. It was around the time of her mother and stepfather's divorce and also right before she went on a summer youth trip to

Israel. She thought converting would make her more acceptable to the Orthodoxy in Israel.

Although she found going to the *mikvah* (ritual bath) a spiritual and cleansing experience, converting didn't make her feel more Jewish. "Conversion was a formality," said Housman. "It didn't impact my Judaism in any way."

In retrospect she has some regrets about having done it at all. "I'm still not Jewish by Orthodox standards," she says of her Reform conversion.

Now a freshman at Georgetown University in Washington, D.C., Housman is active in the Jewish Students Association and occasionally attends Friday night services. Following an anti-Semitic incident where a *menorah* (candelabra) on campus was vandalized, she joined with other students in a community *havdalah* (marking the end of the Sabbath) service, and wore a blue ribbon to protest the anti-Semitism.

Although Housman totally identifies as a Jew and has no question that she will raise her children as Jews, people are often surprised to find out that she is Jewish. With her long blonde hair, she doesn't look it.

"Well, I am," Housman says when people remark on her appearance. "I don't feel I have to qualify it by saying I converted. I am Jewish. Ignore the hair color, and I'm completely Jewish."

She's even dating a Jewish guy who also has blond hair and blue eyes, and she finds that most of her friends are Jewish. "Judaism has such a warm welcoming feeling because it's also cultural," says Housman.

Back in Oakland, her mother feels the same way. Although she is now single, Endicott continues to maintain a Jewish home and is still active in the temple.

Jennifer M. Paquette lives in Toronto, where she works as a software tester, part-time freelance writer, and full-time mother to her two children.

When a Divorced, Traditional Mother of Two Fell in Love with a Non-Jew

JENNIFER M. PAQUETTE

Call it luck. I have unearthed that rare beast, a single guy who loves my kids. In many ways, we're the perfect team. He's too slow in the kitchen to cook for starving children; I do high-speed gourmet. I can't draw; he's a professional artist. But I'm also an observant Jew, while Ted grew up Catholic.

Even so, my kids adore him right back. He tosses them in the air, plays all the "wild" games I refuse to. What impresses them most? As my son, Yerachmiel Meir (YM) told Ted admiringly, "You can eat squirrel if you want to!"—something YM can't do, due to kosher dietary laws.

Okay, so my children (Elisheva, four, and YM, five) lead insular lives. They go to Jewish schools. We share *Shabbat* (the Jewish Sabbath) and holidays with family and friends. They say *brachot* (prayers) with a fluency that I—not raised religiously—secretly envy. Ted, a co-worker I've been dating for a year and a half, has been their first glimpse into an exotic world that contains non-Jews. YM announces to strangers, "Ted's Christian," like he's bragging.

As accepting as they are, the kids are puzzled; they wonder what he's doing here. I overheard YM saying to Elisheva, "You can't marry Ted; he's not Jewish!"

Once, I thought perhaps we could be a "mixed" family. Ted rarely attended church, so we'd only have to deal with seasonal "Christmas/Hanukkah" and "Passover/Easter" issues. And as puzzling as Judaism was to him, he admitted that it seemed good for my kids, and that it made sense to raise any future children in the same way. But as the months passed, I felt less and less satisfied. The relationship was blossoming, but I found myself wishing for more of a shared Jewish and spiritual connection.

Finally, I confronted the truth: I wanted a Jewish family. Or, rather, I needed Ted to join the Jewish family we already had. He'd been holding back, observing our rituals from a distance, like an anthropologist. Finally, I broke down and admitted to him that although his companionship meant so much to me, the picture of our future together could not be complete without one final piece: his *neshama* (soul).

Although Jewish tradition frowns upon encouraging an individual to convert, I said we could only marry if he became a Jew. Finally, after months of painful soul-searching, he asked me to marry him, after he eventually feels ready to convert.

YM told Ted once: "You can come live with us; all you have to do is become a Jew!" To them, Judaism comes naturally. It's just a matter of learning a few new rituals. To Ted, though, this religion is a baffling world, with its own multi-sensory vocabulary: new words, smells, tastes, and images coming at him from all sides. Only recently has he begun to relax and start participating when he's with us for *Shabbat* or holidays.

Every Friday night, after *Kiddush* (blessing the wine), we troop into the kitchen for the traditional hand washing before eating the braided *Shabbat challah* (bread that is traditionally eaten on the Sabbath). Lately, Ted's been joining the knee-high crowd around the sink, where I lead him through the blessing afterwards. One time, though, I was busy, and YM noticed that Ted hadn't "made his blessing yet."

Since they were babies, my kids have known the words that begin most blessings: "*Baruch atah Adonoi*...(Blessed art Thou o God)." I usually just have to prompt them with the single syllable "Ba" to get them going.

YM began coaching Ted. He opened his mouth and said "Ba"— and waited for Ted to continue. Finally, I broke the silence: "Say all the words." Patiently, YM spoke the syllables for Ted to repeat. Ted finished confidently, and YM chimed "Amen!" Together, they headed back to the supper table.

It can be frustrating for Ted, feeling like he's miles from "catching up"—even to the children's level. Elisheva has had almost 250 *Shabboses* (Sabbaths)—Ted has experienced barely a fifth that number. They cannot imagine the difficulties involved.

Encountering Judaism as an adult, Ted was initially swayed by unfavorable stereotypes of the wrathful "Old Testament" God. Now, he says his religious background provides a strong religious footing from which to explore the truths Judaism offers. That open-mindedness is hard-won: lengthy prayers and foreign concepts still daunt him. But now, with the kids' help, he's finding ways Judaism can *add* to his spirituality.

Even with his acceptance of our family's practice of Judaism and respect for our traditions, I worry about the influence Ted's "differentness" will have on our family. He drives on *Shabbat*; eats non-kosher food (though not squirrel!)—my kids are bound to be envious.

Every *Shabbat*, I bless my kids in the traditional way. But first, I whisper to each one my hopes for their Jewish lives—that they raise families, become good people. Sometimes, I ask, "What will you be when you grow up?" and give them a chance to imagine their own future. But one particular Friday evening a few weeks ago, YM was cranky. When I asked him, he raised his blue eyes and laughed wickedly. "I want to be a *goy* (non-Jew) like Ted!"

He was joking, but his statement showed insight: Judaism is a difficult path. Ted's life makes us all aware that we choose to live Jewishly. Observing every *mitzvah* (commandment) is optional, in a sense, and YM knows I'd be devastated if he chose any other way to live his life.

To be totally honest, my kids aren't the only ones feeling jealous. If Ted goes to a movie on *Shabbat* or eats a bacon double cheeseburger, he's careful when he tells me about it, knowing that on some level I'm both cringing and—though I've been observant for almost a decade—drooling at the thought of that burger. Sometimes, with him, I feel like a recovering alcoholic at a party where everybody's drinking.

Still: one foot in front of another, one day at a time, and every day I make these Jewish choices I feel stronger and more confident.

Hesitantly, Ted has begun incorporating Judaism into his own life: he fasted on Tisha b'Av (fast day that commemorates the destructions of the Temples), signed up for a class, is buying tickets for the High Holidays. This year, he's doing more than last year, though neither of us can say yet what he'll be capable of next year or the year after. Like me, he's putting one foot in front of the other, embarking on a path he never anticipated his life would take.

For my kids, keeping kosher, keeping *Shabbat*, these are natural—the pulse of their days and years. I can dream of the day when Ted's heart leaps expectantly when Rosh Hashanah (Jewish New Year) is just around the corner, or when his soul hungers if he forgets to put on *tefillin* (black leather straps for the arm and head, each with a small box containing a scroll upon which is written the *Sh'ma* prayer). But I cannot say when or even if this will ever happen. All I know for sure is this: each step he takes validates the Jewishness of our family, even while blending it with the rich Christian spiritual heritage he will never completely leave behind.

YM's envy—and my own—of Ted's dietary freedom underscore the importance of bringing Ted into our family's religious life. He's not ready to convert yet. That's another long, hard road.

Judaism is a lifelong journey to an unknown destination, but my hope is that my children will see Ted striving to walk alongside them and learn that Judaism is worth the effort. They will watch him struggle with words like *kreplach* (meat pie cooked in soup), choke down gefilte fish, fast for twenty-five hours. Through him, they will feel pride in Judaism, and realize that even though we may have been born into this religion, it's up to all of us to embark on the journey for ourselves.

12. Gay Interfaith Relationships

Lev Ba'esh is rabbi of Temple Israel in Dover, New Hampshire, and chaplain at the University of New Hampshire.

Interfaith at the Top

LEV BA'ESH

When I accepted the position of rabbi at Temple Israel in Dover, New Hampshire, I never expected to find a Jewish partner. The odds of finding the right gay, Jewish man in a big city is one thing. But Dover is a very small town. What I hoped for, however, was what I got. My partner, Andrew, is caring, spiritual, bright, handsome, outgoing, and, although raised a Christian, not predisposed to any one religious choice. Several people—some within the Jewish community—had suggested that I meet him.

Two years later, we are living together, listed in the temple directory together, attending temple services together, praying in English and Hebrew at meals together, celebrating Jewish holidays together, attending Jewish life-cycle ceremonies together, and chaperoning synagogue teen trips and NFTY (National Federation of Temple Youth) camp trips together.

We also visit Andrew's family at Christmas and Easter and celebrate secular holidays with whomever and wherever we may be, together. Who we are, as individuals and as a couple, continues to be enhanced by our shared involvement in each other's religious and family life.

I have often been asked to explain my feelings about being a rabbi in an interfaith relationship. Words can hardly describe the experience. Here are a few glimpses into our lives as an interfaith family.

WE TALK ABOUT WHAT MATTERS TO US, BEFORE, DURING, AND AFTER IT SURFACES

This style of talking things through includes religious observances. We make an effort to respect both families' religious observances, although we observe only one religion within our home, and to also include friends in our plans.

WE PLAN JEWISH RELIGIOUS OBSERVANCES EARLY ENOUGH TO INVITE FAMILY AND FRIENDS

We always plan to see Andrew's parents around Christmas and Easter, usually not on the given day, as my schedule precludes that possibility. It's togetherness as a family that is his parents' highest priority, and they are willing to forgo dates in exchange for total family connection. They are a huge blessing in my life.

As an example of our celebrating with friends, we host a Tu B'Shevat *seder* (ritual meal) in our home. Tu B'Shevat falls midwinter and is loosely translated as the Jewish Arbor Day. We celebrate by inviting several other couples, Jewish and mixed-faith households like ours, asking them to bring dishes that contain at least one exotic fruit or vegetable. Last year we began the meal with a discussion about the nature of relationships, represented by the various types of fruits. For example, someone commented that fruits with hard skins and edible centers represent relationships that are hard to enter, where the reward comes only with determination.

And, as an example of discussing things before they arise, Andrew and I have also begun discussing our personal preferences in death ritual in order to leave no stone unturned (so to speak).

OUR HOME AND OUR BODIES CAN BE SEEN TO REFLECT OUR RELIGIOUS CHOICES

We choose our wall art and the religious articles with which we adorn ourselves with the spirit of Judaism clearly in mind. We gift each other with religious ritual items like candlesticks, *kippot* (head coverings), *mezuzot* (objects placed on the doorposts of Jewish homes that contain a copy of the *Sh'ma* prayer), *chanukkiot* (Hanukkah candelabra), and *tallitot* (prayer shawls). Our bookshelves are filled with titles that relate to our understanding that all of life has spiritual content and that Judaism speaks to that truth. It is clear that we have chosen to embrace one religion for our household, and this is one of the pieces for which I am most grateful to Andrew.

OUR CELEBRATIONS CAN BE SMELLED DOWN THE BLOCK FROM OUR HOME

The flowers and vegetables we grow and the scent of holiday spices welcome our guests.

OUR FAMILY HISTORIES ARE TASTED IN OUR MEALS

We prepare holiday favorites and new twists on old themes to excite the spirit through the palate. Andrew's parents have been particularly adventuresome in eating Jewish foods that have no counterpart in their culture. In exchange for their willingness to experiment, I also prepare foods that represent their history, which adds to my life.

OUR DEVOTION TO HUMANITY AND TO THE PLANET IS ALWAYS FELT

We lovingly hold hands around the table as we bless The Source of Life and all which we hold dear, before we eat. We include blessings for food and the nature of the day. We recognize the blessing of family and friends and people we may have just met. While eating we often have tasty conversations wherein no subject is taboo. Like reading *Torah* (the first five books of the Hebrew Bible) each week, whatever is presented is worth discussing. It all has value and adds to our lives. As we clean up after meals, we bless each other and the earth by composting scraps and sending leftovers, if there are any, home with guests or to Andrew's co-workers.

All in all, our choice to be together has enriched our families, our community, and ourselves.

C. Andrew Martin is a nurse, hospice volunteer, and writer in New Hampshire. His current project, *Through the Mirror of My Mind: Reflective Inspirations for Caregivers,* is a memoir/self-help book.

My Life as the Non-Jewish Partner of a Rabbi

C. ANDREW MARTIN

YOM KIPPUR 1996

The Day of Atonement. A full day of making *yontif* (holiday) in a rural New Hampshire synagogue. I understand little of Hebrew prayer, even when the words are transliterated. Maybe *Baruch Atah Adonai* (Blessed are You God) is becoming familiar. I spend the day reading translations of *tefillot* (prayers of reflection and self-judgment). I cry during the *Yizkor* (memorial) service, having lost my former partner to AIDS seven months ago.

I wanted to do my first "Highest of Holy Days" right: I have fasted from all food and water for twenty-four hours; I am wearing leatherless shoes; I lit a *yahrzeit* (memorial) candle in Gil's memory; and I have said *"Gut Yontif"* (have a good Holiday) to Jewish faces I did not recognize.

After sundown, I force my way through the room, toward the table of food, to finally break the fast. I can see the young, handsome rabbi—the reason I am here. It would be futile to worm my way into that circle of adoring congregants. I reserve our personal relationship for outside of synagogue. Reaching for the first morsel of food to touch my lips in twenty-four hours, the foreign delectable catches in my throat as I distinctly hear a fiftyish woman loudly whisper, "So call me old-fashioned, but don't you think the rabbi's boyfriend should be Jewish?"

YOM KIPPUR 1997

The previous year, I had been Rabbi Lev Ba'esh's gentile boyfriend. However, my presence one year later marks the signs of a lasting, gay, interfaith relationship. I am no longer the rabbi's boyfriend, but the *rebbetzin* (rabbi's "wife"). But is *rebbetzin* an accurate word for the male partner of a male rabbi?

Does our interfaith relationship differ from others? Is our relationship different because my partner is a rabbi? Is the gay issue affected because my partner is a rabbi? And how does being gay impact on these issues?

THE CALENDAR OF HOLIDAYS

I now have twice as many observable holidays in my life. When I left home for college twenty-something years ago, I abandoned my parents' religion. Spirituality took on a solitary peacefulness.

The Hanukkah versus Christmas dilemma is usually an obstacle in any interfaith couple, either with or without children. However, after forty-something years of the commercialism, I was ready to take a break from it all. I respected my partner Lev's sanctuary of home and did not push my holiday traditions on him other than stringing mini-lights—one white, one blue—around our ficus tree. And in a mutual sharing of holiday ritual items, he presented me with a silver and brass Rosenthal Hanukkah *menorah* (candelabra), for which I lovingly made 144 "diversity"-themed, rainbow-colored beeswax candles.

As for the other holidays, we have no conflict. I experience Judaism's religious festivals during a full year's cycle, essentially living a Jewish life. In turn, Lev participates in "my holidays" as I celebrate them, by sharing traditional meals with my parents.

FAMILY

My Congregationalist parents accept our gay, interfaith relationship. You may find them seated at the head table, next to their son and the rabbi, during the congregational Passover *seder* (ritual meal). Or I may be surprised to see them in synagogue, which they drove one hour to attend, accompanied by my mother's non-Jewish hairdresser, along with the hairdresser's inquisitive Jewish husband and their two children—the firstborn approaching the age of *Bar Mitzvah* (the ceremony in which an individual chooses to assume the obligations and privileges of an adult member of the Jewish community).

HEBREW

I want to conquer this mystic tongue to appreciate more of the Friday evening service. You may find me occasionally struggling with a textbook, possibly receiving the benefit of an at-home tutorial from my rabbi-partner.

COMMUNITY OUTREACH

Hospice awareness, gardening, and writing are my passions. Rabbi Lev organized a group of temple congregants to train as volunteers with the hospice organization I support. I helped organize, dig, plant, and maintain a city "Adopt-a-Spot" garden, identifying Temple Israel as its creator. Most of our joint and single endeavors exhibit a melding of our religious lives.

CONVERSION

More of my non-Jewish friends than temple congregants ask me, "So, have you converted?" I believe I live a very Jewish life without the *mikvah* (ritual bath used when people convert to Judaism). However, someday I may take the plunge.

COMMITMENT

I have attended many weddings at which Lev has officiated—Jewish/Jewish, Jewish/non-Jewish, gay, straight, young, old, poor, and rich. Is his credibility compromised by our interfaith relationship that has not yet been ritually formalized? I feel as strongly committed to our relationship as I feel toward living a Jewish life. I am committed to both—at this time in my life—without any ritual ceremony.

YOM KIPPUR 1998

After listening to the haunting *Kol Nidre* service, I finally decided to personally address that woman's comment of two years prior. "You know, I wouldn't call you old-fashioned at all. And personally...affirming life's diversity...maybe the rabbi's life is a little richer with a boyfriend who's not Jewish. *Gut Yontif.*"

13. Creating Jewish Adoptive Families

Marlyn Kress began her adoption journey as a young woman contemplating her future family. In May 1994, as a single parent by choice, she adopted an eight-week-old baby girl from China. Marlyn is the national membership chair for Stars of David International, a support group for Jewish adoptive families, and co-directs Stars of David Chaverim in the Southern New Jersey/Philadelphia area.

With *Chai* You Get Eggroll: Raising a Jewish-Chinese Daughter in America

MARLYN KRESS

Although I didn't realize it at the time, my daughter's integration into Jewish life began before she was even born or chosen for me. My father, adhering to Jewish tradition, asked me to name her after his parents. I had already decided to name her Zoe, as it meant "life." To honor my father's request, I chose the Hebrew names Meira Sigal, meaning "shining treasure," after my grandparents Morris and Mildred Sarah Kress. I also wanted to honor my daughter's heritage and history by giving her a Chinese name.

When I adopted Zoe in May of 1994, adoptive parents were notified that there was a baby waiting for them, but received no other identifying information. I knew I was going to be a mom, period. I first met my daughter via a little piece of rice paper that was put at my place in a hotel restaurant in Nanchang, China. It listed

her name—Fu Mian—her birthdate, and the date of her abandonment. Her first name meant "one who studies hard." The FuZhou
(now Linchuan) Social Welfare House gave every child they
processed the name of Fu, which means "lucky" or "prosperous."
As I stared at that little piece of paper, her name formed in my mind:
Zoe FuMian Suni. I borrowed the Suni from another family in our
adoption travel group because it meant "long-awaited little dar-
ling." Chinese tradition values meaningful names, and Zoe has been
given her share.

Zoe was converted to Judaism in an Orthodox ceremony on her
first birthday. I chose an Orthodox conversion because I didn't want
her "Jewishness" to be questioned as she grew into adulthood. My
father, wearing a T-shirt emblazoned with the Great Wall of China,
carried her into the *mikvah* (ritual bath) and dunked her the requisite
three times. A trio of rabbis joyfully proclaimed her to be a Jew. It
was an incredible experience to see my beautiful daughter become
Jewish from my father's hands. It was as if her new religion was
passed down from her ancestors.

Our daily life is filled with references to Zoe's Chinese heritage.
Her room is decorated with Chinese arts and crafts. Our home is fur-
nished with Chinese antiques and artwork that I purchased before the
idea of a Chinese adoption became a reality. I want Zoe to be proud
of her dual heritage, to appreciate the history and craftsmanship that
went into making these things. I want both her Chinese and Jewish
sides to feel natural and right to her, parts of what make her a whole
person. I also want her to know and understand that I, too, celebrate
her diversity and feel it is a natural part of who she is and what com-
prises our family.

We celebrate Chinese festivals as they come up. I like to draw
parallels between Judaism and Chinese and American cultural celebrations, such as the harvest festivals of Sukkot, Thanksgiving, and
Mid-Autumn Festival. Zoe is growing up in America. She is learning
to speak for herself and to base her opinions on what she is learning
about American life. The fact that she can celebrate the new year
three times—American, Jewish, and Chinese—is fascinating to her.

Showing Zoe the parallels of different cultures and how we are all intertwined is very rewarding.

I have made sure that Zoe has ample opportunity to meet and befriend other Chinese people. We have numerous Chinese friends, and we are members of a Chinese adoption group. Zoe practices her developing knowledge of Mandarin with our Chinese friends and any other Asian who crosses her path. We also participate in our local Stars of David chapter, of which I am the coordinator. Zoe has many occasions to befriend other multinational adopted children and see how their lives fit into the spectrum of being Jewish.

We eat Jewish and Chinese food in our house all the time, and I enjoy pointing out to Zoe their similarities. Think of dumplings and *kreplach* (meat pie cooked in soup) for instance. And what about those old standbys—chicken and wonton soups? From the time she started eating real food, Zoe has had an affinity for anything Chinese. I used to think it was an inborn trait, especially since she learned to use chopsticks proficiently before she was two and a half. But I have since come to believe that her desire for Chinese food showcases a pride and level of comfort in herself even at her young age. Besides, it tastes good!

It has been fascinating to watch Zoe explain being Jewish to our eighteen-year-old Chinese exchange student. Zoe has shown her how to light the candles on *Shabbat* (the Jewish Sabbath), how to celebrate Jewish holidays like Hanukkah and Purim (the celebration of delivery from destruction as recorded in the Book of Esther), and has explained what foods to eat and not eat on Passover. My little six-year-old sees her Jewish Chineseness as her badge of honor.

I understand some parents believe that immersion in Chinese culture—by attending Chinese school and learning Mandarin language—is necessary. I, however, believe that my duty to Zoe is to raise her in a loving home and instill pride in who and what she is. I believe that it is more important to bring our two cultures together as a natural adjunct to each other. I was raised in a Jewish home. Jewish is who I am and what I know. I am sending Zoe to a Jewish day school so that she will have a firm foundation in her Jewishness. This,

I feel, will center her and enable her to meet life's challenges head on. I hope that at the age of *Bat Mitzvah*, when she must reaffirm her life as a Jew, she will choose this path that I have shown her with love.

I want Zoe to have love and respect for both her heritages—the Chinese one she was born with and the Jewish one I gave her. No matter how much Chinese culture I show her, I cannot give her the experience of being raised in China by Chinese parents. She lives in America, as a Jewish child with a Chinese heritage. I cannot give her back what was taken from her in my quest to become a parent. I can only hope that my love of her differences will give her pride in herself as a Chinese American Jew.

Cheryl A. Lieberman, Ph.D., is founder and president of Cornerstone Consulting Group based in Cambridge, Massachusetts, and is co-author of *Creating Ceremonies: Innovative Ways to Meet Adoption Challenges*.

On Adopting Children from a Different Religion and Culture

CHERYL A. LIEBERMAN

I don't know who was more nervous the first night we were together—Eric or me. We had one month to get to know each other before he came to live with me. After about two weeks of brief visits, Eric, who was almost eight years old, had his first overnight at my house. I read him a book and suggested we say a prayer together. He asked me to say it alone, so I made one up quickly, and to signal the end, said, "Amen." Eric quickly corrected me and said I should have said, "In Jesus' name, Amen." I looked at him, smiled, and said, "In this house we just say Amen." "Okay," he said.

I am a Jewish single woman who decided to become a mother through adoption. Anticipating that there would be more non-Jewish than Jewish children available for adoption, and that older children would come exposed to a specific religion, I knew that religion would be an area that needed to be addressed. My children (I later adopted Eric's younger brother Christopher) had been Christian for seven and six years, respectively, when they came to live with me. I wanted to respect both their heritage and mine. This presented a challenge.

In addition to the issue of religion, both boys are part Native American—Blackfeet and Cherokee (although I cannot get either tribe to claim them because I cannot get a long and comprehensive history for them). As I believe that all of one's heritage is important, I asked a friend who was strongly connected to Native American culture to take my children to a special ceremony where they were given Native American names.

We have an open adoption (ongoing contact with birth parents), and right after Eric was adopted his birth mother asked if he was attending church. I said that I was raising him as a Jew because I had a Jewish home, and that I would provide him with a grounding in the religion and values that were part of my home and family. When he grew up, I said, he could choose, as we all can, whatever religion he wants. I explained that I could support him in any religion as long as it was not a group that focused on hurting people in any way. She said she understood, and that that was okay. Eric was relieved to hear this.

Although as a young Jewish child growing up in a predominantly Christian community I had received presents from Santa Claus and candy from the Easter Bunny, I am quite clear today about my Judaism. As a parent, I knew I wanted to make Judaism attractive—especially as an alternative to Christmas. The first year that we celebrated Hanukkah, in addition to buying Eric one major gift, I bought him several little toys so that Judaism would not feel like deprivation. I remember hearing him tell a friend who saw his presents all over the living room, "I got all these presents for Hanukkah," and his friend said, "Wow, are you lucky!" Eric also got something from Santa

Claus, although it paled in comparison to his Hanukkah gifts. At Easter, I put together a basket from the Easter Bunny for him. When he came downstairs and saw the basket, he exclaimed, "The Easter Bunny didn't forget about me this year!"

Every Friday night at dinner, we do a *Shabbat* (the Jewish Sabbath) ceremony. Eric lights the candles and I sing the blessing. I chant the *Kiddush* (blessing over wine) and sing the *Ha-Motzi* (blessing over bread). Then, I always bless Eric. Rather than the traditional Hebrew blessing, I create my own, adding different elements to it each week. I put my hands on his head and hold him close and say, "Dear God, please bless Eric and help him grow up to be a man who is kind to other people, cares about animals, and takes good care of the earth, Amen." I then lean over and kiss him. On the night he received his Hebrew name in a special ceremony in the synagogue, my father gave Eric a *Kiddush* cup, and he surprised all of us by chanting the short version of the *Kiddush* all by himself.

The first time Eric and I went to the synagogue to speak to one of the rabbis about a Hebrew name, we went into the sanctuary, and the rabbi asked Eric to run up and down the aisles to get the feel of the place. The environment was all new and strange for Eric, and yet running up and down the aisles helped him feel more connected. My synagogue, Temple Israel in Boston, was warm and welcoming, and Eric soon felt accepted and at home here. In fact, the first time we went to Friday services, the rabbi invited Eric up to the *bimah* (podium) to open the ark. He was grinning from ear to ear, and I think I was, too. Even though Eric had some behavior problems in public school, the synagogue found a way to successfully integrate him into the religious school and youth program. To this day, my older son feels totally comfortable talking with any member of the staff, including the senior rabbi.

Eric's biological brother Christopher joined us two years later. He had spent the previous three and a half years living with a Catholic foster family. One day Christopher noticed that no other child at the synagogue had his name. I explained why this was probably true and also stated that he had a truly fine name that did not need to be changed. Chris talks about being Christian before coming to live with me and seems to be more conflicted than Eric on this topic. I try to respond casually and tell him, as I told Eric, that he can make a choice about his religion when he is an adult.

About three years ago, my sons were reunited with two other birth siblings who had been adopted by a Catholic family living geographically close to us. Chris decided that when he is an adult, "We [the brothers and sister] will live together the way we should have in the first place. We will all be Catholic, but don't worry, Mom. I will send my children to Hebrew school." After becoming a *Bar Mitzvah* (taken on the obligations and privileges of an adult member of the Jewish community), Chris wondered about becoming either a rabbi or someone who cleans the synagogue when he grows up. A rabbinic friend said, "Those two jobs could be interchangeable!"

During the children's *Bar Mitzvah* training, I gave my undivided attention to them each night as they practiced. Recently, Eric asked me if he could be confirmed. He said his *Bar Mitzvah* experience was one of the most important accomplishments in his life, and if he was Jewish he wanted to do it all.

My children are now fourteen and eighteen years old. They have let go of Santa Claus and the Easter Bunny and identify as Jews. Judaism is only a part of who they are, but it has given them a spiritual base, values, and a community to which they belong.

Rabbi Susan Silverman is co-author of *Jewish Family & Life* (Golden Books). She is currently serving the Multiracial Jewish Network, teaching at the Brandeis University Hillel, and working on a book on the spiritual journey of international adoption. She lives in Newton, Massachusetts, with her husband and three children.

Our Son's Conversion to Judaism

SUSAN SILVERMAN

We are seeking an Orthodox conversion for our son, Adar, a fourteen-month-old we adopted over a year ago from Addis Ababa, Ethiopia. That may not seem like a radical statement, but for us it is. The Judaism that completely permeates our lives is progressive. We are egalitarian. I am a rabbi. Our children have only heard my husband and me refer to God as "She." The women and the men of the *Torah* (the first five books of the Hebrew Bible) come alive for them as God's partners in history through my husband's nightly *Torah* or rabbinic story puppet show and our ongoing *Torah* discussions. The Jewish day school and synagogue communities that envelop us are pluralistic, with a bottom line of egalitarianism. Our two daughters— now six and almost eight—took on the *mitzvah* (commandment) of *tzitzit* (a fringed garment worn almost exclusively by traditional male Jews) shortly after they each turned five, and they have remained committed to it daily since then.

There is clearly spiritual and emotional sacrifice involved in taking the route of an Orthodox conversion. The holy transformation of my son becoming a Jew will not be presided over by loving rabbinic colleagues in an egalitarian ceremony that makes sense in our lives. Instead, both my husband and I are likely to feel the way we do during civil proceedings—like cogs in an administrative machine, going through motions of a process external to ourselves. Such distance from religious ritual is anathema to our daily Jewish life.

So why are we removing ourselves from our natural habitat by seeking the *heksher* (stamp of approval) of a different Jewish community—especially at such a sacred and liminal moment in our lives? We are protecting Adar. He will never know who his birth parents are, or their religion and ethnicity (there are many within Ethiopia). He will never know if he has birth siblings. He will never know the circumstances of his birth and early weeks of life. We do not want to provide any opportunity for anyone to cast doubt on his being a Jew—a fear that projects to his future at the local Jewish high school, which has an Orthodox *minyan* (prayer quorum) as well as progressive ones. We are willing to pay with our own Jewish identities at this moment of our lives for an insurance policy against those who would see fit to question his right to an *aliyah* (blessing and reading the *Torah*) or his credentials as a prom date for their child.

I fear that I am betraying God by casting aside my fundamental relationship with the Creator, and putting on the mask of someone else's. Perhaps God agrees that my son's future relationship with Him/Her needs to be protected when it might be most vulnerable—adolescence—the same time that the doubts of others might be made known to him. To do so, I must take a deep breath, and seek the *heksher* of the community of those who would otherwise reject his Jewish status.

14. Growing Up in an Interfaith Family

Rohanna Gibson Green is currently studying at McGill University in Montreal.

Joyful Family Traditions

ROHANNA GIBSON GREEN

"Sh'ma Yisrael, Adonai Eloheinu, Adonai Echad" (Hear O Israel, the Lord our God, the Lord is One). I have recited this blessing every night before bed for as long as I can remember. It is especially meaningful to me because of the phrase "the Lord is One." Partly because of my interfaith family, that concept has particular resonance, and I believe that all religions bring people closer to the same God that I pray to as a Jew.

Although I have been raised in a Jewish household, my dad's family is Anglican. He has never converted to Judaism, although he does observe many Jewish traditions. I live in Victoria, British Columbia, a city of 300,000 with a fairly small Jewish community. When I was born, Mom and Dad had decided to raise their family according to Jewish tradition. We didn't keep kosher (observe Jewish dietary laws) at that time, or observe *Shabbat*, but I was given a Hebrew name: Chana Mindel Bat Yitah Fegah.

When my younger brother was born, Mom and Dad had to make an excruciating decision. Our rabbi spent many hours with them talking about the commandment of circumcision. I think Mom had more trouble with the idea than Dad did, as she did not want to make a permanent mark on her little baby. Just in time (the circumcision is usually performed eight days after birth), they decided to go ahead with the ritual. I'm sure my brother recovered faster than Mom's nerves. Looking back, I realize that the birth of children is often a major crossroad in a family's Jewish observance.

After my brother's circumcision, we became more observant in several ways. We moved into a new house and decided to keep a kosher kitchen. We did it the easy way, by becoming vegetarian. At four and a half, I was quite thrilled with the experience of pouring boiling water over all our counters. I was probably more interested in the streams of hot water than in the significance of ritual purification.

Every year our family joyfully celebrates the major Jewish holidays. At Sukkot (fall harvest festival), we fumble around trying to fit the two-by-fours together around our backyard picnic table to make the traditional hut called a *sukkah*. There is an excited flurry of scissors and staplers as we put together long paper chains and scribbled flowers to symbolize the fall harvest. Throughout the year, at Hanukkah, Passover, Purim (the celebration of delivery from destruction as recorded in the Book of Esther), Tu B'Shevat (the New Year of the Trees), and other holidays, we savor each other's company with old songs, improvised skits, and good food. We try to observe the rules, but like many other families we know, we often let compromise creep in. Usually one or two of us make it through the fast on Yom Kippur unscathed, but such observances are a matter of personal choice in my family.

Although my Anglican grandparents—my father's parents—go to church regularly, I have attended only a few times, and considered myself a visitor rather than a participant in the service. Christmas is the only Christian holiday we have ever celebrated together. Interestingly, Mom was the one who kept it going; she felt that decorating a tree and giving presents created a wonderful family event that we shouldn't miss out on just because we were Jewish. Dad would have preferred not to celebrate it at all. It was, however, a great occasion to visit with Dad's side of the family, especially when my aunt and uncle moved nearby. In the last few years, however, we have stopped observing Christmas except when relatives are visiting.

My level of Jewish observance is always changing. When I had my *Bat Mitzvah* (the ceremony in which an individual chooses to assume the obligations and privileges of an adult member of the Jewish community), I took responsibility for the commandments in the *Torah* (the first five books of the Hebrew Bible), and I do feel an obligation to fulfill them. I went through Hebrew school, learned to lead services, and have played an active part in Jewish youth activities. For the last four years I have taught *Bar/Bat Mitzvah* preparation classes. I attend services semi-regularly, and occasionally chant the *Haftorah* (reading from the Prophets) in Hebrew, although I do not speak the language conversationally.

People often wonder whether children from interfaith families are less likely to remain Jewish as they grow older. I think that depends on the individual. Personally, I have always been interested in exploring other spiritual paths. For a while I thought about converting to Baha'i. To me, religion is a way of structuring my relationship to God and to the rest of the world. The Baha'i emphasis on the essential unity of all religions fit with my own observations. I liked some of the rules they live by. I'm not sure why I did not convert—I guess it's because so many things about the Jewish tradition appeal to me as well.

Nobody forces me to observe Jewish traditions. Perhaps because of their own background, Mom and Dad leave it to us to decide which commandments to observe and whether to date other Jews. In my case, one out of three boyfriends has been Jewish. I see religion as one aspect of life. If a relationship is really strong, I think it can work despite religious differences.

At this point I feel comfortable dating someone who is not Jewish as long as it doesn't interfere with my ability to observe Jewish traditions. If it comes to a decision about marriage and a family, I know it won't be so easy. In my family, Dad was willing to raise his children in a Jewish environment. In fact, he has studied so much about Judaism that he usually leads our family celebrations. When we ask, he tells us about Christian approaches to life that he learned while growing up, but there is never any doubt that we are a Jewish family. Not all non-Jews would be comfortable with this level of Jewish life.

When it comes down to it, I'm not sure how comfortable I would be raising a family outside the Jewish tradition. It is an issue I would want to discuss seriously before marriage. I suppose I will just search for the right decision if the issue arises. For now, I intend to postpone the matter entirely.

I can't imagine growing up in a family other than my own. The differences in my parents' backgrounds have enriched my experience by showing me that wonderful lives can be lived according to any tradition. Our observance of the Jewish cycle of festivals and traditions has brought us together as a family more than anything else we do together. They have become family festivals, family traditions enriched with our own brand of silliness and joy. I would not have it any other way.

A graduate of Brandeis University, Stephanie Bruce lives in Allston, Massachusetts, and currently attends Harvard Law School.

Growing Up "Half and Half" but Feeling Whole

STEPHANIE BRUCE

Most American seven-year-olds go to Hebrew School or CCD (Confraternity of Christian Doctrine) for their religious education. When I was seven years old, I went to both.

My religious quest began after noticing that while some kids at school celebrated Hanukkah, and some kids celebrated Christmas, my family celebrated both holidays. Upon asking my mother, "What are we?" she replied that she was Jewish, my dad was Catholic, and I was free to choose to be whatever I wanted.

"Free to choose?" I didn't know enough about either religion to choose. And I couldn't look to my parents for much guidance, as neither of them was very religious. Admittedly a rather precocious seven-year-old, I decided to attend both Hebrew School and CCD classes, and to then choose my religion at the end of the year.

That year I was one stressed-out seven-year-old. I felt a great deal of pressure from both sets of grandparents, who were each vying for my religious vote. And I had quite a busy schedule: Hebrew School on Wednesdays and Saturdays, CCD on Tuesdays and Sundays, piano lessons on Thursdays. Some of my friends, whose parents were forcing them to get a religious education, wondered why I bothered to go to even one religious school, never mind two. Why was religion so important to me when it wasn't very important to my parents? Precisely because my parents had such weak religious identities, I wanted a stronger one. Many of my best friends identified with one religious group or another, but I was lost in between—belonging to both groups and to neither of them, all at the same time.

Though this feeling of simultaneously belonging and not belonging will always stay with me on some level, after attending both religious schools that year I began to identify more with the Jewish religion. Though both religious schools were incredibly accepting of me and even encouraged me to share my cross-cultural perspective, I felt more comfortable at Hebrew school, more attracted to Jewish beliefs, and more interested in its language and culture. Also, at the tender age of seven I was a bit overwhelmed by the prominence of the death of Christ in Christianity and was much more drawn to the emphasis in Judaism on life.

Many people, including many Jews, are surprised that I chose to identify with Judaism when Christianity is more mainstream and acceptable in American culture. Why would I choose to identify with an historically persecuted people? How could I resist the allure of the

Christmas season and trade it in for Hanukkah? Perhaps it is because Judaism is not mainstream and is a little bit different that I wanted to identify with it.

But, ultimately, I don't believe that I chose Judaism—rather, it chose me. When I began my quest for religious identity, I wasn't looking to conform to an existing belief structure. Rather, I was seeking a belief structure that most closely matched the one I already had inside. And though I made the decision to discontinue the CCD class and continue with my Jewish education at the end of second grade, my search for a religious identity did not end there. Year after year, through a *Bat Mitzvah* (the ceremony in which an individual chooses to assume the obligations and privileges of an adult member of the Jewish community), confirmation class, and my pursuit of a minor in Judaic Studies in college, I have reevaluated and questioned my beliefs. So far, Judaism has confirmed my own personal beliefs as much as I have confirmed my belief in Judaism.

I am not saying that growing up with an interfaith background and choosing my religion was easy. Though I happened to be very fortunate that my parents and most of my family were open-minded and supportive of my decision, I was unable to practice as many of the rituals of Judaism as I would have liked because my fairly secular family was not interested. I also know that some of my family members and friends who weren't Jewish were somewhat alienated and offended by my decision not to identify with Christianity. On the flip side, I have encountered rabbis and other members of the Jewish community who cast doubt on my Jewish identity and condemn my parents' marriage. In still other unfortunate instances, people mistake me for a Christian because of my last name and reveal anti-Semitic sentiments they would otherwise have kept to themselves.

Ultimately, however, I wouldn't trade the experience of growing up half-Jewish and half-Christian and being given the opportunity to choose one for myself. It was because of this opportunity that I have never taken my heritage and beliefs for granted, nor ever blindly followed them. My dual religious identity has given me a unique perspective on both religions that many do not have. And, having chosen Judaism, I feel that my religion is that much more my own. For me, being "half and half" has not prevented me from feeling whole.

Emily Case is a recent college graduate who works with children with emotional and behavioral challenges and is pursuing a master's degree in social work.

Growing Up Jewish in an Interfaith Family

EMILY CASE

When I was nine years old, my father pulled me aside for one of our routine walks around the block. I remember the beautiful spring day well, the chirping birds and the sweet flower smells that filled our neighborhood. But this walk was not simply a stroll to enjoy the pleasant afternoon; Dad meant business. The agenda of the walk would be my religious identity.

Up until this point, as the daughter of an interfaith couple I had always thought of myself as half-Jewish, half-Christian. According to my childish logic, it made sense to me that I would belong to both of my parents' religions. Even though we were practicing Jews, my mother had never officially converted to Judaism, and we still celebrated Christmas every year. But on that walk, my "half-and-half" logic was forever abandoned.

"You are a Jew," my father told me decisively, externally imposing on me a sense of myself as a religious being. My father's declaration established a mental schema through which I construed my developing religious thoughts and experiences. I wholeheartedly accepted his decree that I was a Jew and never again considered myself to be any fraction Christian.

For many years after this exchange, my religious identity as a Jew continued to be imposed by external factors and created in response to external events. As children, we develop a sense of ourselves in the social realm on the basis of our overt actions and in relation to other people and the beliefs we think they hold about us.

While I was growing up, my religious behaviors were directed by others, primarily by my parents. I attended Sunday school and Hebrew school, observed the Sabbath, and went to synagogue on the holy days because that is what my parents directed me to do. I considered myself to be a Jew and acted as a member of this group in response to external demands and expectations.

Even after I came to proclaim myself as a Jew in middle childhood, as an adolescent I was still concerned about whether others would view me as a member of this religious community. I remember feeling nervous that the family of a very observant friend, who talked of inviting me to *Shabbat* (the Jewish Sabbath) dinner, would look down on me and not consider me to be a Jew. I worried that my Hebrew school classmates would not regard me as a legitimate Jew because I celebrated Christmas each year. In these and many other ways, my religious identity was very much oriented outwards until my late adolescence.

In recent years, my realm of self-definition has shifted away from the social. Internal, personal meaning has become more important to me in thinking of myself as a religious being. I experience my Jewishness more from the inside out than from the outside in, as it was when I younger. I have been working to sort out and define internally what it means to me to be a Jew. There are many questions I ask myself in considering how Judaism informs and enriches my life. For example, what Jewish practices, rituals, and traditions will be important for me to incorporate into my life? What Jewish teachings and morals guide my life and inform my actions? Do I wish to identify with a Jewish community? How can I find a spiritual life in the context of Judaism? Whether or not these questions are more difficult because I am the product of an interfaith marriage, I do not know. Perhaps these are common questions with which people my age grapple.

I do know that sometimes I long for the simplicity I experienced as a child when my religious life was externally defined and directed. Part of me misses the days of being told who I am and what to do as a Jew. Now I must do this work on my own, and the searching often feels as if it is being done in solitary. I struggle to develop a self-concept that incorporates a sense of myself as a Jew. At this point in my life, my Jewish identity is very much a work-in-progress.

Adam Case is a freshman at Northwestern University.

Visiting Israel—a Land I Feel a Strong Bond with, but Where I Am Not Considered a Jew

ADAM CASE

In the summer of 1999 I returned to Israel for the second time on a North American Federation of Temple Youth teen trip with forty-four other teenagers from around America. Each time I have visited Israel, it has strengthened the connection that I feel to the people and especially to the land itself. While there, I feel linked with every Jew around the world. Yet, in the official view of the state of Israel, I would not be considered Jewish.

What troubles me most is that the very land I feel such an intense connection with is the same state that would not recognize me as a Jew. This is because my mother, who practices Judaism, has never officially converted. Jewish law in Israel traces matrilineal descent in deciding who is Jewish.

I have always considered myself a Jew. Though my mother grew up Christian, she has embraced Judaism and is an active member of our synagogue. I, myself, attended Hebrew school for almost ten years, and I can read and write Hebrew. I don't personally consider myself any less Jewish than anyone else, and I think that it is preposterous that anyone would try to tell me whether or not I am a Jew.

I didn't run into any particular difficulties regarding my intermarried background on my trip, in part because NFTY is a Reform organization. The only time that I felt somewhat uncomfortable was on the way to the airport to return to America, when Michael, one of our leaders, was talking about a kid who had told him that he would only date Jewish girls now. Michael congratulated the kid and said something to the effect that the best way to maintain the Jewish people is to marry other Jews. In many ways I agree with this statement. It is much easier to pass on Judaism when both parents are Jewish—yet I don't believe that it is the only way. I am proof that intermarried families can raise Jewish children.

On my trip there were at least nine other kids who came from intermarried families. Their own personal experiences in intermarried families ranged from relatively easy to significantly more difficult. In a few cases the non-Jewish parent had decided to convert to Judaism; in others the parent had not converted. One girl in particular had had a very different and more difficult experience than I had. Her mother, who is a Jew, married her father, who was a Christian, but who now is a practicing Pagan. The Paganism her father practices incorporates many of the ideals of the Iroquois tribe to which he belongs. This girl told us that she has had many difficulties with her father regarding religion. In the past, she said, she had argued with him over the value of each religion. She did not feel that her father accepted or valued her Judaism. Yet, ironically, this adversity may, in fact, have strengthened her connection to Judaism. Her career goal is to become a Reform rabbi.

My visit to Israel was very meaningful for me. I feel a stronger connection to Judaism, but I think that my bond with the land of

Israel is what has really increased. Israel is filled with a history so
ancient that it is impossible not to look in awe and amazement upon
much of it. Three things stand out prominently in my mind: my first
view of the Western Wall, the sight of the two-thousand-year-old
stones the Romans threw off the Temple Mount when they destroyed
the Second Temple, and the sweeping view of Jerusalem I saw as I
emerged from the Yad Vashem Holocaust Museum. It is this mix of
ancient and new that makes Israel such a special place. I know that I
want to return there frequently in my life, and I now have a desire to
learn to speak Hebrew. Yet, it saddens me that in this land I feel such
a kinship with, I am not accepted as a Jew.

15. The December Dilemma

Paula Brody, Ed.D., LICSW, is director of Outreach Programs and Training for the Northeast Council of the Union of American Hebrew Congregations (UAHC, the Reform Movement), where she develops and coordinates a wide range of programs and services to welcome interfaith families into Reform congregations. She is a consultant to, and the "Dear Dr. Paula" columnist for, InterfaithFamily.com.

Happy Holidays? Understanding December Dilemmas in the Context of Jewish Family Memories

PAULA BRODY

"Is it okay if my child sits on Santa's lap?" "What if my child sings Christmas carols?" "Should I let my child decorate a friend's Christmas tree?" "Is it okay for my child to receive Christmas presents from relatives?"

As the December holiday season approaches, I am often asked these questions. Parents want to know, "Will exposure to or celebration of Christmas holiday rituals negatively influence my child's Jewish identity?"

My answer to these questions might be surprising to some. For me, the answer is: "It depends upon how you celebrate *Shabbat* (the Jewish Sabbath) and other Jewish holidays." In other words, the strength, comfort, and joy of one's Jewish identity emerge from a year-long process: Jewish identity is not shaped just in December.

One cannot balance the power of the deep family memories that

Christmas holds for Christians with Jewish memories of Hanukkah. It just doesn't work. For all Jewish families, and especially for interfaith families raising Jewish children, Jewish family memories associated with Hanukkah will not hold a candle—not even eight candles with a *dreidel* (a Hanukkah spinning toy) added for good measure—to Christian family memories associated with Christmas.

First of all, Christmas is perhaps the most significant holiday of the Christian year, filled with family memories for most Christians. Most Jewish families have family memories of time spent together on December 25th, too. After all, as a "national" holiday, most people are off from work, children are not in school, and relatives can come to visit.

So what is a Jewish family to do? Unless it falls right around December 25th, parents are usually working during the eight days of Hanukkah, evening meetings go on, children are in school. So, it is impossible for children, or parents for that matter, to mark this holiday—or sadly, many other Jewish holidays—as "special family time" when the family can enjoy being together without being encumbered by their daily routine.

One solution is: take Jewish holidays off from work. Do not work on Friday evening and Saturday. Teach your children that *Shabbat* and the Jewish holidays are important times for your family to spend together. Make the Jewish holidays and the full cycle of the Jewish year a priority for your family memory bank. Take time off to be together. Special shared family times create family memories.

The Jewish year holds virtually unlimited rich opportunities for family memories. Start the New Year with a family outing to an orchard to pick the sweet Rosh Hashanah apples to be dipped in honey. Together, make a favorite apple dessert for a Yom Kippur break the fast. Build a *sukkah* (a wooden hut) in your backyard so that you and your children can share the fun of decorating it and eating outdoors together during the fall harvest holiday of Sukkot. Participate in a synagogue celebration of Simchat Torah (marking the completion of the yearly cycle of reading the first five books of the Hebrew Bible and the beginning of a new cycle) to witness the *Torah* being fully unrolled, and dance, sing, and study *Torah* together. Keeping the year filled with memories will enable Hanukkah to have its proper place as a minor festival within the context of the Jewish year.

Of course, the most important Jewish holiday for family memories is *Shabbat*. You have a wonderful weekly opportunity to pause together as a family to enjoy and appreciate the family you have created. Make *Shabbat* home rituals a sweet and special time. Create *Shabbat* traditions unique to your family as you welcome the weekly gift of setting time apart from the rest of your busy week. Sing *Shabbat* songs, eat special foods, say the blessings together, and bless each other. Invite friends and family to join you; encourage Christian friends and family to learn about *Shabbat* at your family table, too.

Celebrating *Shabbat* and the full complement of the Jewish year will enable you to build wonderful family memories and a clear identity as a Jewish family. As December approaches, the Christmas season will not threaten the Jewish identity of a family that has built these memories together. Just as a solid Christian identity of friends and family will not be altered if they join you at your *Shabbat* table, so a solid Jewish identity of your children will not be altered if they participate at a Christmas dinner.

Especially for interfaith families, Christmas may provide another important Jewish learning moment for you and your children, teaching how to "honor your father and mother." Helping others to celebrate joy in their lives is a Jewish value. Enable your children to understand that they are helping others celebrate Christmas and learning about an important Christian holiday. However, be clear with yourselves and your children: Christmas is not a Jewish holiday. Hanukkah is not a Jewish Christmas.

Interfaith families will see that as the years go by, as your family has experienced the beauty of *Shabbat* and many other Jewish holidays together, by the end of December you and your children may be looking forward to planting a tree for Tu B'Shevat or may already be anticipating costumes and gifts for Purim (the celebration of delivery from destruction as recorded in the Book of Esther). As years are shared together, the box of homemade *sukkah* decorations may have as much meaning as, or perhaps more meaning than, a box of cherished Christmas ornaments. (Possibly, some of these festive ornaments may even hang in your *sukkah*!)

Optimally, over the years your non-Jewish friends and family have learned about your Jewish holidays, too, and have shared in your *Shabbat* meals, Passover *seders* (ritual meals), and *sukkah* parties; or they have joined you in the apple-picking adventures that launch your family memories of another sweet Jewish year. Hopefully, they have learned to honor you and your holidays and have been a part of your shared family memories, just as you have celebrated with them.

So, "Is it okay for my Jewish child to sing Christmas carols?" I ask the question, "Does your child sing Jewish songs with the same joy and enthusiasm?"

In the question lies the answer. Happy holidays!

Rena Mello lives in the Boston area with her husband and their son. She has worked in the field of international education for the past eight years.

Negotiating Christmas

RENA MELLO

A few months after my husband and I started dating, we had a discussion about religion over dinner. Eric told me that he felt strongly about raising his children Jewish, even if he married someone not Jewish. "Why," I asked, "can't a child be raised with both religious traditions? Wouldn't learning about how Christians and Jews celebrate holidays foster a sense of open-mindedness and acceptance?"

Eric felt that in order to maintain a strong Jewish community, it was essential for children to be raised in only the Jewish tradition. In his mind, being raised with two faiths meant that, eventually, the child might grow up to have no religious or cultural identity.

Once our relationship became more serious, we felt that it was responsible to arrive at a decision about how we would handle raising children before we became officially engaged. Being a non-practicing Catholic, I agreed to raise our children Jewish, since Eric felt so closely tied to the cultural aspects of Judaism. However, the one unresolved issue in our discussions at this early stage of our exploration was how to negotiate the December dilemma. Perhaps we focused on this issue because it was November and my emotions were running high with Christmas around the bend. Or perhaps the issue took on greater importance because it was the most simplistic, tangible interfaith topic to tackle.

I insisted on celebrating Christmas—tree and all—because although I had agreed to raise our children Jewish, I wanted them to have one tradition in the house that was representative of my religious upbringing. I hoped they would cherish the Christmas traditions of my childhood: decorating a tree, singing carols, leaving cookies and milk for Santa. I felt that if my children did not have this, they would be missing something very special, and I would be surrendering the one last vestige of my own family's religious traditions.

Eric thought it important that a Jewish family not have a Christmas tree. He felt that our children would not be truly Jewish if they were to celebrate Christmas in our home. He believed that a Christmas tree represented Christianity in a significant way. I argued that it is a secular symbol and that it would not make our children any less Jewish. Eric had no sense or understanding of the significance of Christmas in my life. Likewise, I had no idea how he could view such an innocuous symbol as a Christmas tree to be an icon as symbolic as a crucifix. We were at an impasse. We had heated arguments, each supporting our own position and not understanding the other's perspective.

Now, many years later, I am married to Eric and the mother of our one-year-old son, Evan. We do not have a Christmas tree during the holiday season, and we celebrate only Jewish traditions in our household. Although I am not formally converting to Judaism, we plan to join a local Reform synagogue that is open to interfaith families.

How, then, did we arrive at this point?

Eventually, Eric decided that he was open to celebrating Christmas, tree and all, in our home if it was *that* important to me. He loved me too much to let this one issue harm our relationship. That was all I needed to hear. I relaxed, the issue became a non-issue, and we became engaged. Shortly thereafter, we decided to attend an interfaith marriage discussion group. It was remarkable how trivial the issue of a Christmas tree became once we delved into larger issues such as our concepts of faith and the values we wanted to pass down to our children. I firmly believe that we would not have reached this stage if Eric hadn't been open to my sharing Christmas in our home. I realized that an attitude of openness and acceptance in my partner was far more important to me than actually getting what I thought I wanted all along. Once he told me the tree didn't matter to him, it didn't matter to me.

I have now gone through two holiday seasons without any trace of Christmas in our home. We go to my sister's house to celebrate Christmas, and we enjoy seeing the tree and opening the gifts my family so lovingly chose for us. In our own home, we light Hanukkah candles. Ironically, I am grateful that I am not lugging a tree up to our apartment and then struggling to keep our son Evan from crawling up to it and tearing it down. I also feel that having a tree would somehow not fit in with our lifestyle these days. Having a baby has changed our lives in so many wonderful ways. It has also made me aware of how insignificant having a tree during December is to us as a family.

Paula Lee Hellman has been active in Jewish education for the past twelve years, working with adults, senior adults, and children. She and her Jewish husband have a blended family that includes children and stepchildren, grandchildren, and a stepgrandchild from their previous interfaith marriages.

The Disappearing Christmas Tree

PAULA LEE HELLMAN

The first year after my Jewish husband and I were married, we still put up a large, beautiful Christmas tree in our living room. Together with our children from our first marriages, we decorated the tree with lights and ornaments, many of which came from the Hallmark store that I had owned and managed.

Christmas trees had been part of our separate lives for more than fifteen years—the time that each of us had spent married to our previous Christian spouses. In each of our homes, a tree—the bigger the better—had greeted our respective children on Christmas day.

My husband had struggled with his first wife's insistence on a tree. Although he tried to enjoy the family trip to the tree farm, and dutifully took along a folding saw to cut down the tree of her choice, he tells me that, brought up as an Orthodox Jew, he had never felt good about bringing the tree into his home.

I, on the other hand, loved the tree—something I'd always wanted when I was a child. The beauty, scent, and glitter seemed to me to be very American, not specifically Christian.

Growing up, I knew I was Jewish and was told that Jews didn't have Christmas trees. But each year my family had walked down New York City's Fifth Avenue, admiring the big tree in Rockefeller Center and strolling past store windows decorated with animated mannequins set in Santa's Toy Shop or in imaginative Victorian homes. I didn't understand why we couldn't bring the sparkle of the season home.

My parents, intellectual and assimilated Jews, attended services at a Reform synagogue on High Holy Days and sent my sister and me to Sunday school. But we did little Jewish ritual in our home. We did light a Hanukkah *menorah* (candelabra) every year. We put on "dress up" clothes and stood close together as we celebrated the minor holiday of Hanukkah, made special and different from the major holiday of Christmas. But the beauty of the tiny lights did not fully satisfy my longing for a tree.

So, when I married a Christian man whose sole connection to his religion was a tree and gifts at Christmas, I was delighted. Each year I looked forward to bringing a tree into my home. My children loved the process of choosing a tree and moving it around to insure that the "best side" faced front. We selected our decorations carefully. Fortunately, Hallmark provides plenty of mice on ice-skates, raccoons peeping out from under pine cones, and bright red cardinals that clip onto tree branches. We were always able to find holiday decorations that pleased our family aesthetic without being overtly Christian.

During the years between my divorce and remarriage, I maintained the tradition of the Christmas tree. It was special and provided continuity "for the children," and for me.

But then my Jewish husband and I married. "We are establishing a Jewish home," he said. "Why should we have a tree?" I replied that, for me, the tree wasn't a Christian symbol, and besides, the children expected one.

And that first year, we did have a tree. But it wasn't the same. That year, the tree really was for the children. I no longer had a desire for it. We decided to tell the children that this would be the last year of "the tree." We held what we called a "great gift-giving bash," and reminded them that the following year we would only be celebrating Hanukkah—with few gifts.

As Christmas approached in the second year of our marriage, "the tree" became a family issue. My daughter didn't really believe that we meant not to have a tree. Although she enjoyed Hanukkah and loved lighting candles and singing Hanukkah songs, Hanukkah couldn't hold a candle to Christmas.

True to my youthful tradition, our family stood close together, reading from a single prayer book as we watched the brightly colored Hanukkah candles burn. The children always looked forward to the nightly decision—multi-colored candles, or uniform? A white *shamash* (helper-candle: the one that lights all the others), or a blue one for Israel? But Hanukkah wasn't Christmas.

While they liked Hanukkah, they anticipated the Christmas tree with glee. With its brightly colored glass balls shining in lights that stayed lit for hours, the tree was very special. And there were lots of presents at Christmastime, which were unwrapped slowly, so we could savor the excitement of guessing what was in each box.

Now, we were telling the children that we were taking Christmas away. The loss of multiple gifts was less significant than the loss of the tree. The children were old enough to realize that we were blessed as a family and able to give them what they needed. They also understood that one or two gifts sufficed. But no tree?

The first year without a tree, my daughter begged for one. Even a little one to keep in her room. My daughter liked celebrating both holidays, as she felt was her birthright as the child of a Christian father and a Jewish mother. We said "okay," but it wasn't the same. Not for her, not for us. Hanukkah that year was less wonderful than it had been. The presents were somewhat bigger, but the feeling was smaller. The loss of the tree loomed large.

That year, we went to the home of my Christian stepson for Christmas. He was the child of my first husband's previous marriage and therefore had no Jewish parents. He and his Episcopal wife celebrated Christmas, and we were invited. There, we could enjoy the tree.

My stepson and his family came to our home for Hanukkah; we went there for Christmas. It seemed like a great system. We enjoyed *latkes* (potato pancakes) and candles in a Jewish home, where gifts were tiny and everyone got chocolate-covered coins, and, on another night, went to a Christian home for turkey dinner and lots of presents under a glittering tree.

That tradition lasted for a number of years, until my stepson moved away. Now, my Jewish husband and I celebrate Hanukkah only. My daughter celebrates Christmas and has a huge, but not real, tree. She's looking forward to making the holiday special. On this, her first year as a single mom, she'll invite us to be with her on Christmas day. My husband's son spends Christmas each year with his Christian mother and family. He does like a Christmas tree. He says it's the "pageantry" that he feels drawn to—and the closeness of being with family. That's what's special for him—the family connection.

Our Hanukkah is bigger now, because we have more lights. When my daughter comes to visit, at least once during the eight days, each of us lights a *menorah* from a collection of Hanukkah lamps that has grown in the fourteen years that my Jewish husband and I have been married. Our extended Christian family also enjoys hearing the story of the Maccabees' fight for freedom that happened 160 years before the Common Era. We eat *latkes* and engage in the complicated pulling apart of the foil wrappers from golden chocolate coins. Every once in a while I look around for the tree, then I remember. We don't have a tree. For just a moment I still miss it.

Jim Keen is a freelance writer based in Ann Arbor, Michigan. He has fifteen years of experience in an interfaith relationship. He is married with two children.

Will Santa Bring Me Presents, Even If I'm Jewish?

JIM KEEN

Ahhh, yes. The "December Dilemma." My wife, Bonnie, and I started talking about how to handle it while we were still engaged. We suddenly had realized that yes, one day we would have children. What to do? We had no clue. We just knew that it was better to go into family life with a game plan. We felt that if we waited to figure it out after our children were born, we would be susceptible to disaster.

Having already decided to raise the kids Jewish like their mother, we knew they would celebrate Hanukkah, and I would *help* them celebrate their holiday. That was the easy part. But I am Protestant and still celebrate Christmas. I also wanted our children to learn about *my* holidays. In addition, Christmas would likely be spent with my parents and my siblings. My brother and sister are both married and would soon have kids as well. We are a close family and all live in the same town. We always get together for the holidays. How would my children react if they had to sit still and watch their cousins open a bunch of presents from Santa? And it's not just the presents. There are a lot of feelings that run wild and free during the Christmas season. The spirit of the holidays is everywhere. There are trees to be decorated, cookies to bake, and lights to be strung. Santa's jolly pink face is ubiquitous—even on your can of Coke. These are all fun things that I grew up with and was not about to give up (not that American marketing would let me). So we decided that Bonnie and the kids would also *help* me celebrate my holidays. We certainly were not going to raise our kids in both religions, yet they were to learn about what Christmas means to me. As Jews, however, they would only be assisting Daddy with *his* celebration.

Bonnie and I knew that whatever plan we came up with would have to be flexible. Not having children yet, we couldn't possibly know what it would be like when they were born and reality hit us. We had to be able to make minor adjustments. The important thing was to make sure we were consistent. The main goal was that the kids knew they were Jewish and celebrated Hanukkah.

Four and a half years ago, our first daughter, Gabby, was born. Last year, Molly came into our world. It was easy when Gabby was an infant. She didn't ask questions. All we had to do was stick to our plan. But by the time Molly was born, Gabby started asking lots of questions.

"Who in our family is Jewish? Which grandparents are Christian? Does Daddy celebrate Hanukkah? Do I get Hanukkah *and* Christmas presents? Will Santa bring me presents, even if I'm Jewish?"

We had been afraid something like this would happen. We didn't want our kids to focus on the differences in our family. Bonnie and I have tried to nurture a sense of identity for our children that they could be proud of, while realizing that their religion and culture are just part of who they are. They are a lot of things. They are girls, they have brown eyes, Gabby likes to dance, Molly likes to laugh at the dog, and, yes, they are Jewish. Daddy is tall, he has green eyes, and he is Christian. Mommy is pretty, she likes chocolate, and she is Jewish.

The next obstacle we had to overcome was keeping a consistent approach to the holidays. My Protestant parents kept asking us what kind of gift, if any, to give the girls on Christmas morning. Christmas or Hanukkah presents? We had to admit that we were slightly unprepared for the question. The gifts had never had an identifying label attached to them. But then again, the girls had never asked—until now. This is why we made our plan flexible. We knew we'd have to adapt to the unexpected.

After we discussed it for a few days, we finally decided how we'd explain things to our kids. Hanukkah was simple; the kids get Hanukkah presents. Christmas, which we celebrate at my parents' house, was a little more complicated.

We decided to tell Gabby, "Santa brings you Hanukkah presents on Christmas, because he knows you're Jewish."

My parents and in-laws give the major gifts to our daughters on Hanukkah. Meanwhile, my parents save one or two smaller Hanukkah presents for Christmas morning. This seems to work well for us. The girls are consistently reinforced that they are Jewish, and they don't miss out on activities during my holiday. My parents, who love to give presents, don't get denied on Christmas morning either.

While working through this not-so-simple problem, both Bonnie and I had felt uncomfortable with various other solutions. Bonnie, in particular, often felt that it just wasn't right to celebrate Christmas at all with the kids. However, I wanted to share with the girls some of the joy and special feelings that I had from my childhood. We both felt emotions that the other one couldn't possibly know. Neither one of us, though, wanted to confuse our children. Fortunately, Bonnie's stepmom offered us a refreshing bit of wisdom. She said, "One day out of the year isn't going to make or break their Jewish identity. It's how you raise your kids as Jews the other 364 days that counts."

In the end, we knew we were an interfaith family and would have to approach this from a different angle than same-faith marriages. We are both comfortable with what we've decided. It may not work for everyone, but it fits our family nicely. In the years to come, I'm sure we'll have to face more surprises and twists. However, we have a sound foundation on which to build. We'll be ready.

Cheryl Opper teaches childbirth education and senior fitness and is the youth group director at her church. She has been married for fifteen years and has one daughter, who celebrated her *Bat Mitzvah* in the spring of 2001.

How Can I Embrace the December Holidays without Offending My Jewish Family?

CHERYL OPPER

I'm Christian and my husband, Neal, is Jewish. We have been married for thirteen years. We have had a lot of experience over the years trying to create our interfaith holiday celebrations. Our holidays have gone from having a Christmas tree in our home, to no tree, to a poinsettia plant instead of a tree, back to a tree. It was easier to create our holiday celebrations before our daughter, Lindsay, was born.

Neal and I made the decision before we were married to raise any future child we might have as a Jew. During our engagement we met with our rabbi and minister about our decision. I remember asking my minister, "As a Christian, how can I not teach my child about Jesus? Jesus is a big part of who I am." The minister said, "You are right, Jesus is a part of you. He lives in your heart. You don't have to talk about him because he lives through your love and your actions."

I remember feeling like a weight had just been lifted from my chest. The minister said that Neal and I had the opportunity as an interfaith couple to reach out to others and show them how two different religions can respect one another's differences and embrace God's love in a special way. I always think about that whenever I have the chance to speak about the many special blessings our interfaith marriage has brought to us. Neal and I have said many times that being married to a person from a different background has helped us to embrace and explore our own religions in a new way.

As we turn to this holiday season, I wonder how I can embrace the Christmas holidays without offending my Jewish family? I think that "fear" often holds us back from embracing our religion and asking for what we want for our holiday celebrations. We are afraid of hurting someone's feelings, if not our spouse's, then maybe our in-laws, or our friends. We get caught up in worrying about what others will think of us. Our fear causes stress and robs us of our ability to enjoy life. Once you are able to find a way to release the fear and tap into your heart to find out what is missing from your holiday celebrations, you will begin to experience the true spirit of Christmas and Hanukkah for yourself and your family.

Neal and I first met at the Jewish Community Center in Houston, where I was the fitness coordinator. He took an aerobics class that I was teaching. We started dating in September of 1984. Our first two Christmases together as a couple were easy. I flew to Indiana to celebrate Christmas with my family. He flew to Boston to be with his family for Hanukkah. We never discussed it much; we exchanged gifts and cards, and it just seemed easy. During our third year together, we got engaged, and I decided we needed a Christmas tree for my new condo. Neal seemed almost excited, like a little kid experiencing something new. It was fun until we had to

wait in long lines to purchase the lights and ornaments. We could-
n't decide what to put on top of the tree. I wanted an angel but Neal
said that would make him uncomfortable, so we decided on a big
gold bow.

We continued to have a tree in our house until our daughter,
Lindsay, was born. Since we had decided that Lindsay would be
raised Jewish, I thought it would be better for her not to be exposed
to Christmas celebrations in her Jewish home. I convinced myself that
flying to Indiana to celebrate Christmas with my family was all I
needed.

My parents, who were very religious, always had a nativity
scene on their end table in the living room. As Lindsay grew up and
began to explore her grandparents' house, she found the nativity
scene. She loved to play with it—especially the manger and baby
Jesus, who fascinated her at age four and five. She wanted to know
more about him. I told her the Christmas story of Jesus' birth. I told
her that is what her mommy and Christian grandparents believe, that
Christmas was our holiday and that she could celebrate it with us. I
pointed out that Hanukkah was her special holiday because she was
Jewish.

Lindsay came home after celebrating one Christmas in Indiana
thanking God for baby Jesus in her prayers every night. I didn't dis-
courage it or encourage it. My Jewish mother-in-law shared with me
that she was surprised to hear Lindsay thanking God for baby Jesus
in her prayers. I said, "Yes, I know she really likes him." After a few
months, she stopped talking about him.

For many years we celebrated both Hanukkah and Christmas on
the surface. We went through the motions, but for me spiritually, I felt
half empty. I was afraid to create my own Christmas celebrations in
my own home. I didn't want to rock the boat. I wanted more, but my
fear held me back. After eight years of doing our routine "safe" holiday celebrations, I decided to listen to my heart and ask for what I
wanted. I stepped out of my comfort zone and took a chance. I wanted to start my own family traditions. I didn't want to fly to Indiana
for Christmas: I wanted to be in my own home. I wanted to decorate

a gingerbread house with my daughter. I wanted to pick out a tree with my family and drink hot chocolate while we decorated the tree with special ornaments. I wanted to go to the candlelight Christmas Eve service and come home and read the story "'Twas the Night Before Christmas." I wanted to leave out cookies for Santa and carrots for the reindeer. Most of all, I wanted to relive my Christmas childhood with my Jewish daughter, whom I was driving to Hebrew school three times a week. I was torn between my needs and the needs of my daughter and husband. I decided to push through the fear and to trust my heart.

My daughter loves our new Christmas traditions. She also loves having a family Hanukkah party, lighting the *menorah* (candelabra), and making Hanukkah cookies. She knows she is Jewish and her mommy is not. She knows Mommy celebrates different holidays. She knows about Jesus' birth. She embraces her Judaism and respects the Christian faith.

My husband acknowledges the sacrifices I have made over the years to raise our daughter as a Jew. He also understands I have needs, too, and he is willing to step out of his comfort zone to help me meet those needs. He has learned to let go of his fears and judgments over the years and really enjoys our new December celebrations.

Emily H. Cappo is a freelance writer and mother of two boys.

My First Christmas

EMILY H. CAPPO

Although my husband and I dated for many years before marrying, it wasn't until we made our relationship "official" that I spent

Christmas with his family. The easy part was that there was no pressure from my own family to spend Christmas with them, since as Jews, of course, we didn't celebrate the holiday. The hard part was that this was all so alien to me. I had never been to a Christmas Mass, decorated a Christmas tree, or eaten a traditional Christmas dinner.

Growing up in a town that was 90 percent Jewish, I always thought of Christmas as somebody else's holiday, celebrated in other places. Sometimes on Christmas Eve my mom and I would drive to the non-Jewish neighborhoods and look at all the houses decorated with bright lights. We discussed which ones were tacky versus tasteful and how we might decorate our house if we were celebrating the holiday.

But now I was going to be faced with the religious aspects of Christmas, participating in rituals that were foreign to me and would accentuate how different my background was from my husband's. My first surprise was when we got to my in-law's house. I was somewhat disappointed to see a fake Christmas tree, rather than the real thing. Even my husband was critical of the imposter tree. Nevertheless, the house looked festive with Christmas decorations, including wreaths, miniature nativity scenes, and Christmas dishes and mugs.

On Christmas Eve, we had dinner with the family, about twenty people that included my husband's four brothers, one sister, and all of their spouses and children. Although the gifts were mostly exchanged on Christmas morning, there was some gift giving that evening so that Grandma and Grandpa could give their presents to the grandchildren, who would be at their own homes Christmas morning. I was shocked at how wildly the kids ripped open their presents. Their parents had to remind the younger ones to say "thank you" to Grandma and Grandpa. The adults did try to reinforce the religious meaning for the children, which meant that after the presents were opened, a birthday cake was served to celebrate Jesus Christ's birthday. I respected this effort, but it was my first of several awkward feelings about the holiday.

Later that evening, I was sort of hoping we'd go to midnight

Mass just so I could see what it was like. I had always heard it was a beautiful service, and to venture out that late would have felt adventurous, rather than religious. But my husband's family preferred going on Christmas day. My sister-in-law insisted that we all go to the late afternoon children's Mass at the church to which her family belonged.

On Christmas morning we exchanged gifts. Amusingly enough, my father-in-law was like an impatient kid, wanting to open gifts as soon as we finished breakfast. Four o'clock came upon us, and although I had been to some Catholic weddings with my husband, this was our first true holiday Mass together. I felt okay about it until it was time to kneel. I continued sitting on the bench while everyone around me kneeled to pray. I looked at my husband and felt so far away from him. He appeared so childlike. It was the only time in all our years together when I questioned, albeit only for a second, our decision to marry. This was the one thing we could never ever do together. I sat very still and waited for him to come back up to the bench. The rest of the Mass seemed fine, and even touching. At one point the children's choir sang, and later on, presents that were brought for other less privileged children were collected at the front of the church. It wasn't until it was time for Communion that that uneasy feeling returned. I remained seated and everyone had to climb over me to get to the aisle to wait in line for the wafer. Again, I had that isolated, far-away feeling that I was so different from everyone else. Suddenly, I heard a whisper to my right. It was my brother-in-law's wife. She had remained seated, too, and said to me, "It's nice to have company for a change." I smiled and felt so much better that I wasn't alone after all. I knew she wasn't Jewish, but she also wasn't Catholic, so she didn't participate in this part of the Mass, either.

After Mass, we all headed over to my sister-in-law's house for the traditional Christmas meal: homemade ravioli, homemade bread, and, of course, a baked ham. While many Jews tend to shy away from or avoid ham altogether, I like it. But, I also felt weird, almost guilty that I was eating it. Before we began eating, grace was said, but I just bowed my head, trying not to stand out by being silent.

My sister-in-law's house was decorated quite beautifully, with elegant but not overdone Christmas ornamentation throughout. I was pleased to see they had a real Christmas tree. It was lofty, smelled delicious, and was trimmed with ornaments that their four children had made themselves through their years of growing up. I was truly moved by this and thought it was a wonderful way to honor the holiday.

Christmas will never be "my" holiday, and I may never feel completely comfortable with it, but I hope that with my husband and our children, it can be our way to affirm love, family, hope, and peace, together.

Sheri Levin McNerthney lives with her spouse, Pat, daughter Terra Joy, and two cats in Leavenworth, Washington—a small town on the east slope of the Cascade mountains, where she and Terra Joy constitute half of the total Jewish population.

December Angst

SHERI LEVIN MCNERTHNEY

Today as I watched a boom truck drape Christmas lights onto the tallest tree in my rural mountain town's Front Street Park, I noticed a familiar angst welling up within me. "Here it is again," I brooded, "the annual December reminder for American Jews that we are 'other,' that we don't 'belong.'" I remember several years ago, before the town acquired a boom truck, when my husband, Pat, climbed to the top of this very same tree to set the lights. Pat is a lapsed Catholic and he doesn't much care about Christmas, but he does enjoy climbing to high places, so he volunteered for the job. That was when our daughter Terra was little, and I had decided to celebrate Christmas. I wanted desperately to see what it was like to be part of the sparkling festivities surrounding me, instead of being perpetually "apart."

That first time, when Terra was a baby, I invited Pat's whole family over for Christmas. It was the first winter in our modest not-quite-finished log home up Icicle Canyon, exceedingly cozy with the influx of all those in-laws. As we sat down to the sumptuous Christmas dinner I had remarkably managed to prepare on our dilapidated kitchen stove salvaged from the dump, my father-in-law asked us all to bow our heads to say grace. I felt a momentary panic in my heart as I looked up and saw him make the sign of the cross (in *my* house!!!) before gently folding his hands in prayer. "Hold everything!" I thought, "I wanted tinsel and lights! *This* was not part of the bargain!!!"

The next Yuletide I did not invite my in-laws. At my insistence, Pat went out and cut a spindly little fir tree that was growing precariously next to our driveway, and hauled it inside. I was momentarily daunted when this Charlie Brown tree seemed to fill up half the house, but I persevered in my quest to finally join the mainstream culture. Terra was my excuse to celebrate Christmas. Pat didn't care— the nostalgia was all mine. I wanted what I had never had: lights and trees, stockings and Santa. Terra and I strung popcorn and cranberries and made brightly colored ornaments. I took many pictures of Terra toddling about, elfin-like in her rainbow-striped jumpsuit, decorating our Christmas tree and tearing open presents. Yet, my vague sense of uneasiness grew with each picture I snapped. I felt as if I were play-acting. I knew that no matter how much I wanted it, this was not an authentic celebration from my inexorable Jewish heart.

The year following my second experiment with Christmas we spent the last half of December with my family in Israel, where December 25th passes by just like any other day, extraordinary in its ordinariness. That year I snapped pictures of Terra making a *menorah* (candelabra) from rocks and shells, in the tradition of Israeli children. At our family Hanukkah party I stuffed myself with *latkes* (potato pancakes) and *soofganiyot* (jelly doughnuts), as ubiquitous in

Israel in December as candy canes are in North America. As I gazed at the collection of the cousins' handmade *menorahs* glowing together in a mass of soft candlelight, I felt suffused with the warmth of true belonging, to a people and tradition that is authentically mine.

Now Terra is nine years old, and there have been no more Christmas trees in my home. Instead, I have a kitchen cabinet filled with *menorahs* she's made for Hanukkah over the years. My favorite is the mama cat with eight kittens that Terra fashioned from Fimo last year in honor of her cat's prolific motherhood. For a week each December we dine on crispy *latkes* smeared with applesauce and sour cream, and play games of *dreidel* (a Hanukkah spinning toy) by the fireplace until we are falling asleep over our piles of chocolate *gelt* (coins).

As American Jews, we each need to make peace with Christmas in our own way. My uneasy flirtation with Christmas led to a renaissance of Jewish identity that has brought great joy to my family. However, this December we will be having some very early *Shabbat* (the Jewish Sabbath) dinners, so that Terra can arrive punctually to sing in her choir's Christmas concerts and I can rush off to play handbells in our town's annual Christmas gala. Others may choose to celebrate Christmas as a secular holiday, or to have a Christmas tree and call it a Hanukkah bush. We each need to search our own hearts and do our best to cope with the relentless December angst.

Dr. June Andrews Horowitz is an associate professor in the Psychiatric-Mental Health Department, School of Nursing, Boston College. She has more than a decade of experience leading counseling groups and workshops for interfaith couples, and she is a member of the Regional Outreach Committee for the Northeast Council of the Union of American Hebrew Congregations (UAHC, the Reform Movement).

Facing the December Dilemma: Guidelines for Interfaith Couples

JUNE ANDREWS HOROWITZ

For interfaith couples involving a Jew and any non-Jew who celebrates Christmas, the December holidays are a yearly reminder that they don't share the same religious, ethnic, or cultural background. From Thanksgiving on, as the Christmas shopping season is in full swing, Jews are faced with daily indications that they are a minority. In response, they ignore Christmas and feel left out of the mainstream, or they participate in Christmas and risk feeling that they've betrayed their heritage. Their non-Jewish partners, in contrast, often want to share Christmas activities. They see requests to avoid or decrease Christmas observance at home as a painful loss. Thus, Christmas and Hanukkah observances can feel more like a crisis than a celebration, truly a December dilemma.

COMMON CONCERNS: "WHY IS HAVING A CHRISTMAS TREE AN ISSUE?"

Although there are numerous issues involved with the December holidays, I would identify three major concerns based on my experience from working with interfaith couples.

CHRISTMAS AS A FAMILY HOLIDAY VERSUS A RELIGIOUS OBSERVANCE

Christmas symbolizes family togetherness for most gentile partners. While the religious significance of Christmas is important for many, the Christian partners I have known clearly differentiate their private religious observance from the shared Christmas activities involving family participation. Decorating the Christmas tree, for example, often is a cherished family tradition that they wish to share with their Jewish mates. Many Jews, on the other hand, tend to see Christmas activities and objects as expressions of Christian religious practice. This difference in perception leads to misunderstanding and hurt.

CHRISTMAS AND HANUKKAH AS IDENTITY SYMBOLS

Each holiday may represent personal identity. When two individuals join in a marriage or significant relationship, their sense of being separate people can be overshadowed by becoming a couple. In interfaith relationships, issues are magnified if one person feels slighted by holiday plans. Thus, each partner's importance or power can seem to be measured by which holiday is given prominence.

CHRISTMAS AND HANUKKAH AS SYMBOLS OF THE CHILDREN'S RELIGIOUS UPBRINGING

When children are involved, holidays take on increased importance. If children are being raised as Christians or brought up in another tradition that observes Christmas, then the family celebrates Christmas without debate. Hanukkah may be included in holiday plans to recognize the Jewish parent's heritage. When the children are being raised as Jews, Christmas becomes a more complex issue. Some parents choose to observe Hanukkah exclusively at home to avoid confusing the children concerning their Jewish identity. They reason that having Christmas at home sends a mixed message that the children are both Jewish and Christian. Others decide to observe both holidays so that the children can appreciate dual traditions and so that they can have the family togetherness that the non-Jewish parent associates with Christmas. Some families who do not observe Christmas at home share Christmas with relatives, particularly the non-Jewish grandparents, in an effort to create a clearly Jewish home while honoring and enjoying the traditions of the non-Jewish parent and extended family. However, when issues concerning the children's religious identity remain unresolved, conflicts during the holidays typically intensify.

GUIDELINES FOR NEGOTIATING THE DECEMBER DILEMMA

Negotiating the December dilemma is seldom simple. Yet, caring, flexibility, sensitivity, and mutual respect can result in an effective plan for your family. These guidelines are based on the experiences of other interfaith couples who successfully negotiated their own approach to the holidays.

- Think about your personal holiday memories. What holiday practices and activities were important to you? What meaning do these observances have to you?

- If you haven't done so, share significant memories with your partner, and ask about his or her family holidays. Your goal should be to understand each other's point of view and the meaning of the holidays rather than to "win" or pressure your partner to agree to do what you'd prefer.

- Talk about your concerns. For example, give voice to worries about confusing the children, upsetting extended family, failing to enjoy your own holiday, or losing a sense of your identity.

- Be open to compromise and to looking at these issues in new ways. Try to work out a trial plan, and evaluate how well it works after the holidays have ended. If children are old enough to express their thoughts and feelings, involve them in discussion and planning. As you try out approaches, keep in mind that plans can change next year, and options you try could be an opportunity to make any holiday observance a creative and personal experience for your family.

- Explain your plans in advance to extended family and selected friends so that they will not feel left out and can know what to expect. Be respectful and inclusive when possible by showing that you have considered their views and feelings, but decide yourselves what is best for you as a couple or family.

- Most importantly, don't use the holiday season as a battleground to struggle over unresolved conflicts concerning your relationship, children, or extended families. Rather, use holiday planning as a chance to learn how to negotiate and resolve other issues in your lives together.

There is no one way to approach the December dilemma that works best for all interfaith couples. Couples reach a variety of successful solutions by trying hard to understand their individual and family needs while jointly creating their own celebrations. Perhaps this year, if you reject confrontation and face the December dilemma within a true partnership, the holiday season will bring you closer. Happy holidays!

16. Celebrating Other Holidays

Jim Keen is a freelance writer based in Ann Arbor, Michigan. He has fifteen years of experience in an interfaith relationship. He is married with two children.

Eggs and Plagues: Handling Easter and Passover in Our Interfaith Family

JIM KEEN

Spring in Michigan is always welcomed. Just ask anyone who has ever spent a winter here. So when the snow melts and the crocuses bloom, everyone tends to get a little giddy. Of course, in my interfaith family we have an extra reason to be elated: It's the Easter and Passover season.

My wife and I each have fond memories of our holidays. For Bonnie, it's *matzah brie* (eggs and unleavened bread fried up in a pan) and getting together with her cousins for Passover. For me, it's Easter eggs and Disney World for spring break with my family. To this day, just the smell of vinegar (used in the dye) reminds me of brightly colored eggs that the Easter Bunny hid for us to find. Like Christmas and Hanukkah, Easter and Passover can also evoke strong emotions in interfaith families.

Instead of letting these feelings be a source of strife for us, we decided to make them a springboard for embarking on a whole new set of experiences. We simply did not want to deny one of us our traditions by trying to pick which holiday would be celebrated in our household. Before we were married, Bonnie and I decided that we would each "help" the other celebrate his or her holiday. We do this for Christmas, Hanukkah, Rosh Hashanah (Jewish New Year), etc. Now that we have kids, we have decided to raise them Jewish. However, like their mother, they "help" me celebrate my holidays. While making certain that they understand that they are Jews, we are teaching them about my Protestant background as well.

One of the most important aspects of these two holidays, for both of us, is being with our families. My wife must be with her family for Passover, or it just isn't the same. The big gathering of her parents, aunt, uncle, and cousins (and now their kids) is an annual happy occasion—even if it is the decibel level of a 747. We all get together in Boston for at least one of the two *seders* (ritual Passover meal, at which the story of the Jews' exodus from Egypt is told). We learn about Moses and the Pharaoh, the ten plagues, and the significance of the Passover food. There's lots of singing and lots to eat. (The food is delicious, but too much *matzah* gives me lead belly.)

For my family, it is important to be together for Easter. As kids, my brother and sister and I used to dye Easter eggs on Saturday night. The morning of Easter Sunday, we'd wake up and scurry around the house looking for hidden eggs to put in our Easter baskets. As we grew older, we started to spend our spring vacation in Disney World. Because this break always occurred over Good Friday and Easter, it became a tradition to enjoy our holiday with Mickey. Today, my whole family, nuclear and extended, makes the trip to Florida. Like my wife and her side of the family, it just wouldn't feel right spending the holiday any other way.

We also choose not to ignore the religious aspects of the holidays. Bonnie usually accompanies me to the Easter church service. I once asked her if all the talk of Jesus made her feel uncomfortable. She replied that, as foreign as it was, she still viewed it as an educational experience. She said that going to church with me gave her an opportunity to learn more about my faith and background. Because we're on the road for Easter, I never quite know what to expect in a different congregation from my hometown. I'm always afraid that the minister will say something that might offend my wife. I don't know exactly what that would be, yet I still worry. Fortunately, my fears have not even remotely come true.

As Bonnie learns from my Easter experience, I, too, enjoy taking in the Passover scene. My first *seder* with her was on the campus of the University of Michigan, while we were just dating. We went to a house with a bunch of friends, where our host proclaimed that, due to our getting together, there were a lot of happy mothers back home. Because we were students, we did a lot more eating and talking than anything. We skipped over quite a bit of the *hagaddah* (book containing the prayers, songs, and story of Passover). I was not intimidated in this setting, but the following year, I wondered how would it be as I went to my first Passover with her big family in a "real" *seder*.

My wife has a wonderful family, and any opportunity to get together with them is a lot of fun. However, I was still worried about fitting in and not sticking out like a sore thumb at the dinner table. True to their form, though, they went out of their way to make sure I didn't feel uncomfortable. I was assigned duties around the kitchen just like everyone else. I can proudly say that I helped grate the horseradish for the Passover plate. (Each food on the plate is symbolic in some way. Horseradish symbolizes the bitterness of slavery the Jews experienced in Egypt.)

The first couple of years spending Passover with Bonnie's family were a huge learning experience for me. There's a part of the *seder* when the leader of the service breaks a piece of *matzah* to create the *afikomen*. In some families, the kids hide the *afikomen* and hold it for ransom. In Bonnie's family, sometimes the leader will hide it in the room and make the kids hunt for it. Now this I could relate to! I did feel out of place when passages were read in Hebrew, or even worse, sung in Hebrew! Not knowing the language is bad enough, let alone not knowing the tune. What was reassuring for me was feeling that everyone there wanted me to be a part of the family.

Over the years, I've gotten to know the different prayers, songs, and symbols of Passover. I've found that I can make this as easy or as difficult as I want it to be. The first couple of Passovers were especially hard, not knowing what was going on. Rather than just sitting there, though, I've discovered that it's much easier on my comfort level—and it's a lot more fun—to learn the material and participate. Bonnie's family has always been welcoming and supportive. I've chosen to make this an experience from which I can absorb a lot about my wife's religion.

This coming Easter and Passover will be our fifteenth together. As we learn more about each other's holidays, we, as parents, are better prepared to impart to our children the meaning of Daddy's Easter and the traditions of their own Passover.

Bonni Goldberg has published several books. She lives in Portland, Oregon, and is intermarried.

Holy Promised Spirit Land

BONNI GOLDBERG

The main focus of my family this time of year is the Passover *seder* (ritual meal at which the story of the Jews' exodus from Egypt is told). My husband was never completely comfortable with his Methodist upbringing, and he's a little wary of organized religion of any sort. But we agreed that children benefit from a sense of identity within a tradition, and I felt strongly that this tradition be Jewish.

We've both hosted and been guests at several *seders* during our relationship. Taking turns this way has given my husband an excellent cross-sectional experience of celebrating Passover. Over the seven years we've been together, he's started to develop not only a familiarity with the *seder* but also a discerning sense of what makes the *seder* both significant and comfortable for him. Every year, whether on the ride home or as we clean up, we discuss the most meaningful aspects of each *seder* we participate in.

The story of Passover is a rich one for renewal on multiple levels: not only as a time to recall slavery and the long journey to freedom suffered by the Jews and many other people, but as a time for reflecting on the subtle types of enslavement we experience today. The *seder* is a powerful opportunity to partake in the catharsis of symbolically acting out the story with ritual foods, chants, and song.

We're fortunate to be an interfaith couple at a moment in history with such an array of theme-based *hagaddahs* (books of prayers, stories, and songs used on Passover). Our friends have passed along many unpublished versions written and compiled by friends of friends (though there are many published ones out there as well). In our family, several have particular metaphoric resonance. One is a *hagaddah* created by a rabbi for Jews in twelve-step programs. Enslavement in Egypt and the Exodus is compared to the slavery of addiction and the road to recovery. Another is a *hagaddah* written by a couple in Oregon that focuses on *tikkun* (repair, social justice) and our stewardship of the earth and environment. I also attend a women's *seder* which uses a special *hagaddah* that affirms the powerful feminine energy of Judaism.

But we don't ignore Easter. Even though my husband isn't a practicing Christian, he did participate in related festivities that were an essential aspect of his childhood and that are an important part of the legacy he has to pass along to his offspring. In past years we've attended a neighbor's Easter egg hunt. In preparation, we decorate hard-boiled eggs to bring to hide, and when the calendar works out just right, we set some of them aside for the *seder*. We talk about the hunt as a way to celebrate spring and the sense of renewal with our non-Jewish friends.

I'm inspired and delighted when I come upon Jewish and Christian rituals and customs that overlap in some way. Sometimes the intersection is because of the universal elements of Judeo-Christian spirituality, and other times it's because of how American culture brings the two together. Whatever the source, the intersection is especially welcome in my interfaith marriage.

This year, I've learned of another Judeo-Christian tie-in through gift baskets. Before our daughter was born, I used to make my husband an Easter basket each year filled with treats. One year I included a variety of black licorice (his favorite); another year, a selection of exotic teas. I thought of the Easter basket as a sort of appreciation gesture for his Valentine's Day gift to me. In my preparations for the Jewish holiday of Purim (the celebration of delivery from destruction as recorded in the Book of Esther), the custom of visiting friends and giving baskets of such things as dried fruits and nuts came up. It's actually written in the *Megillah* (scroll read on Purim) that this is what Jews should do. So at this year's Easter egg hunt we'll refill our Purim baskets, thereby recalling that celebration as we participate in one of my husband's treasured childhood memories.

When our toddler is older we'll be looking out for children's *hagaddahs*. Then we hope to host a second night or weekend afternoon child's seder for her Jewish and non-Jewish friends in the same spirit of celebrating spring and rebirth (of the Jews out of slavery) as the traditional Easter egg hunt.

I think it's because our daughter was born at this time of year that both of us not only feel compelled to honor familiar traditions and create new ones, but also to see them through the eyes of the blessing of our daughter, our young promised land, our growing holy spirit.

Jonathan E. Kraus is rabbi of Beth El Temple Center in Belmont, Massachusetts.

Understanding the High Holy Days: A Primer for Non-Jewish Partners

JONATHAN E. KRAUS

"Why are Rosh Hashanah (Jewish New Year) and especially Yom Kippur (Jewish Day of Atonement) so important to my Jewish partner? He almost never attends services the rest of the year, isn't observant, and doesn't even know what he believes about God. Yet, at this time of year, he insists on attending services. What's the big deal with these holidays?"

There are both "official" and "unofficial" answers to these questions. Perhaps not surprisingly, the unofficial explanations are often the more significant ones. The official answers (to which I'll return shortly) speak in terms like judgment, sin, repentance, life, and death. The unofficial answers have something to do with the complicated puzzle of American Jewish identity.

For many Jews in this country, attending High Holy Day services (particularly, the first evening service of Yom Kippur) is a way of affirming that we still are part of the Jewish people. Finding our way to a synagogue during these days is a way of demonstrating that we haven't yielded to assimilation, haven't broken the ancient chain of the Jewish people's survival and continuity. Being with our people at services says: no matter how far we may have drifted from active involvement with the Jewish religion, we're still proud to be Jews. We still belong. We still care about being Jewish—even if we're not very religious and are not sure how we feel about the content of those services. Many times, our participation also says that we're still connected with the values of parents and grandparents, for whom our attendance (or absence!) is a very powerful symbol.

Notice that these "unofficial" answers have little to do with theology or even with the religious significance of the prayers and rituals. That's because for many American Jews, their "Jewishness" is not first and foremost a matter of religion. Many American Jews will tell you that their Jewish identity is primarily ethnic or cultural or communal. They speak about Jewish holiday customs or Jewish ethical values or a feeling of connection they associate with being Jewish that seems, to them, to be somewhat separate from the Jewish religion. While I take issue with that perspective, I'll save my objections for another time. What's important for understanding this High Holy Day commitment is that in the mind of your loved one, the urgency of attending services may not be primarily about the religious significance of the ritual.

Nonetheless, if you will be joining your partner to sit through an unusually long and crowded synagogue service, you might want to know a little more about what to expect and what the ritual means officially. For most Jews, the term "High Holy Days" is the title given to a period of ten days that stretch between the holy day of Rosh Hashanah—which means, literally, head of the year—and Yom Kippur—the Day of Atonement. Both holy days have their earliest roots in the Hebrew Bible (see, for instance, Leviticus 23:23–32), though the name "Rosh Hashanah" was not used until significantly later in Jewish history.

Rosh Hashanah ushers in the Jewish year and with it a period of profound self-examination and repentance. It is, therefore, a day of joyous celebration balanced against a humbling and solemn consideration of how well (or poorly) we have used the gift of the previous year. Tradition teaches that God judges each of us individually and our community as a whole on Rosh Hashanah. Tradition also teaches that the result of God's judgment will be a matter of life and death (either figurative or literal, depending on your theological orientation). Our prayers, songs, and rituals, therefore, focus on confessing the ways in which we've gone astray, asking forgiveness for occasions on which we've missed the mark, and committing ourselves to acts of repentance (Hebrew word: *t'shuvah*).

Note that we go through this process collectively. We ask for forgiveness and repent almost exclusively in the first person plural! This use of "we" versus "I" reflects Judaism's emphasis on community. Our first concern is how well the Jewish community as a whole has fulfilled its covenant (sacred agreement) with God. Our first responsibility is to live in such a way that we help the community be the kind of holy people God has challenged us to become. Of course, our Rosh Hashanah observances also celebrate the possibility of a new beginning that comes with the new year—God's gift to us if we engage in this cleansing process with sincerity.

Some distinctive observances to watch and listen for on Rosh Hashanah: the extensive ritual for sounding of the *shofar* (ram's horn) during the morning service, which is mandated by the *Torah* (the first five books of the Hebrew Bible) and serves as a deeply moving call to renewed awareness and action, eating apples and honey for a sweet year, and greeting others by expressing the hope that they will be judged for a good year (Hebrew: *Shanah Tovah*). Depending on the congregation you join, you also may participate in *Tashlich*—an outdoor afternoon ceremony in which we symbolically cast away our sins by throwing bread crumbs, or other less traditional things such as small stones, into a body of water.

Yom Kippur begins in the evening ten days later. Its mood is one of deep solemnity, contrition and humility. According to tradition, the judgments begun on Rosh Hashanah are sealed and finalized on Yom Kippur. Because Leviticus (23:27) instructs that self-affliction should be part of this day dedicated to repentance, most Jews will observe a complete fast for at least part of the day. In fact, many Jews will spend almost the entire day at the synagogue (from sundown to sundown) engaged in fasting, prayer, reflection, and repentance. The observance ends with the setting of the sun, a final sounding of the *shofar*—dramatically marking the end of this intensely spiritual day and a reminder of ancient practice in the Jerusalem Temple—and then, gatherings to break the fast together.

The heart of Yom Kippur observances is its liturgy. The opening evening service centers around an ancient formula known as *Kol*

Nidre, which is actually an ancient legal formula that absolves us of vows and oaths we may take between this Yom Kippur and the next one. I suspect that the prayer is revered as much for its haunting and powerful music as for its somewhat complicated message.

While Yom Kippur services may vary somewhat from synagogue to synagogue, all will center around communal confessions and introspection, requests for forgiveness, and the effort to obtain perspective on our present lives by placing them in the context of the past. More specifically, synagogues hold a special *Yizkor* (memorial) service to honor loved ones who have died and to gain important insight from both their lives and their deaths. Many synagogues also honor the martyrs of the Jewish people throughout history and, again, seek to learn important lessons from the humbling example of their sacrifices. Then, as Yom Kippur draws to a close, the observance concludes with the *Neilah,* or locking, service—a final chance to repent before the symbolic gates of repentance are closed and locked to us.

Of course, there are many interesting and important details for which I haven't had room here. I also realize that the details I have provided may raise as many questions as they answer. If you are interested in doing further reading, two of my favorite starting places are *The Jewish Holidays* (HarperCollins) by Michael Strassfeld and *Seasons of Our Joy* (Beacon) by Arthur Waskow.

Jim Keen is a freelance writer based in Ann Arbor, Michigan. He has fifteen years of experience in an interfaith relationship. He is married with two children.

How Jews Can Help Their Christian Partners During the High Holidays: A Protestant Perspective

JIM KEEN

September, for many, brings memories of returning to school, football games, and apple cider. These are the same feelings my Jewish wife Bonnie experiences. However, September, to her, means something much more significant. It is time for the Jewish High Holidays of Rosh Hashanah (New Year) and Yom Kippur (Day of Atonement). This is a time spent with her family, going to services, dipping apples in honey, and atoning for her sins.

In interfaith families, both partners may be experiencing warm fuzzy feelings during this month, but for different reasons. While I am thrilled about the beginning of the football season, my wife is reliving memories of family High Holiday celebrations. As with any religious holiday, observance can bring stress to the interfaith home. The fact that I, as a non-Jew, have no previous emotions attached to her holidays only compounds the problem. I feel it's important for her to remember that and to help me build memories that we can call our own. Fortunately, Bonnie has always been understanding and has eased me into the Jewish experience at a pace that has been comfortable for me.

The first time I experienced the High Holidays with my wife, I wasn't sure what to think. We went to her dad's house for Rosh Hashanah. I loved being with her family and eating the tasty food that was served nonstop for two days. Going to temple, though, was a different story. It was my first time ever in a synagogue. It's not like going to a different church, where a few minor details are changed around. At my in-laws' temple, not only was it a foreign holiday, but there was a lot of Hebrew spoken in the service. I didn't know what was going on. The fact that I had to sit there for three hours did not help my restlessness. Most Protestant services are only one hour long and in English. I felt lost, even though Bonnie did her best to explain what was happening and what some of the Hebrew meant. I also felt like I stuck out like a sore thumb.

Looking back on it, I probably fit in fine. Nonetheless, I joked to myself that at any moment I was going to be "discovered" and kicked out. Were these ridiculous feelings? Of course. Was everyone I was introduced to as nice as can be? Of course. It was helpful that Bonnie's parents tried to make me feel as welcome as possible.

Each couple needs to decide for itself whether each partner will accompany the other to their respective houses of worship. In our case, Bonnie and I decided that I would go to temple with her on her holidays, and she would travel to church with me on mine. We feel this is extremely helpful in learning about each other's religion— especially when it comes time for us to teach our children. Just as important, it is a show of support and love for each other.

After temple that first year, we went back to Bonnie's parents' house, where Bonnie helped me learn more about her holiday. She explained the meaning of the *Torah* (the first five books of the Hebrew Bible) portion read that day. We dipped apples in honey "for a sweet New Year." Even though my wife had all her friends and family around, I was really happy that she spent extra time with me that day. The Christian partner can have feelings of being alone on Rosh Hashanah. A little handholding can go a long way.

Eight days after Rosh Hashanah is Yom Kippur. To a Christian, this can feel like a double whammy—first the Jewish New Year, and then the Day of Atonement. Yom Kippur is a serious and somber holiday. Protestants don't have anything like this. Catholics have confession, but not a whole day devoted to atoning, praying, and fasting.

We had talked about the holiday in advance so that there would be no surprises. I did not fast, but felt it was important to respect my wife's situation. While Bonnie did not expect me to fast along with her, she was still unaccustomed to being around someone who was eating.

At first, I didn't think my wife could fast all day. Bonnie loves food, so I didn't know how seriously she would take the fasting. In fact, I was sure she wouldn't make it. But I learned a lot that day. I developed a newfound respect for her and her religious convictions. Not only did she make it, but she never complained.

Once again, I went to services with Bonnie—actually, twice that day. Being at the temple was not my idea of fun. Where I enjoyed myself was watching and admiring my wife during this most holy day for her. I was not about to complain. This was my wife's day, and I would see her through it. To my great surprise, she slipped me a Power Bar during the service and told me to go take a break outside. I was floored. I was speechless.

About the only thing I could do was give her a peck on the cheek and head for the door. When I came back ten minutes later, she had a big smile on her face. I think it was caused by a combination of giving me pleasure and knowing that it would soon be time to break the fast.

Yom Kippur can feel like a long holiday, but they reward you with a big spread of food at the end. The best thing we learned was that it is important to be respectful of each other's feelings on this day. Giving each other the support to make it through strengthened our relationship that much more.

In short, when it comes to the High Holidays, Jewish partners can help by remembering that their Christian partners may feel insecure, or like they don't fit in, whether at temple or at family gatherings. Sometimes the non-Jewish partner might just be plain ignorant of traditions, feelings, and experiences and needs to be guided. Also, I know at times I felt conflicted inside. What was proper for me to be doing at this moment during services? Would Jesus see me as, somehow, less of a Christian? For me, temple can be both fascinating and boring. Fascinating in the sense that I am learning about my wife's culture. Boring in that most of it is in Hebrew, and it is long.

It takes time to build memories together. Gradually, thanks to Bonnie's help, I've found myself feeling more and more comfortable with her holidays. I have learned the rituals of the different services. I have made friends at the temple. I have even learned some Hebrew. I now look forward to Rosh Hashanah and Yom Kippur. I actually get a warm fuzzy feeling over these holidays. After nine years of marriage, it's getting to be that September can't roll around without me breaking out my football, fall clothes, and *shofar* (ram's horn sounded on the High Holidays).

Andrea King is the author of *If I'm Jewish and You're Christian, What Are the Kids?* (UAHC Press) and supervises preschools for the Santa Monica School District.

Rosh Hashanah, Yom Kippur, and the Non-Jewish Partner

ANDREA KING

Ben and I had been married for a couple of years when I asked him to take me to a High Holy Day service. As a regular church-goer who enjoyed the ceremonies and rituals of worship, I thought I'd appreciate the service. Besides, I wanted a glimpse into Ben's background.

It turned out to be one of the most disconcerting experiences of my life. Yom Kippur (Day of Atonement) was a blistering September day, and the temple was packed. When we arrived, the service was already in progress, but no one looked askance as we (and several other late arrivals) found seats. I noticed that many people seemed to be comfortable talking and walking around during the service. The music, instead of being joyful and uplifting, was downright mournful. To top it off, when the service ended, it just ended. No triumphal procession down the aisle and out of the building to carry the message of faith into the world. People simply left. This was not how we Episcopalians worshipped!

Suddenly I felt distanced from Ben; maybe we didn't share as much as I had thought. This was the one service of the year he was willing to attend, and I wanted to share it with him, but I could not. It was simply too different.

Twenty-some years later, I know that my reaction was predictable. Interfaith couples tend to build their relationships on their similarities rather than on their differences. What the couple shares is much more important to each partner than the ways in which they differ. Couples tend to identify the parallel threads in their ceremonies and holidays, while playing down the differences.

It's easy, for example, to find all the ways that a christening is like a *bris* (circumcision ceremony) or baby naming. The Jewish *Shabbat* and the Christian Sabbath are both designed to be days of rest and worship, set apart from the rest of the week. Christmas and Hanukkah, because they occur at the same time of year, are easy to link. Passover and Easter also have the calendar in common, and because the Last Supper was in all probability a Passover *seder* (ritual meal), the bond between the two holidays is especially strong.

This comparability can be convenient and comfortable for the Christian partner: for each new Jewish holiday or event, there seems to be a familiar Christian parallel. That, in a nutshell, is why Rosh Hashanah (New Year) and Yom Kippur are so difficult for non-Jewish interfaith partners. There is no Christian analogy to the High Holy Days.

The two Christian festivals that most American Christians celebrate are Christmas and Easter, which go nicely with Hanukkah and Passover. All four have messages of hope and freedom; all four have home-based customs that focus on children; all four are essentially fun. For many interfaith couples, the "Four-Holiday Calendar" fills their need and/or desire for religious observance.

Rosh Hashanah and Yom Kippur do not make it onto this top-four list, despite the central role that the High Holy Days play within

Judaism. Why? First, there is no big Christian holiday in September to balance them. Second, the whole tone of High Holy Day services is foreign to most Christians. If you haven't grown up with them, Rosh Hashanah and Yom Kippur are not easy to understand and appreciate. Somber self-reflection is seldom the theme at Christmas or Easter services. Third, there are few home-based customs in connection with the High Holy Days, so it's difficult to include young children in the observance. Finally, even though it's the one time of year that many Jews are drawn to services, the Jewish partner may not be able to articulate why the High Holy Days are meaningful to him or her, and it's hard to share what you can't talk about.

So why bother with the High Holy Days? Because, even for the non-Jew, there can be meaning in the services and value in the exercise of self-reflection.

Through twenty-odd years of Rosh Hashanah, *Kol Nidre* (evening of Yom Kippur), and Yom Kippur services, I have grown to appreciate them. I see them now as an opportunity to take a break from the hectic demands of family and work, a time to look honestly at my goals and progress, my shortcomings and strivings. The cycle of High Holy Day services is a progression that offers me a chance to clear the dust, cobwebs, and disorder from my mind; re-focus on my priorities; and start fresh. Rosh Hashanah and Yom Kippur give us a couple of family days without having to entertain, travel, shop, or even cook much. We can spend time together and, if we choose, take stock of where we've been and where we're going.

I didn't grow up with the High Holy Days. Hearing the *shofar* (ram's horn, which is blown on the High Holidays) or the *Kol Nidre* prayer (haunting chant that is offered on the evening of Yom Kippur) will never transport me back to my childhood as it does Ben. For me, the High Holy Days are an adult expression of my continuing growth as a thinking, feeling, caring human being. At High Holy Day services I am part of a community engaged in the process of self-examination. There is meaning in this uniquely Jewish observance, even for this non-Jew.

Paula C. Yablonsky serves as co-chairwoman of Congregation Gates of Heaven's Outreach Committee in Schenectady, New York. She is currently chairwoman of the Regional Outreach Committee for the Northeast Council of the Union of American Hebrew Congregations (UAHC, the Reform Movement). A meal site manager at her local Jewish Community Center, she plans meals and programs for senior citizens. She and her husband, Mark Gibbons, have a daughter, Erica.

How I Used My Christmas Tree Decorations to Light Up My *Sukkah*

PAULA C. YABLONSKY

One of the questions that I am asked as a Jew-by-Choice is the inevitable "Do you miss Christmas?" The other question, asked by people who know I converted years after my marriage and the birth of my daughter, and who knew we had previously celebrated Christmas in our home, is "What did you do with your Christmas decorations?"

During the first years after my conversion, I would quickly change the topic and just say the Christmas decorations were in the attic. But I always felt a twinge of sadness knowing that part of my life was over, sitting collecting dust. Every once in a while, I would be in the attic and run across the box holding all the decorations. Sentimentalist that I am, I would slowly lift each item and reminisce, as each was laden with memories. One had been given to us by neighbors the first year we moved into our house; one was a handmade gift my younger sister gave me when she was a little girl; one had been given to us by my mom during our first year together. Lovely memories, lovely items, lovingly packed away.

As a Jew-by-Choice I had made a decision not to celebrate Christmas any more, but I still had decorations in my attic that I was attached to and couldn't easily give up. One year I brought the issue to our synagogue's outreach group (a national Reform Judaism project that helps and encourages families to make Jewish choices). My rabbi told a wonderful story of how he was in Israel during the holiday of Sukkot (fall harvest festival) one year and saw many *sukkot* (plural of *sukkah*, a small wooden hut constructed during Sukkot) with lights decorating them. He spoke of the lights twinkling in the night—of families gathered for meals in their *sukkot* and of some even sleeping in them!

It was an interesting coincidence: my husband, daughter, and I had decided to erect a *sukkah* in our backyard for the first time when the holiday next arrived. Although I liked the idea, it felt very strange and foreign. Suddenly I had a thought—perhaps I would use the lights and decorations from my Christmas tree to decorate my *sukkah*.

The next year when Sukkot rolled around I went to work, carefully looking at the decorations that had remained upstairs for so long. The lights were still in their post-Christmas jumble, the ropes of beads—golden, wooden, and such—were there, as well as little grapevine wreaths and bird nests. I took them downstairs, gave Mark the jumbled lights to untangle, and went off to decorate. While we had a lot of Christmas decorations, many—such as candy canes, reindeer, and Santas—were inappropriate for our *sukkah*. So, off to the nearest craft and garden shop I went, rationalizing that for so many years I had purchased decorations to make our tree look lovely, and that this year and in the future I would buy decorations to do the same for our *sukkah*. Laden with leaves, grape vines, gourds, pumpkins, and colored corn—symbols of harvest in the Northeast—I made my way back home to finish.

That night when the sun went down we turned on the lights. My heart stood still as I saw our *sukkah* glowing in the backyard. Going outside, we brought our cups of tea and plates of cookies, recited the *Shehecheyanu* (blessing said in times of joy, thanking God to have been able to reach this season), and munched our dessert in our *sukkah*.

Looking through the corn husks and pine branches that made our roof, I could see the stars in the autumn sky. A sense of peace enveloped me as I remembered how these very lights once wound around my December tree, and I picked out various decorations—the beads, bird nests, and such—each with a December memory. Suddenly, the strange *sukkah* we had constructed felt like mine.

Over the eight days of Sukkot, I would sit in the *sukkah* and gaze around me. I would think about my new ancestors, wandering in the desert, dwelling in their *sukkot*. I wondered if the women would try to make their temporary homes comfortable and familiar for their families. I wondered if when the Israelites hurriedly packed to leave Egypt, the women took a small memento to remind them of the homes they were leaving, something to bring a small dose of comfort when going into the unknown.

Now the question arises, did my *sukkah* become my replacement Christmas tree? While I did use the decorations to make the *sukkah* seem more mine, more familiar, and while I experienced similar feelings of peace, one cannot replace the other. My *sukkah* had become a symbol of my Judaism—of thanksgiving and of remembrance—but I have managed to integrate some of my past into this new identity.

Christmas memories will forever live in my heart. I am thankful that I had the memories to draw upon, that I could use them to make the unfamiliar familiar and to help make a connection to my Jewish present.

Rachel Goldsmith lives in Boston and still celebrates *Shabbat* with her friends.

Shabbat Becomes My Own

RACHEL GOLDSMITH

Part of what makes being Jewish special is that every week you are given the gift of *Shabbat* (the Jewish Sabbath). It is a day set apart from all others to do with as you please—to rest, reflect, celebrate, study, and enjoy the company of family and friends. When this gift is given to you all of a sudden, how do you make it part of your life in a meaningful way? One way I make *Shabbat* an enjoyable and significant part of my life is to celebrate *Shabbat* dinner with the same group of friends once a month.

Two years ago, I took an Introduction to Judaism class with about forty other people—some couples considering interfaith marriages, some Jewish individuals wanting to learn more about how to live their religion more fully, and some people like me, as part of the conversion process. There were eight of us who sat together for the two-and-a-half hour session every Monday night: Michelle and Jim, a couple preparing for an interfaith marriage; Steve and Mary Catherine, an interfaith couple expecting their first child; Michael and Jacque, an interfaith dating couple; Marta, the daughter of a former Catholic nun and a Jew, who wanted to explore Judaism for herself; and me, a single woman preparing to convert to Judaism.

We were a talkative group. A constant stream of commentary, stories, questions, arguments, and jokes flowed among us and out to the rabbis and the other students. Our enthusiasm for the material, and for each other, was apparent. When the six-month course was over, we felt happy to have our Monday nights back, but reluctant to give up something that had started to seem like a mini-tradition. We decided to have a *Shabbat* dinner together at Michael and Jacque's house the Friday after class ended, and we have made a dinner togetherer one *Shabbat* a month ever since.

We do most of the planning via email, alternate hosting, and take turns bringing wine, salads, desserts, and, of course, *challah* (a braided bread traditionally served on the Sabbath), of which we are all serious connoisseurs. At first, we took turns on who said which blessing, but we have settled into a bit of a routine: Michelle and I bless the candles, we all chant *Kiddush* (blessing over wine), and the guys say the *Motzi* (blessing over bread). Along the way, we have practiced our Hebrew, shared stories of *Shabbats* growing up, and extracted bits of crucial *Shabbat* information from each other (Example: Why is the *challah* covered? So it won't be jealous that it is blessed last!).

Our *Shabbat* friendship has pushed happily outside its bounds, as these things will do. I share season Red Sox seats with Jim and his family; Steve recently gave them some crucial help in buying their first home. Michelle and Mary Catherine are both social workers and are able to relate to the frustrations and triumphs of each other's work. I was the backup *ketubah* (marriage contract) signer at Michelle and Jim's wedding, in case a friend coming from Europe couldn't make it. I was honored to be considered for this important job and thrilled that I could accept the responsibility of witnessing their marriage.

Over the past year, we have had culinary highs (Michael's brisket) and lows (the night I ordered pizzas), as well as emotional ones. The birth of Steve and Mary Catherine's baby, Max, last summer, gave us all much joy, as well as our first new group member. We gave Jim and Michelle an *aufruf* (wedding blessing) in October and threw Halloween candy at them in their kitchen. We had a special Hanukkah dinner together, after which my apartment smelled like burning oil for several days. We listened to Max's reminiscent wails as we watched the video of his *bris* (circumcision ceremony) together.

Claiming *Shabbat* as one's own means creating traditions that make that night and day more meaningful to you. In addition to my dinner group, I attend Friday night *Shabbat* services regularly and *Torah* (the first five books of the Hebrew Bible) study on Saturday mornings (irregularly). I occasionally join a friend for *challah* baking on Friday afternoon, and am still experimenting with other ideas— meeting friends for Saturday lunch, not carrying money, meditation. A study session with friends can turn into a favorite pastime: what begins as one dinner may become a lifetime tradition of Friday nights together.

Each time my *Shabbat* friends and I get together to light candles, recite the blessings, and eat together, we share the events of our lives and add a little more to our tradition, still new to most of us. Our *Shabbat* dinners give us time to reflect on our memories and to create new ones, and add a certain continuity for those of us to whom Judaism still feels a bit new.

17. Death and Mourning in Interfaith Families

Anita Diamant has written six guides to contemporary Jewish practice, including *Saying Kaddish: How to Comfort the Dying, Bury the Dead and Mourn As a Jew* (Schocken).

Till Death Do Us Part

ANITA DIAMANT

When my father died three years ago, Jewish tradition gave me the words and a way through a terrible and chaotic period. The first week after his death had a name: *shiva*. The first month was called *shloshim*. The first year ended with a *yahrzeit* (yearly memorial) candle, lit in his memory.

The Jewish rituals and customs for death and mourning are guided by two basic principles: respect for the dead and comfort for the bereaved. Respect for the dead (in Hebrew, *kevod ha-met*) is expressed with an almost Zen-like simplicity; the body is viewed as the soul's vessel, which deserves to be returned to the earth in a pure and natural state. Comforting the mourner (in Hebrew, *nichum ave-lim*) means both encouraging the bereaved to take the time and space to confront their loss head-on and leading them back into the world of the living in a step-by-step process.

RESPECT FOR THE DEAD

Judaism mandates that the body be treated with awe and reverence. Embalming or viewing of the body are usually not permitted because they tend to turn the person into a "thing." The corpse is cared for tenderly, washed, wrapped in plain cotton or linen shrouds, and buried in an unadorned wooden casket. The simplicity of shrouds and caskets may have been a way to avoid Egyptian excesses, and also to protect the poor from embarrassment.

While the idea of handling the body as little as possible is important, the *mitzvah* (commandment) of "saving a soul" (in Hebrew, *pikuah hanefesh*) is considered paramount, and nearly all Jewish authorities now support organ donation and permit autopsy in the service of medical research.

According to Jewish custom, the body is buried quickly—within twenty-four hours if possible. This is both a token of respect and a way of sparing the mourners' feelings, since the healing work of grief cannot begin until after the funeral.

Jewish funerals are simple, even austere—the tradition considers flowers and music too festive for such a somber occasion. The funeral focuses on the loss of a unique soul, and thus the core of the service is the eulogy (in Hebrew, *hesped*).

In marked contrast to Christian funerals, the Jewish funeral liturgy does not speak of death as a "better place." There is no one, single Jewish view of the afterlife: Jews have embraced beliefs that range from simple decomposition to reincarnation, from elaborate depictions of heaven and hell to humanistic metaphors about the tangible legacy of good works. The liturgy, however, makes no mention of the afterlife, or of a reunion with God or with family members who have passed away.

Perhaps the most powerful custom of the Jewish funeral comes after the casket is lowered and family members shovel the first clods of earth onto it. That terrible sound makes it virtually impossible to deny the reality of death. Painful as that sound is to the bereaved, it makes the healing work of grief possible.

COMFORTING THE BEREAVED

From the moment the funeral ends, all attention shifts to the care of the bereaved. Only close family members—spouses, siblings, children, and parents—are required to "sit *shiva*" (mourn for seven days). Sometimes, other family members choose to do so as well. *Shiva* (from the Hebrew number seven) is a time for facing the whole complicated gamut of emotions that follow a death: fear, anger, sorrow, terror, emptiness, even relief. The bereaved are taken care of by family and friends, who come to share memories and to make up the *minyan* (prayer quorum of ten adults) that recites the *Kaddish* (prayer usually said when mourning, which extols God).

Traditionally, mourners "say *Kaddish*" for their loved ones daily during the week of *shiva* and the month of *shloshim*. Children are required to say *Kaddish* for parents for a full year; bereaved spouses, siblings, and parents often do so as well.

Kaddish, a prayer recited at virtually every Jewish worship service, makes no mention of death or mourning. Like the Christian Lord's Prayer, *Kaddish* is a doxology—a litany of praise for God. However, the centuries-old association of *Kaddish* with bereavement, and the familiar sound and cadence of the prayer, make its recitation a form of comfort that transcends language.

The fact that *Kaddish* must be said in a *minyan* is a powerful, almost behavioral, element in the Jewish approach to death. Community support is fundamental to the Jewish response to bereavement; the tradition seems to know that, without the support of others, the burden is often too heavy for the mourner to bear. So, mourners who might otherwise withdraw from the world are required to become part of a group which probably includes other mourners who can provide companionship and understanding.

MOURNING A NON-JEWISH LOVED ONE

The whole range of Jewish mourning customs is open to anyone mourning for a non-Jew. For example: Jews-by-Choice say *Kaddish* for their non-Jewish parents; the death of a non-Jewish friend may prompt the wearing of a torn ribbon *(k'riah)* that denotes a mourner; and anyone can light a *yahrzeit* candle on the anniversary of a dear one's death. And of course, any synagogue member can request bereavement counseling from his or her rabbi, regardless of the deceased's religion—or his or her own.

A death in an interfaith family can expose unreconciled issues and profound differences. Old feelings of abandonment and loss may rise to the surface. But do not assume you're the first person to face a dilemma of this sort. Some rabbis can act as thoughtful sounding boards, and it's always a good idea to seek out others who have had similar experiences.

For the most part, however, the disagreements that divide interfaith families when death comes are not all that different from the ones that cause conflict in all-Jewish or all-Christian families. Most extended families are split over religious observance and practice; some members are more traditional than others, some are affiliated with congregations while others are not. Many interfaith families have found ways to honor both traditions and meet everyone's spiritual needs: for example, attending the Catholic funeral Mass for a parent with siblings and other family members, and then returning home to sit *shiva* with synagogue members and friends.

Paula C. Yablonsky serves as co-chairwoman of Congregation Gates of Heaven's Outreach Committee in Schenectady, New York. She is currently chairwoman of the Regional Outreach Committee for the Northeast Council of the Union of American Hebrew Congregations (UAHC, the Reform Movement). A meal site manager at her local Jewish Community Center, she plans meals and programs for senior citizens. She and her husband, Mark Gibbons, have a daughter, Erica.

Mourning My Episcopalian Mother as a Jew-by-Choice

PAULA C. YABLONSKY

How does a Jew-by-Choice mourn a non-Jewish loved one? I struggled with this question as my mother lay dying.

My family has a rich and varied spiritual history. My father, born in the Ukraine, was brought up Ukrainian Catholic. When arriving in this country, he found no Ukrainian Catholic churches in his area and chose to affiliate with the Roman Catholic Church. My father married my mother—an Episcopalian—in the Episcopal Rectory. They brought their six children up in the Roman Catholic faith, after having done what many families did during the sixties and seventies—rejected, explored, and found their way back to organized religion. My father finally found a Ukrainian Catholic Church in which to worship. Older siblings re-grasped Roman Catholicism with a born-again fervor, and I found rhyme and reason in Judaism.

As my family gathered at my mother's bedside for what turned out to be her last illness, we all were in tremendous pain at the thought that she was dying. During this time, I said many *mi she-beirachs* (prayers for the sick and their caregivers) for my mother and for my family. My older siblings and my father had their various priests in to give my mother the "last rites." She was in a coma at the time and very much unaware of what was happening—which, considering that she was Episcopalian, may have been a blessing, as it was Catholic priests, Roman and Ukrainian, who presided.

I watched as the various priests came in to offer comfort to my father and siblings, and, knowing that I had left the faith, ignored me. An older brother read the New Testament out loud to my mother. When he needed a break, my older sister took over the reading. I quietly read psalms to myself, and when I did speak, it was to tell my mother that I loved her and to thank her for everything she had given me, for being a wonderful mother and a fantastic grandmother.

On a *Shabbat* (the Jewish Sabbath) evening, my mom died. The next day her funeral was planned. As we sat around the funeral home, decisions were made about the service. It was not up for discussion: a Roman Catholic Mass was to be said for this Episcopal woman. Again, I saw how my father, brother, and sister seemed to derive comfort from choosing songs and readings that were meaningful to them. My request was to be able to read the twenty-third Psalm—a request that was ignored.

The wake was short compared to others I have attended: one day only, and, once again, priests, rosaries, Our Fathers, and Hail Marys. I sat quietly, remembering all the words to the prayers, remembering all the motions—when to bow a head, when and how to make the sign of the cross. I remembered and listened and felt alone: knowing that, as a Jew, I could no longer say the prayers. I sat listening to the cadence of the words as they were recited, remembering when I had learned them, how I had said them with my parents as a child.

Sitting alone, I wondered how I would find comfort. How could I honor my mother and still remain true to myself as a Jew? These questions weighed heavily on my heart and mind.

After speaking with my husband, I decided that once all the Catholic rituals and rites were over and my non-Jewish family had departed, I would watch my mother's coffin be lowered into the ground and put the customary shovels full of dirt into the grave. I would ask my Jewish friends, who I knew were coming to the funeral Mass, to stay and recite *Kaddish* (the prayer extolling God that is said by mourners) with me.

Sitting in the church, smelling the flowers and incense, once again hearing all the familiar prayers of the Mass, the songs of my childhood, all the memories of my Catholic girlhood came back—and remembering gave me a bittersweet sort of confusing comfort. Confusing in that as I looked around the same marble altar of my childhood, I saw the statues, the flowers, knew which pew was the pew we all had stuffed ourselves into so many Sunday mornings. The smell of the incense, as familiar to me as my mother's Shalimar perfume, drifted through the church, and I felt myself a child again.

For a moment I pretended that we were at a regular Sunday morning Mass, Ma was home cooking a big roast, and we would all soon be eating and arguing over our Sunday dinner. I allowed myself a small dram of comfort in taking in all the sights, smells, and sounds. I also experienced a hefty dose of guilt: Was I betraying my Judaism—my newfound faith—by letting myself find comfort in a Roman Catholic church?

Looking back, I now know that the comfort I found in church that day was derived not from reciting the prayers or believing in the rites that were performed, but from the memories of childhood—the memories that recalled my mother young, healthy, and whole; my father smiling, not broken over the death of his wife; and all of us children, young and naturally blonde.

I know that finding comfort in remembering my childhood, especially in a place where I had spent so much time, was not wrong, and that my love of Judaism was in no way diminished or negated. I know that what helped me in the days that followed was Judaism—the prayers and rituals for mourning and the community and acceptance I found in my Jewish friends.

Rabbi Paul J. Citrin is spiritual leader of Temple Sinai, Palm Desert, California.

Jewish Burial and Mourning Practice for Non-Jewish Relatives

PAUL J. CITRIN

Mixed marriage between Jews and non-Jews raises questions about the application of Jewish rituals and privileges to the non-Jewish relatives. These questions can arise when a death occurs even after decades of harmonious family life. Among the concerns of mixed-married couples are the following issues surrounding funeral practice:

1. May a non-Jew be buried in a Jewish cemetery? May a Jew be buried in a non-Jewish cemetery?
2. Who officiates at services for a non-Jewish spouse or relative?
3. May Jews observe Jewish mourning rituals for non-Jewish relatives?
4. May Jews participate in non-Jewish funerals? May non-Jews participate in Jewish funerals?

The following responses to these questions are a summary of American Reform Jewish opinion expressed throughout the twentieth century. Orthodox Judaism has very different approaches.

CEMETERY BURIAL

It is accepted practice to bury a non-Jewish spouse in a Jewish cemetery. The opinion of Reform thinkers is that the entire cemetery is not consecrated ground, rather only the individual grave where a body rests is sacred. When others disallow the burial of a non-Jew in a Jewish cemetery, they are adhering to custom, not law. The *Talmud* (a body of texts of Jewish law) states that for the sake of peaceful relations, we may bury the gentile dead (see Gittin 61a). Thus, Reform practice has been to permit non-Jewish relatives to be buried in Jewish cemeteries as long as there are no non-Jewish symbols on the person's grave marker. Generally, clergy of other faiths are not permitted to officiate at the interment in a Jewish cemetery.

The concept of a Jewish cemetery is an extension of Jewish communal identity and cohesion. It is, therefore, desirable for Jews to be buried in a Jewish cemetery. Yet, when a Jew is buried in a non-Jewish cemetery, a rabbi may officiate nonetheless.

WHO OFFICIATES FOR A NON-JEWISH SPOUSE?

If a non-Jewish spouse was a practicing member of another faith, a clergyman of that faith officiates at the church or funeral home. If the interment for the deceased is to be in a Jewish cemetery following the funeral, a rabbi officiates at the graveside. If a non-Jewish spouse has been part of Jewish family and communal life, but has never converted, a rabbi may officiate at the funeral and at the interment, if such was the wish of the deceased.

OBSERVING JEWISH RITUALS FOR NON-JEWS

Jewish mourning rituals are observed for a deceased spouse, parent, sibling, or child. If the non-Jewish deceased stands in one of these relations to the mourner, the mourner should observe Jewish mourning customs. Such practices are intended to support the living and to help them express their grief. They also serve to honor the memory of the deceased by those to whom they were beloved. *Kaddish* (the prayer extolling God that is said by mourners), then, may certainly be recited for non-Jews. Converts to Judaism may say *Kaddish* for deceased non-Jewish relatives.

PARTICIPATION IN FUNERALS

Jews mourning non-Jewish relatives and friends may attend funeral services held in a church or funeral chapel. Jews may serve as pall bearers and may accept an invitation to speak about the deceased. In a Roman Catholic funeral, the Eucharist (Communion) may be included. Of course, Jews do not participate in receiving Communion, nor do Jews kneel during the service. In certain Protestant denominations, the funeral is an occasion to witness for Jesus, with less emphasis on the life of the deceased.

Non-Jewish participation in a Jewish funeral should be limited to serving as pall bearers, and, if desired, sharing in the eulogy.

CONCLUSION

In Jewish tradition, burial of the dead is sometimes referred to as *hesed shel emet* (true loving kindness). This term expresses the idea that what we do for the dead is the most sincere and selfless act of caring we can perform, since the dead cannot repay us. Burying our non-Jewish relatives in our midst and expressing our grief through Jewish mourning practice is no less an effort of true loving kindness. The act of *hesed shel emet* stands as a memorial to relationships in life that bespoke love, devotion, and caring. Further, our openness promotes peace among the living. If we want our beloved deceased to rest in peace, we, their survivors, must find wholeness and completeness in their death through sharing our tradition.

Rabbi Elias Lieberman has served the Falmouth Jewish Congregation in Falmouth, Massachusetts, since 1990.

Bereavement and the Interfaith Family

ELIAS LIEBERMAN

A story attributed to the Buddha tells of a mother desolate with grief over the death of her young child. Distraught, she comes to the Buddha, begging him to bring her child back to life. "You must bring me," he tells her, "a mustard seed from a home that has never known sorrow." The bereaved mother begins the search for such a mustard seed and soon learns that loss and bereavement are universal experiences. She returns to the Buddha better able to accept her child's death.

This tale underscores the reality that we all experience death and loss. Our responses to death, however, are culturally defined. The Hindu cremation pyre, the Catholic wake, the *shiva* observance in Judaism are all manifestations of our need to mourn a loss, and we turn to familiar rituals to help us do so. For interfaith families, the death of a loved one can give rise to questions, and the solutions we come up with can either facilitate, or impede, a healthy grieving process.

As the rabbi of a Reform congregation, I serve the needs of many interfaith families. I am also called upon to help bereaved interfaith families who are not affiliated with any synagogue. I am frequently asked about the "proper" role of the non-Jewish survivor in mourning rituals. In responding to the grief of mourners, regardless of their religious identity, I try to remember that one of the more significant *mitzvot* (commandments) in Jewish life bids us to bring comfort to mourners.

My primary responsibility is to help the family constellation begin to process its grief appropriately. To the non-Jewish survivors of a deceased Jew, I explain that, according to Jewish law, the obligations of mourning fall upon first-degree Jewish relatives: parents, spouse/partner, siblings, children. These responsibilities include the observance of *shiva* (the initial seven-day mourning period), *shloshim* (the thirty-day mourning period, which includes *shiva)*, and *yahrzeit* (the observance of the anniversary of the death).

A non-Jewish survivor is neither required, nor expected, to take on these obligations, but may choose to do so. Not infrequently, the non-Jewish survivor is estranged from the faith tradition of his or her upbringing. He or she may have been living for years within the orbit of Judaism and Jewish practice. When death intrudes, the non-Jewish survivor may feel bereft of the traditional sources of comfort that a faith tradition provides, or that survivor may naturally look to Judaism for guidance.

I must often simultaneously find ways to meet the needs of both Jewish and non-Jewish survivors in an interfaith family. This involves presenting clear explanations of Jewish funeral and mourning practices. It means explaining what the non-Jewish survivor may or may not do from the vantage point of Jewish tradition.

Two examples may be helpful. Before a Jewish funeral service begins, first-degree Jewish relatives engage in the act of *kriah* (tearing one's garment or pinning a black ribbon to one's lapel). It is a powerful and ancient reaction to the harsh reality of death and an acknowledgment that death tears an irreparable hole in the fabric of our lives. The *kriah* ribbon (or the torn garment) is worn for the *shloshim* period. Traditionally, it is removed on *Shabbat* (the Jewish Sabbath).

What if a non-Jewish partner or child asks to wear the *kriah* ribbon? I respond that, while this is an obligation for Jewish mourners, I understand that, like a black armband, the *kriah* ribbon is a symbol that communicates a universal message about the status of one who wears it. I therefore leave such a decision to the mourner.

What if there are not enough Jewish adults to constitute a *minyan* (a prayer quorum of ten Jewish adults) for the worship services held in the house of mourning? The lack of a *minyan* precludes the recitation of certain prayers, including the mourners' *Kaddish* (a prayer most closely associated with the Jewish mourning experience).

May a non-Jew be counted in the requisite ten? Insofar as the *minyan* symbolizes the Jewish community, which is mourning the loss of one of its members and which is drawing together in support of the mourners, I do not count a non-Jew in a *minyan*. That non-Jew is welcomed into that circle of prayer and comfort, but may not, by definition, help constitute it. This underscores the importance of connecting to a Jewish community which may be called upon to provide a *minyan* of support. It is among the many reasons people decide to affiliate with a synagogue.

Every family and every death are unique. The challenges which interfaith families often face come most sharply into focus at liminal moments: spiritual thresholds such as birth, marriage, and death. As autonomous entities, Jewish communities can, and will, decide for themselves where boundary lines will be drawn. The phenomenon of interfaith marriage, especially when mixed-faith couples must contend with death, requires Jewish communities and their leaders to decide when and to what extent those boundaries may be made more permeable, so that the blessings of Jewish tradition may be brought to those bowed in sorrow.

David Horowitz is immediate past president of Temple Beth David of the South Shore, Canton, Massachusetts. Currently, he serves on the Northeast Regional Board of the Union of American Hebrew Congregations (UAHC, the Reform Movement). He is married to Dr. June Andrews Horowitz.

My First Wake

DAVID HOROWITZ

The first wake I attended was for my friend's father. Although I had learned something about wakes from Christian friends and had witnessed facsimiles of wakes in movies, I really didn't know what to expect. Although I wanted to be supportive to my friend, his mother, and sister, I was uncertain what was expected and how I was supposed to participate.

To be really honest, my greatest fear was how I would react physically to the presence of an open coffin. I had attended funerals for Jewish relatives (where the coffin remains closed) and thought about the physical appearance of the deceased relative as I looked at the coffin. However, the prospect of viewing the body of my friend's father was unsettling.

While there are many challenges facing interfaith newlyweds, one advantage to marrying a Catholic woman was that I was able to draw upon her knowledge of Christian funerals and wakes. I followed her lead as we attended the wake of my friend's father.

Unlike the Jewish tradition I had grown up with—in which the burial takes place as soon as possible, and friends and family then visit the grieving family at their home over the next seven days— Christian traditions commonly call for visiting with the grieving family in the days following the death and up until the time of burial. The wake typically takes place in a formal funeral home. Upon entering the building, there is a sign indicating in which room the wake is being held. The room has the appearance of a formal living room or parlor with plush carpet, classical window drapes, and upholstered chairs.

When we entered the room where the wake for my friend's father was being held, we joined the end of a line of visitors. As we solemnly proceeded through the room, we first stopped at a podium holding a visitor's sign-in book. Next, we came to the coffin, which was surrounded by many sprays of long-stemmed flowers as well as pictures of my friend's father and some of his certificates of accomplishment. A padded kneeler was located beside the open coffin. The visitors who preceded us were kneeling beside the coffin and appeared to be speaking to my friend's father or imparting one final prayer on his behalf.

As we walked by the open coffin, I glanced at my friend's father, who was dressed in a black suit, white shirt, and necktie. His hair had been trimmed, and his hands were folded on his chest, clasping a string of rosary beads. Beyond the coffin, my friend and his family were waiting in a receiving line. Despite my apprehension over approaching an open casket and viewing a dead person for the first time in my life, I learned that there was no expectation that I walk up to the coffin.

When we reached the head of the line of mourners, we embraced our friend and his family and shared with them our deep sorrow over their loss. We then waited in the funeral parlor until the line had ended and we were able to speak with our friend at length.

Since my first wake, I have attended wakes for my mother-in-law, relatives, friends, and neighbors. Although the specific details of wakes may vary, each takes place within specified visiting hours during the days preceding the funeral. When the members of the family in mourning are close friends or relatives, one may wish to remain at the funeral home to meet with other friends and relatives or to spend more time with the grieving family. However, in the case of a wake at which you are not a close friend or relative, there is no expectation that you remain at the funeral home after speaking with the grieving family in the receiving line.

Although the setting and the rituals around mourning are not the same as those I grew up with, I have come to appreciate that the structure and formality of the wake bring a degree of comfort and reassurance to the grieving family. Each wake I have attended has been a celebration of the life of the deceased.

Dr. June Andrews Horowitz is an associate professor in the Psychiatric-Mental Health Department, School of Nursing, Boston College. She has more than a decade of experience leading counseling groups and workshops for interfaith couples, and she is a member of the Regional Outreach Committee for the Northeast Council of the Union of American Hebrew Congregations (UAHC, the Reform Movement).

My First *Shiva*

JUNE ANDREWS HOROWITZ

When someone we love dies, we are hit by a waterfall of emotions: shock, anger, pain, sorrow, sadness, fear, anxiety, guilt, loneliness, emptiness, and sometimes even relief. Although our reactions may vary depending on the situation of the death, experiencing a loss is never easy. Rituals and customs can help us through the early days of mourning by providing structure and meaning.

For Jews, the immediate period of mourning is known as *shiva*, a period of seven days (from the Hebrew number *sheva,* or seven) that include and follow the funeral. During this seven-day period, mourners refrain from their usual activities. Some people observe a shorter period, but at least three days usually are designated. The phrase "sitting *shiva*" often is used to describe this period of intense grieving because of an ancient custom of sitting on the floor to symbolize being struck low by the loss. Today, some mourners sit on low stools or benches, or remove cushions from furniture to be closer to the floor. There are other traditions that may be observed, such as covering mirrors and washing hands before entering the house of mourning after coming from the cemetery.

LEARNING FROM MEMORIES

When I think back to my first *shiva* over twenty-five years ago, I remember that I didn't understand very much about Jewish mourning practices. I was not Jewish when my husband's uncle died. We were newly married ourselves, so I had not yet experienced the loss of any of our Jewish relatives. I was somewhat anxious because I did not know what to expect and feared that I might offend someone by making a false move. I approached the funeral and *shiva* like a visitor to a foreign country.

My husband gave me a crash course in what to do and how to act. I learned that in Jewish tradition the burial takes place quickly, followed by a time of mourning that was not unlike what I was used to during a wake. At first, it felt as if the funeral was taking place too soon. I was used to a slower pace following a death because Catholic practice involves a wake being held before the funeral and burial. It also seemed strange to me to have the funeral in a funeral chapel or funeral home rather than in a synagogue. Although I was familiar with having wakes in funeral homes, I was used to having the funeral service in a church. The service was new to me, too: There were no familiar prayers or melodies to help me feel a part of what was happening.

On the way to the family's house for *shiva*, I wondered how people would act and hoped that we would encounter family members I knew. Once we arrived, my anxieties melted away because the relatives welcomed me as part of the family. As people gathered to share food and reminisce about my husband's uncle, I realized that our presence was supportive to the immediate family. My attention shifted to their needs, and I knew that being together eased the sadness of this difficult time.

My first *shiva* experience taught me that although specific practices among religions differ, the primary purposes—to provide comfort to and show concern for the mourners and to show respect for the person who has died—are the same. To me, that's the ultimate goal of mourning rituals—to help us cope with the sorrow death brings, and to provide support for others. After these many years, what I remember most is that it was comforting to spend time with the family in the mourners' home during *shiva*.

For those who want to learn more, some helpful books that explain Jewish practice are *The Jewish Book of Why* and its sequel, *The Second Jewish Book of Why* (Jonathan David), by Alfred Kolatch, or *Living a Jewish Life* (HarperCollins) by Anita Diamant and Howard Cooper.

18. Interfaith Families and the Synagogue

A former congregational rabbi, David Regenspan is currently a writer. His main project at the moment is a novel about the medieval Hebrew poets Shmuel ha-Nagid and Shlomo Ibn Gabirol, set in eleventh-century Andalusia.

Sojourners among Us: Non-Jews in Jewish Life

DAVID REGENSPAN

They are models for the rabbi's sermon about how to lead a good Jewish life. They light Sabbath candles and send their children to Hebrew school. They attend adult education classes on Jewish subjects. They sing boisterously at Jewish services and know the Hebrew words of every prayer. They serve on synagogue committees; they even become synagogue officers.

And they are not Jews.

The American Jewish community is filled with participants who are not Jewish according to the rules of anyone in organized Judaism, be it Orthodox, Conservative, Reconstructionist, or Reform. Having never undergone conversion, they are Jews in practice but not in name. They have no "church" other than the synagogue, no home rituals other than Jewish rituals.

Why do they not convert to Judaism, yet live as Jews? Here are two stories.

CATHY

Cathy Currier is not Jewish and has no plans to become a Jew. Yet, Jewish life is very important to her. Her husband, Ted, is committed to Jewish practice; her son, Yossi, and daughter, Hannah, are being raised as Jews. Cathy's family holds an honored place in a medium-sized Conservative congregation in Ithaca, New York, where her husband serves as membership chairman.

Cathy freely admits that her marriage brought her to synagogue life. Having studied Hebrew and lived in Israel, Cathy is comfortable with Conservative Jewish worship. Raised a Unitarian, she is at ease with a religious environment that is not Jesus-centered or dogmatic. She now considers her synagogue to be a key element of her community life, and feels welcomed even though the rules exclude her from ritual and certain other activities.

Bringing up her children as Jews "was never a question," because it was a condition of her marriage to Ted. Both children underwent conversion in an effort to insure their Jewish status; both attended Hebrew school and became a *Bar* or *Bat Mitzvah* (took on the obligations and privileges of adult members of the Jewish community). Judaism, Cathy feels, provides them with a sound moral code, and she is happy that they are being raised as Jews. As a day care professional and social activist, morality is high on Cathy's priority list.

Why does Cathy not intend to become a Jew? "Even if I converted I wouldn't be Jewish in any meaningful way," she explains. The product of a home in which religion did not play a major role beyond Unitarian church membership, Cathy does not feel that she can embrace any religious doctrine. Furthermore, she feels that unless she were born Jewish, she could not be an "ethnic" Jew. Being part of a Jewish community, however, is central to Cathy's life—a paradox she accepts.

CHARLIE

Charlie Wilson married into the Jewish community, but, unlike Cathy, may some day convert. For now, he is content with participating in his small Reform congregation.

An intensely moral man, Charlie gave up a lucrative defense industry career due to his horror at the Vietnam War. But organized religion did not interest him after he became disillusioned with his Catholic upbringing. He felt a void in his life where the Church had been.

His marriage to public school educator Denise represented the start of his gradual approach to Jewish life. Denise, a born Jew, felt alienated from Jewish religious life. The birth of their daughter, Elsa, however, forced the couple to rethink the question of religion in the home. "I was concerned," says Charlie, "that she should have an education in a religious system." Judaism, at least of the liberal variety, seemed to be the logical choice. Later, Charlie was stunned to discover that his father's mother had been Jewish, a fact she had never discussed. He suspects that some Jewish values were quietly transmitted to him down through the generations.

Charlie and Denise began to attend Jewish worship when Elsa's religious school class was participating in the Sabbath service. Charlie enjoyed the rabbi's historically oriented explanations of the weekly *Torah* (the first five books of the Hebrew Bible) portion. He found himself learning the Hebrew words to the prayers and hymns, and began to feel at home.

Charlie does see conversion as a possibility in his future, but he is still dealing with his old fear of organized religion. He is not ready for that ultimate step.

ISSUES FOR NON-JEWISH PARTICIPANTS
IN JEWISH LIFE

Some non-Jewish participants will never convert, while others might and do. For many, family-of-origin issues come into play. As one rabbi observes: "My guess is that there are many whose delay in conversion is linked (consciously or unconsciously) to family affection, not theology." In other words, some may feel that they will hurt their parents' or siblings' feelings by formally embracing another faith.

HOW SHOULD JEWISH COMMUNITIES RESPOND TO THE NON-JEWS IN THEIR MIDST?

More liberal congregations allow some ritual participation for non-Jews. As one rabbi describes the practice in her synagogue: "We allow non-Jews to read parts of the service in English, to open the ark, and to stand with their spouse when they do an *aliyah* (recite the blessing over the *Torah* reading)." A good rule of thumb may be to bar non-Jews from reciting or performing such non-universal rituals as the *Torah* blessings, which are designed to celebrate Jewish particularity, but to permit them certain more universal expressions of public prayer, such as reading many of the psalms.

Some synagogues allow non-Jews to assume certain leadership roles—here again, it seems advisable to be very cautious about which roles are permitted. It may be more appropriate for a non-Jew to work with the social action committee, an activity that transcends religious denominations, than to work with a committee on religious or ritual matters.

Yet, perhaps the most important thing is the presence of a general sense of welcome rather than the specific rules and restrictions that are applied. Like anyone else in the community, non-Jews wish to be treated with warmth and kindness. Synagogue leaders must ensure that such treatment is the norm.

As the Jewish community continues to battle assimilation and attrition, welcoming non-Jewish participants may prove to be one key to its survival. As it says in the *Torah:* "But the stranger who dwells with you shall be to you as one born among you, and you shall love him as yourself; for you were strangers in the land of Egypt."

TEN RECOMMENDATIONS FOR DEALING WITH NON-JEWISH SYNAGOGUE PARTICIPANTS

- Treat non-Jewish participants as honored guests, even though they may be restricted from many activities and decisions. They have chosen to be with your community.

- If non-Jewish participants in your synagogue make you uneasy, try to understand your feelings. Do not behave in a hostile manner; uphold Jewish principles in a humane way.

- Make congregational decisions concerning non-Jewish participants in a rational and fair-minded manner.

- Make sure that non-Jewish participants have a voice (if not a vote). Allow them to share their perceptions and suggestions.

- Only place limits on the ritual and leadership activities of non-Jewish members that reflect the greater good of Judaism, and not petty and insignificant matters.

- Welcome non-Jewish participants as potential converts, but do not badger them to convert.

- If you must turn down a non-Jewish participant's request to perform a specific ritual, such as saying the blessing over the *Torah* reading, do so in a gentle manner and explain the reason for the refusal.

- Do not be inclined to suspect non-Jewish participants of having ulterior motives, such as Christian missionizing. This is very unlikely.

- Go out of your way to ask non-Jewish participants how they feel about their reception in the congregation. Is there some way that they could be made to feel more welcome?

- If your rabbi or other leaders seem unaware of the importance of the issue of non-Jewish participants, then be sure to raise the issue. You will be doing the community a service.

Wendy Case has been a clinical social worker for over twenty-five years. She works with individuals, couples, and families in a private psychotherapy practice.

Is There a Place for Me in Judaism?

WENDY CASE

I have been part of a Jewish family for over twenty-five years. I practice Judaism exclusively, and I would call Judaism my spiritual home. Both my daughter and son have become *Bat* and *Bar Mitzvah* (taken on the obligations and privileges of adult members of the Jewish community) as well as confirmed. I am very active in our Reform congregation and have acted as co-chairperson of our Social Action Committee for many years. However, I have not formally converted to Judaism, and I do not believe that I would feel any differently if I did. Having learned Hebrew over twenty years ago, and with the practice of repetition at services, I have learned many of the prayers and songs in the *Shabbat* (the Jewish Sabbath) and High Holiday liturgies and have participated fully and joyfully in services.

Recently our temple's religious practices committee has been grappling with the issue of the participation of non-Jews in ritual practices, specifically the issue of *aliyot* (blessings over the *Torah*, the first five books of the Hebrew Bible) at *Bar* and *Bat Mitzvah* ceremonies. The emotional debate surrounding this issue has created a personal crisis for me, even though my children are already past that *B'nai Mitzvah* stage.

In our congregation's debate over the *aliyot* issue, some people have said, "What would be the motivation to convert if non-Jews could do the same things as converts?" Conversely, some say, "if non-Jews want to perform certain rituals which are reserved for Jews, why don't they just convert?"

I do not believe that people convert to Judaism in order to be able to perform specific rituals. I view conversion as a highly complex psychological process that is tied closely to each person's very unique sense of identity. Each person brings his or her individual needs and motivations as well as personal circumstances to the process. In no way do I mean to diminish the meaning and value of conversion. However, I am interested in the relationship between identity and practice—between, on the one hand, "being Jewish," and, on the other hand, practicing Judaism or being involved with Judaism as a faith-based religion.

I have always been fascinated by how the fact of being born Jewish seems to be so compelling. Many people just feel that they "are" Jewish. I have heard the bewilderment of non-Jews in interfaith relationships when their Jewish partners, who ostensibly have had no involvement in Judaism, insist that their children be raised as Jews. Even though they do not "practice" Judaism, they "are" Jewish, and this is important to them.

Certainly, I realize that some people need the sense of "being Jewish" before they can involve themselves in the "practice of Judaism." For those people, conversion may be a necessary step to involvement in Judaism. For me, however, actions have always "spoken louder than words," and it is not sufficient to just "be Jewish." I want to know what you are doing if you are Jewish—whether or not you celebrate *Shabbat* (the Sabbath), attend services, study *Torah*, perform *mitzvot* (commandments), engage in *tikkun olam* (repair of the world), etc. I can honestly say that I would not be doing anything differently if I "were" Jewish. For my own idiosyncratic reasons, I do not feel that the identity of Jewishness is attainable by me through conversion.

It seems to me that Judaism encompasses a broad spectrum of individuals, from those who solely identify themselves as Jews, with no involvement in Judaism as a religion, to those whose involvement with Judaism infuses all aspects of their lives. I wonder whether there is room in Judaism for people like myself, who involve themselves in Judaism as their sole religion but do not possess the identity of "being Jewish."

Jonathan E. Kraus is rabbi of Beth El Temple Center in Belmont, Massachusetts.

Walking the Tightrope: Dilemmas a Rabbi Feels with Interfaith Families

JONATHAN E. KRAUS

On Monday, my phone rings. A Jewish member of my congregation, who is in an interfaith marriage, has called to inform me his family is leaving the temple. It seems that our outreach programs (activities to support interfaith families and those interested in becoming Jewish) have been too aggressive for them. Our attempts to create a safe and welcoming environment for interfaith families feel like pressure to them. Our programs to address the needs of interfaith families place unwanted attention on their religious difference. They are uncomfortable, and they are leaving.

On Wednesday, I am meeting with another interfaith couple from the congregation. In angry and hurt tones, the Jewish partner complains of our failure to reach out to her spouse. No one in the congregation (including the rabbi) has actively encouraged him to convert to Judaism. No one has recognized that he is ready to become a Jew, if only someone would ask him. Apparently, our failure to reach out more aggressively makes him feel unwelcome and unwanted by the Jewish community.

A rabbi who works with interfaith families walks a tightrope. Should I give more attention or less attention to the needs of interfaith families in my congregation? If I lean too far toward an active outreach effort, I may offend those who are sensitive to being identified as interfaith families. If I lean too far the other way, I may hurt those who feel that our lack of programming reflects a lack of concern, or worse, an implicit criticism. If I take the risk of asking non-Jewish partners whether they've ever thought about becoming Jewish, my inquiry may be received as a welcoming invitation or an offensive invasion of privacy.

A rabbi who works with interfaith families must become adept at giving what may be perceived as mixed messages. I want to say to non-Jewish partners: you are warmly welcome in our synagogue, exactly as you are. I am grateful for the compromises and sacrifices you have made by choosing to make your family's spiritual life in our community. You are a treasured member of our temple family, whether or not you are Jewish.

At the same time, I want to tell non-Jewish partners: if becoming Jewish ever seems like the right choice for you, I would consider it a privilege to help you explore that possibility. If I don't ask you, my silence does not reflect a lack of interest. It doesn't mean that I think you're not "good enough" to become Jewish. Rather, my silence grows out of my respect for the extraordinarily personal nature of such a decision. My silence reflects my fear lest you interpret my invitation to consider becoming Jewish as a statement that you are not welcome as you are.

A rabbi who reaches out to interfaith couples struggles to articulate many such mixed messages. How can I tell interfaith families: we are honored to have you among us, but we feel the need to reserve certain roles in the life of our religious community for those who have made a formal, personal commitment to Judaism? How can I explain the awkward double standard that often accepts nonobservant and uneducated Jews without condition while telling more committed and knowledgeable non-Jewish spouses that there may be some limits to their full participation in Jewish rituals or the leadership of our synagogue?

I have now worked with interfaith couples for a number of years. I know that my perception is not always penetrating enough to intuit which message a particular family needs to hear. For fear of alienating families or making the wrong choice, I sometimes err on the side of caution. I sometimes lack words that are sufficiently eloquent and sensitive to communicate the complexity and pain of this rabbinic balancing act. I sometimes unintentionally hurt the very people I am trying so hard to help. And I frequently require the support of interfaith families who help me find my way, even as I try to help them find a place in Jewish life.

A rabbi who works with interfaith families walks a tightrope. But increasingly, I realize that interfaith families live on that same wire, doing their own balancing acts. I continue to look for better ways to help these families understand my struggle. And I continue to listen as carefully and openly as I can, trying to help families with the issues that seem difficult for them. I begin to see the possibility of joining hands, helping each other to achieve more balance and security (yes, rabbis need help, too). I begin to hope that we can find the courage to be open with each other and the patience to build understanding and trust, if not always agreement.

Though the rope sometimes wobbles beneath us, though we sometimes inadvertently throw each other off balance, I feel more and more certain we can find a way to reach our destination together in safety, fulfillment, and joy.

Samuel N. Gordon is rabbi of Congregation Sukkat Shalom of Wilmette, Illinois, and holds an M.B.A. from Northwestern University's Kellogg Graduate School of Management.

Interfaith Families and Synagogues: A New Approach

SAMUEL N. GORDON

Begin with a couple from your congregation—she is Jewish, not very religious but strongly identified as a Jew; he is Christian, nonobservant.

Today, Jews marrying non-Jews are not doing so in order to

escape from their Jewish roots. They do not consider themselves to be Jewish failures and are often resentful of their condemnation by much of the organized Jewish world. Most significantly, the non-Jewish partner is often seeking a spiritually dynamic life and is quite open to Jewish living and observance. The partner is often not a practicing Christian and finds Jewish observance, values, and traditions appealing and meaningful.

Intermarriage is dramatically changing the American Jewish culture. New Jews-by-Choice as well as those non-Jews actively living a Jewish life require new institutional responses to their needs. In addition to a new population of those not born as Jews, many unaffiliated Jews are seeking a newly defined spiritual home but feel unwelcome or uncomfortable in the traditional synagogue.

INSTITUTIONAL CHANGE

The traditional program and design of the American synagogue is not conducive to welcoming and integrating these new members of the Jewish community. The American synagogue has been built around an assumed collective ethnic memory, experience, and loyalty. In the past, Jewish identity was largely determined by birth, and few leaders or thinkers anticipated an American culture in which significant numbers of non-Jews would seek to become part of the Jewish world, whether through formal conversion or voluntary lifestyle.

Today, even in synagogues where an active outreach program is in place, outreach is seen as a specific program that has no real effect on changing the culture of the synagogue itself. One cannot expect a radically different population within Jewish culture to fit into a traditional institutional model. Significant institutional change is necessary in order to create a synagogue that is welcoming to these new members of the American Jewish community. Traditional forms of Jewish education, worship, and funding often act as entrance barriers to this group. Their low affiliation rates indicate that the primary institution of Jewish identity, the synagogue, must be transformed.

EDUCATIONAL CHANGE

The traditional Jewish supplementary school is widely recognized as a failure. Better textbooks, higher salaries for teachers, or improved curricula cannot solve endemic problems based on fundamental design. The supplementary school program does not work for most Jewish families. It is even more of a problem for families in which one parent was not born as a Jew. Only the American synagogue maintains a Sunday morning program that actively separates children from parents. No person born as a Christian knows a model of parents dropping off their children for religious education.

Indeed, throughout today's American culture, parents are spending more time with their children in weekend activities. Dual professional couples seek opportunities to participate in programs with their children. Children's museums, cultural centers, and art and natural history museums all have successful family education programs, usually meeting on weekends. The synagogue has an opportunity to build upon this trend and create exciting educational opportunities for parents and children to experience Judaism together.

Rather than a drop-off religious school, synagogues must offer quality family-based religious learning. In particular, parents need to be empowered to transmit Jewish values and traditions to their children so that the educational process can be centered on the home, with the religious school as supplementary. This kind of education program must develop beyond holiday workshops for families. The ideal curriculum should engage all age groups in challenging learning on the same or complementary topics, but at age-appropriate levels. The goal is to have the family unit continue its learning, discussion, and engagement after it leaves the synagogue building. Serious adult learning models the notion of Jewish study as a lifelong enterprise. The synagogue must also transmit the spiritual power of learning. Separately or in coalition with other synagogues, serious text study should be offered.

SUKKAT SHALOM AS MODEL

Congregation Sukkat Shalom offers a model of a synagogue dedicated to transformation. Sukkat Shalom was formed initially from an outreach support group that had been meeting for eight years. By 1995 that group had grown to approximately twenty households and had offered support group discussions, family educational programs, holiday and *Shabbat* (the Jewish Sabbath) observance, guest scholars and discussions, and occasional worship events. Our synagogue was established with the clear mission of being a congregation of welcome and acceptance to a diverse community. Sukkat Shalom has attempted to transform the nature of the American synagogue in areas of outreach, family education, worship and observance, and funding.

EDUCATION

Sukkat Shalom's education program involves the entire family. Parents and children join together twice a month to explore stories, values, and traditions. A combination of parallel and joint study deepens the learning experience for all. The primary goal is to establish a model in which the family is the key learning unit. The curriculum is largely text based, with children learning the key biblical stories while parents are exposed to serious text study complementary to their children's learning. Older children explore values and ethics through the same biblical tales. The goal of the Family School is to enable the entire family to find stimulation and challenge within Jewish thought.

WORSHIP

Worship is experienced in an intimate setting conducive to meditation, poetry, and song. Creative readings in both Hebrew and English are intended to deepen the spiritual search. At least once a month the community gathers for a *Shabbat* meal. With songs, blessings, prayers, and food, *Shabbat* as sacred meal is shared. The worship service may include elements of Reform, Reconstructionist,

Conservative, Orthodox, Hassidic, and Renewal traditions. A key goal is to foster a spirit of *Shabbat* as an intimate home observance through the synagogue as model. Shared meals within the congregation allow all members to experience *Shabbat* as sacred time.

FUNDING

Members are asked to make voluntary yearly pledges to support the work of the congregation. Guidelines are suggested, but each family is free to determine its own level of giving. Our leadership feels that this system has produced financial results similar to the more traditional dues system without the resentment often expressed by synagogue members elsewhere.

MISSION

Sukkat Shalom is attempting to transform the nature of the traditional American synagogue. As a community built on inclusiveness and respect for diversity, the congregation has gone far beyond individual and specific programs of outreach or support. All aspects of the congregation are affected by the mission to imagine a radically new synagogue for a new community.

Rabbi Mark Hillel Kunis has been rabbi of Congregation Shearith Israel in Atlanta, Georgia, for the past twelve years.

Welcoming Intermarrieds in *Shul:* An Ordained Orthodox Rabbi's Perspective

MARK HILLEL KUNIS

Do you remember the TV series of the 1970s named *Bridget and Bernie?* Their lives depicted an interesting mixture of two cultures— kosher salami and Virginia ham. What the viewers did not see in this series or in most other Hollywood depictions of such relationships is how they dealt with their spiritual lives. Perhaps it is typical of the way many mixed marriages avoided the issue altogether. But there are now many mixed marriages that do want to make God and tradition a part of their lives.

More than ever, interfaith couples (if the non-Jewish spouse converts, it is not an interfaith couple) are coming to the synagogue. One might think that this is merely a reflection in the rise in interfaith marriages among Jews. But the Jewish rate of intermarriage has been high for some time now (52 percent in the 1990 Jewish population survey). I think it reflects a spiritual undercurrent in our society, a longing for the divine, and a search for our inner selves that is so strong that it emerges despite the obvious complications of an interfaith marriage. Despite what many Jews may think, Jews in interfaith marriages have not given up on God or Jewish tradition. In fact, the opposite may often be true— they may need this spiritual connection now more than ever.

My congregation, Shearith Israel, is a "Traditional" congregation. Its service is lively—filled with song and spirit—and it follows the traditional liturgy that has remained the same for hundreds of years. There are *mechitza* sections (for men and women who choose to sit separately), but most of the congregation sits in the larger mixed seating section.

When I came to Shearith Israel twelve years ago, if an interfaith family wanted to join the synagogue, only the Jewish partner would be accepted, and he or she would then be listed as a "single" membership. This was typical of Orthodox, Traditional, and even Conservative congregations. I had a problem with this policy and insisted that it be changed. If we, as a congregation, would have any spiritual impact upon these families, we needed to approach them as a family.

Yes, the non-Jewish spouse cannot be buried in our cemetery or lead the service or become an officer of the synagogue, and most of them understand that. But he or she is invited to be a full participant in congregational programs—*Shabbat* (the Jewish Sabbath) dinners, Friday night family services, adult education, socials, religious school programs, etc. Non-Jewish spouses are encouraged to become active on committees to help plan and carry out programs. In my first year at Shearith Israel I began an interfaith couples support group to meet at holiday times and discuss the inevitable holiday conflicts that arise and how best to deal with them. I make myself available to interfaith couples for marital and family counseling. I wanted both the non-Jewish as well as the Jewish spouse to feel comfortable in Shearith Israel and to know that they have a spiritual home here.

This may seem strange coming from an Orthodox rabbi—I received my *smicha* (ordination) from Yeshiva University. The prevailing belief in Orthodox, Traditional, and even Conservative circles has been that by making interfaith couples feel welcome in the synagogue, we are, in effect, encouraging intermarriage. This argument may have had some validity—probably not much—fifty years ago when the intermarriage rate was less than 5 percent, but now we know better.

Sitting *shiva* (mourning) for a child who intermarried, as was done by some in the past, never brought a child or his or her children back to the fold. But what has helped keep the Jewish family members of an interfaith family in the fold has been the support and embrace of the extended Jewish family. Whether or not a synagogue will welcome a non-Jewish spouse into its midst is simply not an important consideration for the overwhelming majority of those contemplating intermarriage. But once the intermarriage has taken place, how we welcome them can make a huge difference in the Jewish life of this family and whether or not it will have Jewish children.

In Shearith Israel, non-Jewish spouses have become regular attendees of *Shabbat* services. Many attend our adult education classes in order to learn more about Judaism, and some have decided to convert (no pressure, I promise) after a few years of participation—others after as much as fifteen years of marriage! If the mother is not Jewish, I will convert the children providing the mother sign a declaration promising to raise her children as Jews, faithful to Jewish tradition.

The children of interfaith couples are thus full participants in synagogue life. They attend our religious school, participate in youth services and programs, and regularly lead services and read *Torah* (the first five books of the Hebrew Bible) after their *Bar* or *Bat Mitzvah* (the ceremony in which an individual chooses to assume the obligations and privileges of an adult member of the Jewish community) as do other children. No stigma is attached to them, and disparaging remarks are not tolerated.

How often, in the wake of the Holocaust, have we agonized over our declining numbers and the decline in Jewish observance? My revered teacher, Rabbi Joseph B. Soloveitchik, may he rest in peace, taught that we are called the Children of Israel, who was Jacob, and not the Children of Abraham or Isaac, because it was only Israel who had a lasting relationship with his grandchildren. The barometer of Jewish survival is perhaps through our grandchildren. Several years ago there was a survey of intermarried grandparents in Philadelphia. Not one of the grandparents surveyed had a grandchild who was being raised as a Jew today. Perhaps this has something to do with the attitudes of that past generation. My experience has shown me that this does not have to be!

I'm not saying that synagogues should promote or condone intermarriage. Quite the contrary. But the truth is that intermarriage is not going away, and we cannot afford to abandon any Jewish soul.

The non-Jewish spouse is not our enemy. He or she also has a soul created in the image of God and might have been attracted to marry a Jew because of a conscious or subconscious affinity for Judaism. Only if we welcome these families and show them the joy and the beauty of Jewish life will we have a chance that all our grandsons and granddaughters will be Jewish.

Formerly director of education for Congregation Beth El of Sudbury, Massachusetts, Sheila E. Goldberg is now a Jewish education consultant.

Will Christopher McNulty Feel "at Home" in a Jewish Religious School?

SHEILA E. GOLDBERG

THE CHALLENGE

A generation ago it was not unusual to hear a parent or a grandparent identify someone as a Jew based on their last name. Today, this no longer holds true. In many of our religious schools we find children named McNulty, Wong, and Fitzpatrick. Through intermarriage, the Jewish community has greatly expanded.

PARENTS PROVIDE A FOUNDATION

The successful integration of children from interfaith families into religious schools begins long before the child is born. It is the parents who must provide the foundation for success. In the decision to enter an interfaith marriage, it is important that the couple address the religious upbringing of their children, as this issue only becomes more difficult after the child is born. Many interfaith couples take the "easy" road by giving a child what they consider "the best of both worlds" and then letting that child make his or her own decision. As I see it, the problem with this approach is that this child ultimately has only a superficial knowledge of both religions and lacks a solid religious identity to hold on to as an adult. In addition, if the child later chooses one parent's religion over the other, she or he could be viewed as favoring that parent. Confusion around religious identity often results.

SITUATIONS WE CONFRONT IN RELIGIOUS SCHOOL

A number of years ago, one of my third-grade teachers came to me quite concerned about a student in her class. It was December, and whenever she attempted to have a discussion about Hanukkah, the child would chime in with "I'm only half-Jewish and I celebrate Christmas, too." He was part of an interfaith family that had decided to expose the children to both religious traditions. Knowing that this was a delicate issue, I went into her class to facilitate a discussion on what it feels like to be Jewish at Christmastime. I had barely begun when he let me know that he was "half and half." In a loving way I told him that since his parents had enrolled him in our religious school, we understood that to mean that he was being raised as a Jew. He was quiet for most of the remaining discussion, but at the very end he raised his hand and said to me, "There are times I'm just not sure what I am." In a non-judgmental way, I told his parents what had happened that day in class. They agreed that what they had attempted to do didn't appear to be working. Once they made a firm commitment to raise their children as Jews, the child's confusion ceased, and he ultimately became one of our most knowledgeable and enthusiastic students.

The following December I had a very different experience with a fifth grader whose father, a non-Jew, agreed to create a Jewish home for their children. It was right before winter break, and the mother was delayed at work. I offered to drive her son home. On the way, we talked about the approaching holidays. He told me that they had a Christmas tree in their home. I was taken aback for a moment, and then I commented that it must be hard for him living with two religious traditions. "Oh no," he replied. "My mother and I are Jewish and we celebrate the Jewish holidays. But we also help my dad and my grandparents celebrate their holiday too. It's sort of like helping someone celebrate their birthday." It was evident that he has a strong Jewish identity and does not see this as in any way undermining the love he feels for his father or his non-Jewish grandparents.

The key to success clearly depends upon parents being united in their commitment to raising their child in one religion and jointly reinforcing his or her identity. Children need to know that this is not about choosing one parent over another or loving one parent more. It is about doing what you ultimately believe will be in the best interest of your child.

CONGREGATION AS "SUPPORT SYSTEM"

If parents have made the decision to raise their child as a Jew and to provide him or her with a Jewish education, the next step might be to join a synagogue. Selecting the right synagogue is crucial. It must be a place where both the Jewish and the non-Jewish spouse feel welcome, comfortable, and supported. To make this determination, couples need to take the time to meet with the rabbi and the Jewish educator. If they have school-age children, they should ask to sit in on a class to get a feel for the atmosphere of the school. It's also important to find out how the congregation welcomes interfaith couples.

Congregations that open their doors to interfaith couples and families must be prepared to do more than merely accept them as members. They must find ways to integrate and support these couples. This could entail mentoring programs where interfaith families who have successfully raised Jewish children and created a Jewish home help couples who are just starting out on this path. For couples who are ready to think about conversion, the natural mentor would be someone who has just recently become a Jew-by-Choice.

Several years ago I did a session with preschool families who were either interfaith or where one spouse was a Jew-by-Choice. Midway through the workshop, a young woman, a Jew-by-Choice, shared her pain with us. She had gone through a traditional conversion and felt that she had a very strong Judaic background: "My husband says I know far more than he ever did." But somehow that wasn't enough. Not having grown up in a Jewish home surrounded by tradition, she had no experiences to draw on and, as a result, felt she had no choice but to repeat the traditions of her husband's family even though they were not meaningful for her. She and her husband needed to know that it was okay to create their own family traditions and know that we, the professional staff, were available to help them in this process.

Our congregations must be sensitive to the issues and feelings of our interfaith families. We must also be aware of and ready to help couples with additional unresolved issues.

THE RELIGIOUS SCHOOL EXPERIENCE

In congregations where interfaith families are welcomed and a support system is in place, it is not unusual to find an education director who is sensitive to the needs and feelings of these families. Educators must also work with their staff to uncover any prejudices or ambivalence on the part of the teachers. One way of doing this is to invite interfaith parents who have created a Jewish home to meet with the staff and share their experiences and successes. As educators, we need to dispel the myth that if both parents are not Jewish, then their children will not ultimately become Jews.

It is important that interfaith families meet with the education director to discuss their commitment to the education of their children and to provide any information that could be helpful to teachers. In order for religious education to be meaningful, it is important that all families, interfaith or not, make a commitment to be a "partner" in their children's education. This involves participation as a family in services, holiday celebrations, and family education programs, as well as "at home" rituals such as *Shabbat* (the Jewish Sabbath) dinners.

With the family involved, the scene is then set for Christopher McNulty to have a meaningful religious school experience.

Rachel Barenblat is co-founder of Inkberry, a literary organization in Western Massachusetts, and holds an M.F.A. from the Bennington Writing Seminars.

Is Judaism Necessarily Insular?

RACHEL BARENBLAT

Recently my husband and I attended his first Conservative *Shabbat* (the Jewish Sabbath) morning service.

For me, the service was familiar. I loved hearing the chanted *Torah* (the first five books of the Hebrew Bible). I studied religion in college; I'm a writer by trade; the *Torah* is a resonant symbol for me.

I'd forgotten how long a *Torah* service takes when the portion is broken into pieces, each book-ended with *aliyot* (people going up to say blessings over the *Torah* reading). But even as I fidgeted, I hummed the *Torah* blessings, which are as familiar to me as breathing.

For my husband, the morning was frustrating. Most churches, he pointed out, do everything they can to make the outsider welcome. Services are in English, hymnals pair words with music, often there's a pause in the service where congregants are urged to greet one another.

In contrast, this service was mostly in Hebrew; prayers were only partially transliterated, or not transliterated at all; melodies weren't notated; and we sang things that weren't even in the prayer book, like when the *Torah* processional took longer than expected and the cantor led us in *"Al Shlosha D'varim"*—which the congregation, unlike my husband, knew by heart.

This service, he said, did not make him feel welcome.

My response: it wasn't designed to. Which speaks to a really profound difference between Judaism and Christianity, one that I'm still working on articulating.

When the *Shabbat* liturgy was written and codified, the only people who encountered it were Jews. If you were Jewish, you learned this stuff from birth; and if you weren't Jewish, you never encountered it. Judaism was insular, a closed bubble.

Why *is* Judaism so insular?

Perhaps because, unlike Christianity, Judaism traditionally hasn't proselytized. In fact, tradition held that a potential convert should be turned away three times.

Perhaps because we call ourselves "chosen"—though chosenness is a mixed blessing. There's a *midrash* (an interpretative story) that God offered the *Torah* to every nation in the world before offering it to the Jews; but it was so difficult, no one else wanted it.

Perhaps because of persecution. Are Jews insular because we were persecuted, or persecuted because we were insular? Hard to say.

Part of what makes us insular is Hebrew, which, my husband knows, some Jews can't read; and many who can sound out the words, don't know their meaning.

"Doesn't that strike you as strange?" he asked.

"Well," I said, "I'm the wrong person to ask, because I do understand. I've learned what the prayers mean."

For others, the words are a mantra. This is true for my friend L, a feminist who resists feminizing Hebrew God-language. If we change the words, she says, she can't lose herself in their sounds. For her, the words are a ladder to the divine. What's important is their familiarity.

But I know that she and I are relative rarities. Most people don't regard the words as a mantra or as a ladder to God. Many people don't know what they're saying when they recite passages in

Hebrew, and for some, like my husband, Hebrew might as well be Martian.

So is Hebrew the tool he needs to find the service meaningful and welcoming? I'm not sure it would be enough. This year I attended *Kol Nidre* (a service held the evening of Yom Kippur, the Day of Atonement) with four Israelis. After the service (almost all in Hebrew), I asked what they thought. "It was...nice," one said game-ly. "You really do this every year?" another asked. They smiled. They did not return.

The Israelis had no access to our service. They understood the language, but the framework—the repetition of the same prayers and melodies year after year, the association of the prayers with family and repentance and God—wasn't there. The service made literal sense, but it wasn't spiritually accessible.

Language is a barrier for my husband and for Jews unfamiliar with the liturgy, but lack of cultural and familial context is the larger problem. Yet if I'm right, then what? I have context; he doesn't. Now what do we do?

Reform Judaism is one answer. Reform has transliterations, translations. Reform Judaism allows the vernacular. Reform Judaism holds that, while *Torah* and *Shabbat* and Israel are still fundamental, multiple interpretations are possible. It's the Reform Jew's responsi-bility to engage with Judaism for him- or herself.

But is traditional Judaism's closed-ness somehow vital? Is insu-larity inherently Jewish? Does Reform's openness make it less Jewish?

Reform Judaism isn't perfect, either. It is open-minded, and has politics and policies I can support, but the flipside of the liberal reli-gion coin is that it can also lack *kavvanah* (focus). Repetition of familiar prayers can calm one into transcendence—or it can become rote and meaningless. Reform services make the prayers more acces-sible, but that doesn't guarantee that people enter into the prayers with complete heart, soul, and mind.

Create your own Judaism, my friend D would advise. Do you really think that the Infinite Radiant Is—a term for God—cares what kind of Judaism you practice?

No, I have to admit, I don't. God is God, regardless of whether I light *Shabbat* candles six minutes before sundown or two hours later, regardless of what I practice or what I believe.

So what's important about preserving Judaism? The relativist in me doesn't think any one religion is inherently better or worse than any other, but the Jew in me wants to remain Jewish, and I'm not sure how to resolve that contradiction.

The best answer I've come up with is that the contradictions, the tensions, are themselves important. Judaism is full of people arguing with God and wrestling with angels; this struggle is my variation on that. I'm commanded to be a Jew; my arguing with the implications and interpretations of that commandment is a quintessentially Jewish enterprise.

This doesn't answer whether Judaism must be insular, but it gives me grounds for continuing to explore what upsets me about my tradition. Lately, I'm choosing to regard "insular" as descriptive, not prescriptive. That is to say: Judaism has been insular, but I don't think it necessarily needs to be. Are we not commanded to be "a light unto the nations"?

In *Pirkei Avot,* a collection of rabbinic wisdom, there's a proverb, "It is not incumbent upon us to finish the work. However, neither are we free from beginning it."

It is not incumbent upon me to solve the contradictions between Judaism and modernity. The tension they embody generates the tradition's richness. But the sages were right: even if I can't solve them, that doesn't free me of the responsibility to try.

How can we make Judaism less insular? Bringing English into the service is a start. Providing good transliterations and translations is another. We can offer resources which explain Judaism to the non-Jews among us—the "other half" of each interfaith couple—in the form of books, lectures, classes, and magazines.

But the most important shift is a conceptual one. We need to stop thinking of ourselves as a closed system, and of non-Jews as outsiders who are "infiltrating" our community. Focusing our energies internally made sense in previous centuries, but it is time to take our place in the larger world. That means redefining our relationship to non-Jews, including the ones who have married into our families and our congregations.

Letting go of insularity doesn't mean letting go of our uniqueness, our heritage, or our traditions. It means interacting with the entire world, whether Jewish or gentile, in what Martin Buber calls an I-Thou relationship. This isn't a departure from Judaism; to my mind, it's the most Jewish thing of all.

Rose L. Levinson writes and teaches in Northern California. Her work is included in the Jewish Lights Publishing anthologies *Lifecycles, Vol. 1: Jewish Women on Life Passages & Personal Milestones* and *Lifecycles, Vol. 2: Jewish Women on Biblical Themes in Contemporary Life.*

The Synagogue as Village: Will It Welcome Interfaith Villagers?

ROSE L. LEVINSON

For about ten years, my Conservative synagogue has functioned as a village, an intimate small town.

Like many Jews, I live in a highly urbanized area. All around me are the stresses and demands of the modern metropolis. The requirements for belonging to and succeeding in that culture exact a high price. Within the Jewish community, and particularly within my synagogue, I have an identity which rests on a different set of assumptions, and in which my worth is determined less by what I do than who I am. The synagogue provides a sense of place and grounding not to be had in the larger world.

Primarily for these reasons, the response of my synagogue when

I brought in my non-Jewish partner was of paramount importance. I had been on my own for many years. For a good portion of that time, I sought a suitable partner, and had looked long and hard within the confines of the Jewish world.

When my yearning for a life-companion was fulfilled, it came in the form of someone who is not a Jew. After working through my own profound questions and sorting out, as best I could, my internal contradictions, I presented him to my synagogue-village with joy and excitement. I wanted the blessing of the community, which served, so strongly, as my ballast and my home base.

Instead, I experienced the message that it was not possible to grant this relationship full support because of my partner's not being a Jew. We were, for example, not permitted to join together at the *bimah* (podium) to express publicly, within a Jewish context, the gratitude we felt at coming together.

It is life-cycle observances which highlight the isolation that interfaith couples face. Non-Jewish parents committed to rearing a Jewish child are not permitted to be part of the synagogue naming ceremony. The non-Jewish parents at the *Bar* or *Bat Mitzvah* (the ceremony in which an individual chooses to assume the obligations and privileges of an adult member of the Jewish community) of their child are greatly restricted as to what they can do to participate in the *simcha* (joyous occasion).

Intellectually and rationally, I understand the boundaries that the synagogue draws. I understand that Conservative Judaism articulates those boundaries for reasons of *halakha* (traditional Jewish law). I struggle with knowing that opening the village gates to non-Jews will have profound implications, negative as well as positive.

But it is one thing to understand intellectually and another to grapple with the emotional implications of being an interfaith partner. My relationship to my synagogue has undergone a profound shift. The place upon which I had stood in my synagogue-village will never be as solid as it once was, and I do not feel as safe and whole there as I once did.

In fairness, mine is a relatively new synagogue and has not had to confront such realities as the increasing presence of interfaith couples. There have been, and continue to be, attempts to address the role and place of interfaith families. Furthermore, most of the synagogue members, and the rabbi in particular, address this issue in a spirit of openness. And the interfaith situation does not yield easy answers.

That said, the ambiguities surrounding the role of the non-Jew in my synagogue still serve to confuse my relation to what was always a warm and welcoming home. There is not yet clear articulation about the ways in which the non-Jew shall have a place—or shall not—in the life of my village-synagogue. There tends to be a "don't ask, don't tell" approach.

And there is no stated recognition that interfaith couples are part of the fabric of the synagogue; often there is a sense of being invisible. This lack of validation leads me to feel a need to make excuses for myself, to be secretive. At the least, it would help if the synagogue addressed the interfaith issue forthrightly and articulated the boundaries more clearly.

Because the synagogue means so much to me, I choose to stay within the village walls and to take an active stance. I was instrumental in forming a group for interfaith couples. This group is beginning its fifth year together. There are nine couples, and we have become a meaningful support system for one another as we grapple with the various permutations of being a committed Jew partnered with a person who is not a Jew. Equally important, we are making our presence felt and raising the need for the synagogue to acknowledge and define our role.

Each of us, Jew and non-Jew, feels connected to the synagogue and wishes to work out our relationship to it. We recognize that a Conservative synagogue confronts institutional impasses and difficulties in dealing with intermarriage. None of us tries to simplify a complicated situation. What we are doing as a collective is, we hope, helping our synagogue work toward clarifying its stance on mixed partnerships.

It would be easier sometimes to walk away, to seek a Jewish home elsewhere. There are alternatives. But we came together within the confines of this particular Conservative synagogue in this particular time and place. We have roots, friends, ties, history within these walls. Home is the place one goes for shelter, succor, meaning. May it be so in our synagogue-village.

Myrna Baron is executive director of the International Federation of Secular Humanistic Jews. She serves as co-director of The City Congregation KidSchool, facilitator of the *Bar/Bat Mitzvah* program and a member of the congregation's board of directors.

Intermarriage Has Our Blessing

MYRNA BARON

Humanistic Judaism sees intermarriage differently from most Jewish organizations. We celebrate differences, and welcome non-Jewish partners as full members of our community.

Nearly ten years ago, the Leadership Conference of Secular Humanistic Jews, the organization that represents rabbis and certified leaders in the Humanistic Jewish movement, released its position statement on intermarriage, stating unequivocally, "We...strongly affirm the right of individuals, including all Jews, to choose their own marriage partners...the obligation of Secular Humanistic Jewish leaders to serve the needs of couples with different cultural and religious backgrounds and the right of such leaders to officiate at their wedding ceremonies...[and] the responsibility of all Jews to welcome the non-Jewish partners of Jews into the Jewish family circle and to offer them acceptance and respect."

At The City Congregation for Humanistic Judaism, a non-theistic alternative for Jewish education and celebration in New York City, this means promoting a humanistic, pluralistic environment where all members of an intermarried family feel welcome.

We have no requirements or recommendations for how inter-cultural families should celebrate with us or rear their children. We believe that the reason so many intermarried families leave Jewish community life is that they don't feel welcome—sadly, they often feel alienated. But when they are welcomed without reservation, their family can have a wonderful Jewish community.

At The City Congregation, the non-Jewish partners are welcome to be fully involved in the community, or not participate at all, as they choose. We believe involvement in a Jewish community is a personal decision to be made within the family—and we understand and support the decision families make.

Our congregation has become a home for many intercultural families who have searched for a comfortable place to educate their children. As the facilitator of The City Congregation's *Bar/Bat Mitzvah* program and classroom teacher for eleven- to thirteen-year-olds, I have spoken with many families in their search for a Jewish community that is consistent with their beliefs and embraces their non-Jewish spouse. Our program makes certain that the non-Jewish parent and in-laws are comfortable and included in the adolescent's rite of passage.

Our *Bar/Bat Mitzvah* program focuses on heritage, culture, values, social responsibility, heroes, and role models. As part of the program, our students complete an extensive independent study project in addition to the twice-monthly classes they attend. Our students work closely with an adult mentor and take responsibility for choosing and researching a major topic of inquiry, which they present at their ceremony. The independent study portion becomes a family project in order for our adolescents to gain a greater understanding of their heritage and how they fit into both the Jewish and the larger world community.

The students from intercultural families are encouraged to equally investigate their non-Jewish heritage and to include it in their *Bar/Bat Mitzvah* ceremony. The ceremony consists of a series of essays in addition to humanistic liturgy—and the resulting rite of passage becomes very personal.

One of my students titled her research project "The Streets Were Paved with Cement." She investigated Jewish immigration to the Lower East Side, as well as the immigration of her father's non-Jewish forebears to early California, and compared and contrasted the two. The information she learned was extraordinary. Her mother commented, "Her larger study of Jewish history became infused with immense personal meaning.... Molly's response was electric; she saw she was committing to a lot of work and a lot of responsibility, but she loved the fact she'd be making choices."

Another student, the child of a Jewish mother and an African-American father, researched how Jews and African-Americans worked together in the civil rights movement to make the world a better place. She interviewed her mother's and her father's families to find out how each participated in the civil rights movement, how they were affected by it, and what it meant in terms of their values. She researched the three civil rights workers who were murdered in Mississippi. For my student, this was history. For many of us in the room, it was current events. Her family and the congregation were moved—some to tears—by her presentation. She gained a strong connection and respect for her heritage in both cultures. This teenager is firmly rooted in her Jewish identity—she now teaches younger children in our KidSchool—and equally respects her African-American heritage. This family, like so many others, has found a way to embrace its various heritages in our Jewish home.

Debora W. Antonoff facilitates discussion groups for interfaith couples in the Atlanta area. She is the creator of the "Pathways to the Synagogue" and "Bridge to the Home" courses designed for interfaith families.

First Steps into Synagogue Life

DEBORA W. ANTONOFF

"As an interfaith family, will we feel comfortable participating in the synagogue we plan to join?" wonder Ellen and David. "We are both supportive of our decision to raise the children Jewish and have found a synagogue that we enjoy. We have so many questions, so much to learn, and don't know where to begin. We want to be involved, but will people look at us differently? Will we ever both feel at home in the synagogue?"

Ellen and David's concerns are common to many interfaith couples as they consider joining a synagogue. It's one thing to join, yet it may be another matter to feel like you belong to this new community. What can an interfaith couple do to develop this sense of belonging?

For a moment, think of yourself as involved in a journey to a Jewish family life, composed of a series of "stepping stones." You may want to write down your individual responses and then share these notes with your spouse. First, consider the early steps you have already taken. This includes decisions made before marriage, courses for interfaith couples, conversations with clergy, deciding upon the children's religious identity, and Jewish experiences you have shared as a family. Next, think about more recent steps. This may include becoming a member of a synagogue, sharing a Jewish experience that is new to your family, or enrolling your child in religious school. Share what you wrote with your spouse, taking some time to reflect on what you already have accomplished as a couple. Finally, discuss what steps you might consider next.

A vast array of Jewish experience is available to you: from adult learning opportunities, to initiating a new family ritual in your home, to participating in a synagogue program, to learning how to perform some aspect of Jewish living. Focus on building your own pathway, step by step. This approach may help you avoid feeling overwhelmed by all that is a part of Jewish life. Try out a new experience, and over time it will likely feel more comfortable. Perhaps it will become an integral part of your family life. If you are not ready for that "step," seek another.

This is an ongoing process that can enrich your own and your family's life. Let's turn back to your arrival at the synagogue doorstep. What are some ways in which an interfaith family can begin to feel a part of synagogue life? Consider the following:

Connect with others. Begin connecting with people who make you feel welcome. Develop a network of those who can assist in finding the resources you are seeking, including members who are familiar with adult education programs, a clergy or staff person who is particularly supportive of interfaith couples, or other interfaith couples who have "been there."

Participate in synagogue programs that will help you on your journey. Inquire about programs specifically created for interfaith couples. For example, the Reform Jewish Outreach programs offered in many communities include discussion groups for interfaith couples ("Times & Seasons" and "Yours, Mine and Ours"), basic Judaism courses, and one-session programs on topics pertinent to interfaith couples. Look for specific information about programs in your community and/or contact local congregations.

However, do not limit yourself to programs for interfaith couples. Consider adult education courses, programs for families to experience Judaism together, events the preschool or religious school sponsors for parents, and more. One "secret": Do not presume that others know all the answers! Many Jewish adults come to courses because they, too, feel there is some gap in their knowledge of Judaism. Consider volunteering in an area that interests you. Becoming active will aid in developing your network of members with similar interests. You may feel comfortable participating in the congregation's community service projects, volunteering to help at a synagogue event, or supporting your child's education by helping at a school program.

Explore the opportunities. Begin to share new Jewish experiences as a couple and as a family, taking the next small step along your journey. The best way to learn about Jewish living is to experience it. Do not wait for members to invite you in; rather, pursue your next step. Judaism thrives both in the home and through the connection to a living Jewish community. I have had the privilege of working with many couples like Ellen and David over the course of many years of facilitating programs for interfaith couples. I have seen couples grapple with the difficult decisions as they begin their life together. Many then sought out resources, learned the information they needed, and became an integral part of their synagogue's life. You, too, have the power to create a fulfilling environment for yourself and your family. Enjoy your journey as you begin to take those important first steps!

How can an interfaith family begin to feel a part of synagogue life? It may seem like a daunting task at first, but each family can build its own pathway by beginning to share new Jewish experiences. Taking the next small steps becomes a process that can enrich your own and your family's life. Through making the connection to a community and by exploring the opportunities available, you have the power to create a fulfilling environment for your family as you develop your path along the interfaith journey.

Eleanor W. Jaffe, M.S.W., M.Ed., has been a teacher, counselor, and psycho-therapist. She is the mother of two children; both are in interfaith marriages.

A Challenge to Action

ELEANOR W. JAFFE

This is our family's story of love, marriage, personal accommoda-tions, and some subtle institutional changes as well.

Three years ago our daughter married a fine Christian man after a long courtship and considerable discussion and counseling about the religious and personal dilemmas that lay ahead of them. They were married in a Jewish ceremony, conducted by a Reform rabbi, with her uncle acting as *chazan* (cantor). Like many interfaith mar-riages, this one evoked many mixed emotions within the extended families, creating emotional turmoil as well as rejoicing for these two young people who so obviously loved and found joy in one another.

Family and religious loyalty issues felt threatening to many members of our families, especially among the more traditionally inclined. Nevertheless, we worked with these issues in as loving and respectful a way as we were able, and today we are delighted with our children's loving and solid marital relationship, and with our new baby grandson, who, we hope, will be the richer for his dual heritage.

As members of our Conservative synagogue do on the occasion of a *simcha* (joyous occasion), we submitted an announcement of our daughter's marriage to the temple bulletin. We have been members of this temple for twenty-five years. This is the same temple where our children attended religious school, and where they became *Bar* and *Bat Mitzvah* (took on the obligations and privileges of adult members of the Jewish community). We did not anticipate any difficulty with an announcement because a rabbi had officiated at the wedding and the couple had agreed that their children would be raised as Jews.

However, neither factor mattered. Indeed, no one even inquired about the circumstances of the marriage. We discovered, astonishingly, that our temple would not announce our *simcha*, that it was temple policy not to announce any mixed marriage involving any member of the congregation or their progeny.

My husband and I were dismayed, frustrated, and angered by this policy. Its effect was to make us feel that the temple was punishing us and our family for what seemed to be viewed as our daughter's indiscriminate, religiously illegal, and certainly wrongful marriage. It was at this juncture that I decided to transfer membership to a Reform congregation. If my synagogue could not accept a marriage that was now an integral part of my family, then I refused to be a part of the synagogue. My husband, the take-charge optimist, asked, "Why not—before we resign our membership—go to see our temple's new rabbi, tell him how we reacted to this bulletin policy, and test the waters?"

We did meet with the rabbi in his study. We shared our deep disappointment and chagrin with him about the bulletin policy, which seemed to strongly suggest that in the future our children and grandchildren would be pariahs to the congregation. To our great amazement, the rabbi listened sympathetically to our comments and thanked us for them. He said that it was his intention as the newly appointed rabbi to modify attitudes and some policies within the temple and to make our congregation one that welcomed interfaith couples. He asked us if we would be willing to participate in this change. In fact, he asked us to be the chairs of a *keruv* (reaching out and drawing near) committee.

At this same time, the Combined Jewish Philanthropies of Boston was making seed money available to Conservative synagogues wishing to begin *keruv* work, and our rabbi suggested that we apply for a grant. Our synagogue was one of five in the greater Boston community to receive funding for our programs. The synagogue is a very large (more than 1,400 families) and influential congregation, so when we began advertising programs in the secular press that invited all interested people to attend lectures by authors like Anita Diamant and Gabrielle Glaser, who spoke about interfaith issues, we believe it made a difference. We have also run several workshops at our synagogue for interfaith couples, and other workshops for the parents of interfaith couples, so that they can process and discuss the changes within their families. These workshops have been run by social workers, and our rabbis visit the group during the final session in order to respond to questions and to firmly assert that interfaith families are welcome at our Conservative synagogue. This same message has gone out from the pulpit: Jews need to extend a welcome to the strangers in our midst, the rabbi says, for we were once strangers in many strange lands. These are positive steps, but we are aware that a lot more action is needed within the temple to create this sense of welcome.

One thing has not changed, however—our temple still does not announce interfaith marriages in its bulletin. As we have come to understand the larger picture, the Conservative Rabbinic Assembly strongly advises against such publication, although a rabbi would not be officially sanctioned were he to allow it. Currently, we know of only one rabbi in the Boston area who allows these announcements to be published.

Thus, the bulletin issue remains deadlocked at present. Passions run very high and deep, and what seem like reasonable compromises to some do not seem so to others. We have spoken and written publicly in our temple bulletin on an almost monthly basis about a heretofore mostly taboo subject. We have arranged public forums where interfaith issues are discussed. We have added books and pamphlets on interfaith marriage to our temple library. We have let other congregants know that their friends and neighbors are deeply affected, are involved in interfaith dilemmas, and need their compassion. And we have let our fellow members know that we need their help in order to create a welcoming community at our temple where interfaith families may be integrated and made to feel that they belong.

We do not want more young families lost to the Jewish faith because of high walls and intolerance. We have begun making changes in our community, and we believe we are making a difference.

We urge others to take activist positions in their own communities and synagogues. Working together, we should be able to make an even greater difference.

Dru Greenwood is director of the William and Lottie Daniel Department of Outreach at the Union of American Hebrew Congregations (UAHC, the Reform Movement).

Judaism Is Not a Closed Club

DRU GREENWOOD

Among the first stories I remember hearing from my husband's family is the one about my father-in-law becoming the second Jewish accountant in Toronto. As a young man he bided his time until the man who was the first Jewish accountant was fully certified and had set up his own practice. Only then could my father-in-law serve the apprenticeship he needed in order to become a chartered accountant himself. In subsequent years, the Greenwood firm proudly brought many more young Jews into a profession that had once been closed to its founder.

There was a time, not long ago, when Jews and gentiles did not mix in America. Intergroup segregation and outright anti-Semitism were powerful deterrents to assimilation in either direction. Quotas limited the number of Jews who could attend prestigious universities or enter various professions. Jews were prohibited from living in particular neighborhoods and joining certain country clubs. For their part, of necessity and desire, Jews built a rich infrastructure of institutions including synagogues, social clubs, and old age homes that paralleled gentile institutions but served the Jewish community and kept it coherent and self-reliant.

Marriage between a Jew and a Christian, while not unheard of, was rare, and, when it did occur, was seen as verging on the pathological. Entering such a marriage meant trying to bridge a social chasm and met with severe sanctions on every side. The Jewish partner was seen as turning his or her back on Judaism, and the family might have sat *shiva* (observed seven days of mourning as if their child had died) on the occasion of the marriage. The Christian partner might be considered rebellious or eccentric. Social scientist Kurt Lewin categorized their children as "marginal persons," at home nowhere.

In mid-century America the social fabric included many "closed clubs." Getting into them required determination and good luck; sometimes it also demanded subterfuge or a willingness to carry a social stigma. "Passing" was one common way to circumvent the system. Jews often "passed" as gentiles by changing their looks or their names. In my family, "Cohen" became "Coleman." Interfaith couples who found their way into the Jewish community and raised Jewish children, and even those who converted to Judaism, acknowledged a non-Jewish past only in the most private relationships. The compassionate rabbinical dictum against reminding converts of their "pork-eating past" was a favored rationale that protected individuals, but also effectively hid the whole topic.

Converts and non-Jews "passed" as best they could, often experiencing such personal characteristics as blond hair or the name Mary as liabilities, embarrassing give-aways. Upon close inquiry, one could discover that indeed there were converts and non-Jews who were part of the Jewish community, but everyone knew that the eleventh commandment for Jews was "Thou shalt not proselytize." One result was the appearance of Jewish communal life as a "closed club."

Thankfully, times have changed. Although remnants of earlier barriers and prejudicial attitudes remain and show themselves in sometimes painful events, the common experience of most Jews in America is to feel welcomed in schools, in communities, in professions, and as marriage partners. No Jew coming of age today could tell my father-in-law's tale. Jews can participate fully in American life and at the same time, without hiding, celebrate their distinctiveness as Jews. American life is enriched, and Jewish life is flowering here.

Similarly, the experience of interfaith families and seekers looking for a place for themselves in Judaism is also much more likely to be "welcome." For the past twenty years, the Reform Movement has promoted formal outreach programs to Jews and Jewish institutions. Programs geared to interfaith families are now being developed by the Conservative Movement, as well as by Jewish Federations and other community agencies.

Rather than keep the presence of converts and interfaith families secret, programs now help introduce and integrate newcomers into Jewish life. For instance, "A Taste of Judaism: Are You Curious?" is a three-session class run by the Reform Movement, which is designed to introduce the ideas of Jewish spirituality, ethics, and community. The course is widely advertised and offered free in cities across North America, reaching more than 35,000 people since 1994.

"Introduction to Judaism" classes teach Jewish belief and practice, not only to individuals interested in becoming Jewish, but also to interfaith couples exploring the possibility of raising Jewish children. Synagogue outreach committees are evidence of institutional commitment to welcome interfaith families. They sponsor programs specifically for interfaith couples and their families and work with other committees to help raise awareness of special sensitivities and needs. Congregational policies directed to the role that family members who are not Jewish can play in synagogue ritual and governance take intermarriage further out of the closet and welcome appropriate participation as a normative part of community life. Time after time, the result of Jewish openness and outreach is profound enrichment and increased vitality, both for interfaith families who choose to partake and for Jewish communal life as a whole—again a double blessing!

Judaism is the distinctive, precious heritage of the Jews, reflecting the sacred covenant between God and the people Israel. However, it was never intended to be a closed club. Abraham, the first Jew, is praised in rabbinic tradition for his hospitality to strangers and his zeal in bringing them near. The most often repeated *mitzvah* (commandment) in the *Torah* (the first five books of the Hebrew Bible) is to love the stranger and treat him or her with the same dignity and respect as the home-born. Isaiah calls Israel to be "a light to the nations" and to make God's house "a house of prayer for all peoples." And the Passover *seder* (ritual meal) begins with the words, "Let all who are hungry come and eat; let all who are in want share the hope of Passover."

The door is open for you.

19. Conversion

Anita Diamant has written six guides to contemporary Jewish practice, including *Choosing a Jewish Life: A Handbook for People Converting to Judaism and for Their Families and Friends* (Schocken).

My Conversion Story

ANITA DIAMANT

Sixteen years ago, I sat in my parked car on a residential side street, staring at the door of a substantial brick home, which also housed the office of a urologist and *mohel* (person trained to perform ritual circumcision). Jim, my fiancé, had gone through the door a few minutes earlier, accompanied by our rabbi. Inside, Jim was undergoing *hatafat dam brit* (the ritual taking of a drop of blood), required by Jewish law of already-circumcised male converts. There was nothing for me to do but wait.

Nearly three years earlier when I first fell in love with Jim, I realized that I'd found a life partner, someone with whom I could imagine having a family. But that made me suddenly aware of my need to raise any child we might have as Jew.

This was not an issue for Jim. A lapsed Presbyterian, he had no objection to raising Jewish children. The problem was mine. Not only was I non-observant and unaffiliated, I had almost no knowledge of Jewish traditions, history, or ritual.

Even so, I was unconditionally Jewish. Although there was little religious practice in my childhood home and even less formal Jewish education, I am the daughter of Holocaust survivors. My grandparents spoke Yiddish. Still, I knew that I could not impart a purely ethnic or historical Jewishness to another generation. I would have to teach my child how to be a Jew on my own terms, whatever those might be.

Jim joined me in the search. Together, we learned the blessings for lighting candles on Friday night. Jim found an ad for a Jewish study group, "no prior knowledge necessary." When we started talking about a wedding date, he made an appointment with Rabbi Lawrence Kushner to discuss the possibility of conversion.

His conversion curriculum became the core of my remedial Jewish education. We met with the rabbi regularly, read the books he assigned, attended an "Introduction to Judaism" course with 100 other people, and made our first attempt at learning Hebrew. As we planned our wedding, we discovered the joyful wisdom of Jewish ritual.

Waiting for him that spring morning sixteen years ago, I counted off the days until our marriage. Jim smiled at me as he got back into the car. He told me that it was nothing he ever wanted to do again, but it had gone okay. Then we drove to the *mikvah* (ritual bath), where we met Rabbi Kushner and two other rabbis for his *beit din* (court of Jewish law). After a spirited fifteen-minute conversation, the rabbis nodded their approval and sent Jim to the *mikvah*.

I stood in the hallway and listened to the quiet splashing as he walked into the water. The rabbi asked if he was ready to enter the covenant between God and the Jewish people—freely, without reservation, forever, and to the exclusion of all other faiths. Jim answered "Yes" and recited the Hebrew blessings for conversion.

A few minutes later, we all walked out into the bright sun. Rabbi Kushner said, "Welcome, brother." Jim's hair was still wet. Neither of us could stop smiling.

Catherine Brennan Rein is a clinical social worker at an elementary school in Hingham, Massachusetts. She is married and the mother of twin boys. She grew up in New York as the fourth of seven children in an Irish-Catholic family.

Becoming Jewish in the Eyes of My Parents

CATHERINE BRENNAN REIN

"Your people shall be my people; your God my God." These powerful words in the Book of Ruth have pointed the way for many new Jews. But as we are becoming one with a different people, what do we do with our original family?

For me, the search for this answer has been one of the most challenging parts of becoming Jewish. My Irish-Catholic parents do not believe in choosing a religion. You are what you were born, and that's that. My parents are "good" Catholics. It was unimaginable to them that their daughter would be anything but Catholic, always. Perhaps not observant, but Catholic, nonetheless. They were, therefore, unprepared for the discussion I needed to have with them.

Facing my parents meant facing the past I was leaving. My parents envisioned grandchildren who would be baptized and celebrate First Communion and Christmas. With my news, I would be taking that dream away from them. There might be grandchildren, but they would be Jewish, as would their daughter. Knowing I was precipitating that loss for them was profoundly painful.

I married my husband, who is Jewish, without talking too much about our religious differences. After several years of marriage, and a few hundred miles distance from my parents, I began to fall in love with Judaism. I began to see my future more and more tied with the Jewish people. My parents and I needed to talk, but I dreaded the conversation.

My mom and I were having lunch in a local diner in New York. I had come in for the weekend to visit and "talk." I told her that Rich (my husband) and I had been talking more about religion, and espe-cially as we began to think about having children, we wanted to decide what we would do as a family. I knew that many interfaith couples tried to celebrate both religions as a family, but I didn't think that worked well. I then told her that we had decided to raise our chil-dren as Jews and that I had decided to convert to Judaism. I can still hear her response:

"You're not asking my opinion, right?"

"Right."

"I don't get a vote, right?"

"Right."

"Then I'm old enough not to worry myself about things I can't change. You're still my daughter. Nothing can change that."

"Thanks, Mom. You're a wise lady."

She then shared her appreciation that we weren't going to "do both." For her, that seemed like a belittling of both traditions. Obviously, she wished Rich was Catholic. She wondered whether I was sure about my decision, and asked if I was doing it "for Rich." She also had practical questions about holiday celebrations.

The one unfortunate request my mother made was that I not tell my father about my decision to convert to Judaism, because "he wouldn't understand." Both of us were afraid of his reaction. People in his family had stopped talking to each other for smaller infractions. Reluctantly, I agreed not to share my decision with him. It was a mis-take. Unfortunately, the secrecy didn't work and made things worse.

A few months after talking with my mother, my father acciden-tally learned of my conversion. He confronted me about it, and I tried to explain my decision to convert as well as my reasons for not hav-ing told him. It was useless. He was too angry to listen. Unfortunately, he launched into an attack and assured me that "the Jews who you want to join don't want you. They know you're not really one of them. You'll learn the hard way. You've turned your back on your family, so you'll have no one." He then cut off all con-tact and refused to speak with or see me.

No one could persuade him to reconsider his position, which

was dictated by his rules and his fear of a vengeful God who would punish him for failing to raise a good Catholic daughter.

My father's response, while extremely harsh, is, unfortunately, not unique. His angry threat that the Jews will not accept me has, at times, worried me. His banishment of me lasted a few long and painful years, but not forever. Ultimately, he acknowledged the truth of my mother's loving response, that I was "still [his] daughter."

Despite my conversion, my parents and I know that we are inextricably connected to each other. I am learning what it means to be a good Jewish daughter to my Irish-Catholic parents. They are learning to cope with what was once unimaginable—having a Jewish daughter.

Myron S. Geller is rabbi of Temple Ahavat Achim in Gloucester, Massachusetts, and is director of the Gerim Institute of New England. He is a member of the Committee of Law and Standards of the Conservative Movement's Rabbinical Assembly.

Sanctifying Waters: The *Mikvah* and Conservative Judaism

MYRON S. GELLER

Ever since the days of the Bible, the use of a *mikvah* (bath for spiritual purification) has been a widely practiced ritual among the Jewish people. The *mikvah* is a natural or constructed pool of water that conforms to very precise specifications in both its minimum size and the source and characteristics of its contents. When the Jerusalem Temple still stood, immersion in the waters of a *mikvah* conferred ritual purity on those who had come into contact with the dead, allowing them re-entry into the precincts of the sanctuary. After the Temple was destroyed, the *mikvah* was used primarily by three groups of people: married women following menstruation, who could resume marital relations after immersion; proselytes as part of their ceremony of conversion; and those seeking a measure of spiritual uplift, particularly before the Sabbath or on the eve of festivals.

Although in the past the *mikvah* may have served occasionally as a bathhouse, its true significance was spiritual and ritual. After the loss of the First Temple, the biblical prophet Ezekiel used the *mikvah* as a metaphor of restoration, spiritual and political. "I will sprinkle clean water upon you, and you shall be clean: I will cleanse you from all your uncleanness and from all your fetishes" (Ezekiel 36:25). And almost two millennia later, Maimonides wrote, "Ritual purity and impurity are based on Scriptural law and are not rationally understood categories. So too immersion after impurity. Impurity is not mud or filth that can be removed by water but is based on Scriptural law and depends entirely on human intention" (Yad, Mikvaot 11:12).

Some aspects of ritual *mikvah* immersion have retained their importance among observant Jews to this day, but the spiritual implications of *mikvah* are now being appreciated by growing numbers.

The practice of sexual abstinence during the period of menstruation and the use of *mikvah* by women several days afterwards is widely observed amongst the Orthodox because the resumption of marital relations without immersion is a particularly serious offense to *halakha* (Jewish law).

Conservative Judaism had largely ignored this practice in the past, but recently has begun to re-evaluate its silence in this area and to consider the spiritual implications of *mikvah* immersion for human sexuality and for women. As Rabbi Elliot Dorff has written, "...some couples have made [sexual abstinence during menstruation followed by ritual immersion leading to a resumption of sexual relations] part of their sexual practice...some women find this to be one of the distinctly female rituals by which they can affirm their Judaism and reconnect with Jewish women through the ages...In general, these rationales, taken together, add a sense of ongoing holiness to the marital relationship."

Conservative Judaism's outreach activities have, in recent decades, resulted in increasing numbers of people seeking to convert to Judaism. The Conservative Jewish process of conversion requires candidates, after a significant period of study, to appear before a *beit din* (rabbinic court) to explain their reasons for choosing Judaism and to commit themselves to live as Jews, observe the Commandments, and raise any children with whom they may be blessed in the Jewish community and faith. Male candidates are required to undergo circumcision or, if already circumcised, to have a symbolic ceremony. All converts complete the rituals of conversion by immersing themselves in a *mikvah*.

Jews-by-Choice tend to recall the *mikvah* ceremony as an experience of heightened spirituality, leaving a permanent mark on their religious awareness. I have received many comments about the *mikvah*: "It made me feel closer to God." "Rich and rewarding." "An emotional highlight of my life." "Excellent experience... It was inspiring." "When I came up from the waters all was quiet, my eyes wanted to cry. My soul was still...I am still in a state of peacefulness and love fills me." "An experience I shall never forget." "Probably the most moving event ever in my life." These observations, written by converts to Judaism several weeks after the event, reflect the powerful impact of the *mikvah* ritual on Jews-by-Choice and the profound importance they attach to its spiritual significance.

At a time when New Age enthusiasm is persuading numbers of people, disenchanted with traditional religious expression, to seek fresh ways of discovering spiritual meaning in their lives, Conservative Judaism has found in an age-old practice a metaphor for rebirth and renewal that retains its power to uplift, cleanse, and inspire.

Kerry M. Olitzky is a rabbi and executive director of the Jewish Outreach Institute, the only national organization dedicated to providing a network of programs and services to intermarried families and children.

Doing the Conversion "Two-Step"

KERRY M. OLITZKY

We at the Jewish Outreach Institute (JOI) believe that the conversion process has two steps, one that is external and public, and one that is internal and unseen. But we wonder if the organized Jewish community puts too much emphasis on the external (formal) conversion—in order to categorize "Who is a Jew" and better quantify our numbers—without recognizing that, like most things in life, the transition into a new religion includes varying shades of gray.

Rabbi Bernard Felsenthal, a spiritual leader in Chicago during the late part of the nineteenth century, and one of the earliest rabbis in America, said it rather succinctly: I consider a Jew anyone who calls himself one and is considered by others to be one. While we might make his statement more "gender neutral" to fit the tendency of the times, we are pretty much in agreement (though *halakhic*, that is, Jewish legal authorities, would disagree). After all, what is a conversion anyway? It is a ritualized process to confirm the existing circumstances that Rabbi Felsenthal identifies.

When a person formally converts, only that person is sure of the order of those two steps. One step, the public ritual of conversion, is marked in time and follows a certain procedure controlled by a *beit din* (rabbinical court). There is relative control of the process, including study, ritual immersion, and, for males, circumcision or the release of the ritually required drop of blood. The other step is what I and others call "conversion of the heart." This is when the individual has an internal conversion, when he or she effectively casts his or her lot with the Jewish people. There is no way to control this process. It happens when it happens—sometimes before the other step, sometimes after, and sometimes never. But to us, this is the real conversion, the most important.

For many interfaith families, a formal, ritualized conversion for the non-Jewish parent is not appropriate or not possible. But they may have cast their lot with the Jewish people anyway. Why else would they raise their children as Jews, even when they themselves do not convert? To exclude these people from feeling fully a part of the community is, we believe, a mistake. Even if there is no official conversion, we should honor and welcome those non-Jews who have dedicated themselves to the continuity of the Jewish people by raising their children Jewishly. In many cases, they may have already undergone a "conversion of the heart," which would go unrecognized by a *beit din* but should be celebrated by the Jewish community nonetheless.

Take, for example, the non-Jewish wife who was so actively involved in raising her kids as Jews that, when a friend of hers found out theirs was an intermarriage, the friend remarked, "I didn't know your husband wasn't Jewish!" (The only reason the wife hadn't converted was because she feared it would devastate her parents.) At JOI, we hear many such stories.

This is not to take away from conversion as the ultimate expression of identifying oneself with the Jewish people, and most Jews would still agree that conversion of the non-Jewish spouse is the "best case scenario" of intermarriage. Too often, however, institutions within the Jewish community are heavy-handed about promoting conversion, or wary of non-Jewish seekers rather than welcoming of them. It's like saying, "First join our club, then we'll welcome you into it."

JOI's research shows that conversion rates are not keeping pace with the rise in intermarriage. Therefore, the community needs to adopt new strategies of welcoming non-Jews who want to join our "club"—without us requiring "membership" up-front.

In an article in InterfaithFamily.com, Dr. Egon Mayer, JOI's co-founder, has argued that a "conversionary agenda inevitably sends the message to interfaith couples that they are welcome in the Jewish community only if they will be prospects for conversion. That is the surest way to insure that our efforts at welcoming will not be reciprocated." Interestingly, a woman replied to his article with the tale of her own conversion process, and pointed out how badly she felt that—pre-conversion—she was unable to kiss the *Torah* (scroll containing the first five books of the Hebrew Bible) during synagogue processions.

If we take a step back and put this in historical perspective, it seems quite remarkable and somewhat ironic that we have the luxury of asking non-Jews to refrain from kissing our holy scrolls (that they would even want to!) when, within a half-century—one generation really—Jews were running into burning synagogues to save those very scrolls, and were murdered simply for belonging to a community that we now have the opportunity to open to all who genuinely want to join. Perhaps it's more than remarkable—it's miraculous, and it's as much a test of survival for the Jewish people as any in the past. We hope the community can identify and applaud those "conversions of the heart" as much as we do the more formalized conversions. Let's work together to measure up to this great test.

Rabbi Daniel Siegel is the rabbinic director of ALEPH: Alliance for Jewish Renewal and, with his life partner Hanna Tiferet, co-spiritual leader of B'nai Or of Boston.

Welcoming Initiates to Judaism: Why I Prefer the Term "Initiation"

DANIEL SIEGEL

We were in the sitting room of the *mikvah* (ritual bath). There were the required three rabbis for the *beit din* (rabbinic court), the husband of the woman "converting," and the convert herself. Since I was the rabbi who had been the teacher, my job was to stay in the background while the other two rabbis asked questions to make sure that she knew what she was doing (and that I had taught her well).

At first, the conversation was about the usual details—when do we light candles, blow the *shofar* (ram's horn), and what are the outlines of keeping kosher. Then, one of the rabbis asked her why she wanted to be Jewish at all. Her answer was something like this: "I am a smart woman and I am choosing Judaism as the spiritual path I want to walk. This gives me two wonderful opportunities. The first is to show my non-Jewish family that Judaism is a wonderful thing and not to be feared. The other is to show the same thing to those who were born Jewish." I was deeply moved by this answer and realized why I as a rabbi always feel so close to those Jews who have chosen Judaism as adults. The response of the other two rabbis, when she had gone into the inner room to prepare for her immersion, was to continue to wonder why someone would choose to be Jewish at all. I wondered why they had chosen to be rabbis.

In the same room, with a similar cast, at another time. Now the rabbis wanted to know what the potential convert would do if her family invited her for dinner on December 25th. They wanted her to refuse the invitation. Instead she said, "If the meal is kosher, then of course I'll go." They did their best to convince her to refuse the invitation, arguing that even a secular Christmas still had its origins in an exclusive Christianity which had no place for Jews. Again, I thought her response was wonderful and had the unintended effect of completing a process of my own.

Until quite recently, it was dangerous and even illegal to "convert" from Christianity or Islam to Judaism. It made perfect sense, then, that the rabbis would be very suspicious of someone wanting to become Jewish. After all, why would anyone want to join a persecuted community, no matter how wonderful its spirituality and values might be? Perhaps the potential convert was really an informer seeking to infiltrate the Jewish community in order to seed the next pogrom. The only way to protect themselves against this possibility was to insist that the convert break all ties with his or her family and friends and come completely inside the Jewish community.

Now, thank God, things are very different. Those who choose Judaism as their path and Jews as their people serve as bridges. They are links to our non-Jewish families and inspirations to Jews by birth, who so often fail to see the richness and profundity of their own tradition. Nor is there a need for new Jews to deny their families of origin. Instead, there is a new opportunity to bring a tolerant and respectful Judaism into the homes of our non-Jewish relatives. Remember that our tradition has always claimed to believe that "the righteous of all the nations have a share in the world to come." What a wonderful moment this is when we can actually practice this teaching, learning to model a strong commitment to Judaism while recognizing the beauty and depth of other traditions and paths at the same time.

The end of this particular part of my own journey was to stop using the term "conversion" to describe this process and ritual. In the days when it was impossible for a person who chose Judaism to continue interacting with his or her family of origin, perhaps it made sense to speak of a conversion. Now, however, a person who chooses Judaism both can and should continue to be connected to his or her family of origin. Further, since Judaism has never laid claim to sole possession of "truth," there is no need to use this word "conversion" any longer, and I have come to prefer "initiation." Full initiation into Judaism and the Jewish family means the conferring of all the benefits and responsibilities of membership in our people. These include financial commitments, being included in a *minyan* (the ten people needed for public worship), and being called to the *Torah*. Today, there are many non-Jews who like to be around Jews and synagogues. Without initiation, however, we usually don't include them in a *minyan* or ask them to come up to the *Torah* and say the blessings ("who has chosen us...and given us the *Torah*"). To decide to "take the plunge" and be immersed in the living waters of the *mikvah* is to become an initiate, one who is a full participant in all the rituals, joys, and responsibilities of this wonderful people.

Afterword

EDMUND CASE

Something very important is happening in the North American Jewish community: Jewish interfaith families are engaging in Jewish life. That is the message of the moving personal stories that fill this book.

- Non-Jewish partners are participating in Jewish life, choosing Judaism as the religion of their family and their children—people like Annie Modesitt, who teaches Judaism to her children as she learns along with them and creates a Jewish home that honors her own religious heritage, and like Jim Keen, who feels at home at his daughter's Jewish baby naming and at so many other Jewish moments in his intermarried life. Non-Jewish partners are even finding spiritual fulfillment within Jewish worship—like Andrea King, who feels part of a community engaged in self-examination at the Jewish High Holy Days; and Wendy Case (my wife), who has found a home for her spirituality within Judaism.

- Jewish partners—like Cheryl Opper's husband, and Sheri Levin McNerthney—are experiencing a deepened commitment to their religion *because* of their intermarriage, which causes them to evaluate what their Judaism means to them and to not take it for granted.

- Children are being raised exclusively as Jews while learning about and respecting the backgrounds and traditions of their non-Jewish parent and relatives—like six-year-old Zeke, who, after delivering food to a soup kitchen with his non-Jewish mother, exclaims,

"Mom! We did a *mitzah*!" and like Morgan Caplane, a teen who says, "I couldn't raise my children anything but Jewish."

- Both Jewish and non-Jewish extended family members are accepting and supporting the Jewish choices of their relatives—like Jim Keen's Jewish *Bubba*, who says, "You're my grandson now," and Cheryl Opper's non-Jewish mother, who is looking forward to her granddaughter's *Bat Mitzvah*, and Reena Judd's non-Jewish mother-in-law, who says, "Why shouldn't I be supportive…I am only happy for you…."

None of this suggests that achieving the kind of Jewish interfaith family life that these families experience is easy. Our writers realistically portray the multiple complex issues that interfaith families encounter, but their stories, and our experts' professional advice, offer many helpful guidelines.

- The exercises in Paula Brody's essay, "Opening Up Communication in an Interfaith Relationship," can start couples on the road to the open, clear, and direct communication about religious differences that establishes a solid foundation for a satisfying interfaith family life.

- Couples can help each other on their journeys—think of Jim Keen's wife slipping him a Power Bar to eat on a break from his first Yom Kippur service! And they can compromise—as did Rena Mello's Jewish fiancé, who said he loved her too much to let the issue of celebrating Christmas in their home harm their relationship. She then realized that his acceptance was more important than what she thought she wanted, and lost interest in having a Christmas tree.

- Honoring and respecting the traditions of each partner, and integrating them into a couple's family life—while still choosing one religion for children's identity—is very important. For Jewish interfaith families, participating in the Christmas celebration of the non-Jewish partner and his or her family is a way to acknowledge and honor that family's traditions. Jews need to understand that such participation does not compromise the Jewish identity of a Jewish interfaith family or its children; as Jeri Zeder says, "Judaism is compassionate enough, warm enough, and strong enough to withstand intimate exposure to another religion."

- Many of our writers describe flexible adaptations to traditions, rituals, and ceremonies—weddings, baby namings, *Bar* and *Bat Mitzvah* ceremonies, and holiday observances (like Paula Yablonsky's Christmas tree lights now used to decorate her *sukkah)*—that are welcoming and inclusive for all family members.

- Finally, the stories of many of our writers show that emotions and attitudes change over the course of a relationship. Feelings a partner never expected to have often develop later; practices that once seemed strange become comfortable.

The attraction of Jewish life expressed by our writers is undeniably powerful. So we encourage and invite you, our readers who are involved in interfaith families yourselves, to continue your exploration of Jewish life. You too can experience the personal meaning and the enrichment of your family life that engaging in Judaism offers. On the virtual "pages" of InterfaithFamily.com, you will continue to find firsthand accounts of people like you, grappling with the issues that you face. You can discuss those articles and issues with others like you in our online community, and you can contribute your own stories. And on these online pages you can find local programs offered by inclusive Jewish organizations that welcome your participation.

The goal of this book is not to promote conversion by intermarried non-Jews. We view conversion as a wonderful option for those who choose it, and it will be a wonderful result if this book leads readers to give positive consideration to conversion. But we say first that you are very welcome in the Jewish community, just the way you are. We recognize conversion to be a very personal choice and understand, as Rabbi Kerry Olitzky points out, that transition into a new religion involves varying shades of gray, with many people experiencing "conversion of the heart" before they undergo—if they ever do—a formal "external" conversion. We frankly are more interested in having intermarried non-Jewish partners "live Jewishly" and raise Jewish children than we are in having them "become Jewish." Instead of first asking, "Are you a Jew?" we think the first question should be, "Is your family living Jewishly?" It is a question that also might be asked of families with two Jewish partners.

Finally, to our readers who are leaders in the Jewish community, we have an additional message. This book is not intended to glorify, promote, or encourage intermarriage. We acknowledge that most interfaith families today do not choose Judaism as the religion of their family or their children. That is a matter of great concern to us, and the impetus for our work. But those Jews and Jewish leaders who respond to statistically low rates of affiliation with a strategy that seeks only to promote in-marriage by demeaning intermarriage are, we think, misreading the evidence.

Such a strategy underestimates and undervalues the potential impact of a truly welcoming response to intermarried couples. If more rabbis, educators, and Jewish communal workers expressed the sensitivity and genuinely welcoming attitudes of the professional contributors to this book, there is every reason to believe, based on the personal stories in this book, that we would see increased engagement in Jewish life by interfaith families. We believe that that would be a very good thing. Jewish interfaith families living Jewishly—even without conversion—can enrich and enliven the Jewish community as a whole, raise Jewish children who can then go on to create new Jewish families, and ultimately represent a positive contribution to the Jewish future. But this will only happen in larger numbers if interfaith families are genuinely welcomed and accepted by the Jewish community.

Glossary

Afikomen: literally, dessert. The *matzah* (unleavened bread) that is hidden at the beginning of the Passover *seder* and which children look for and ransom back to the adults.

Al Shlosha Devarim: "on three things," the first words (and name) of a song in some worship services.

Alef-bet: the Hebrew alphabet, of which *alef* and *bet* are the first two letters.

Aliyah: going up. Used to refer to someone who is going up to say the blessing over the *Torah* reading, or to that blessing itself.

Aufruf: celebration on Shabbat prior to a wedding.

Bar/Bat Mitzvah (plural *B'nai Mitzvah*): son/daughter of the commandment. Usually refers to a ceremony in which an individual chooses to assume the obligations and privileges of an adult member of the Jewish community.

Baruch atah Adonai: "Blessed are You, God," introductory words to many Jewish prayers.

Beit din: rabbinic court, involved in conversion and divorce procedures.

Bimah: the raised platform in front of the sanctuary which holds the ark in which the *Torah* is kept.

Birchot erusin: engagement blessings, part of Jewish wedding service.

Birchot nisuin: wedding blessings.

Brachah (plural *brachot*): a blessing.

Bris: colloquial for a *brit milah*, or covenant of circumcision ceremony.

Brit: covenant.

Brit bat (plural *brit banot*): naming ceremony for girls.

Brit milah: covenant of circumcision ceremony.

Bubba: grandmother.

Challah: braided bread, over which the *Motzi* (blessing recited before meals) is said, usually on *Shabbat* and holidays.

Charoset: mixture of apples, nuts, and wine, traditionally eaten during Passover.

Chazan: cantor.

Chuppah: wedding canopy.

Communion, or *Holy Communion:* in Christianity, when wine and a wafer, symbolic of the blood and body of Jesus Christ, are consumed.

Dreidel: a spinning toy used during the holiday of Hanukkah.

Eretz Yisrael: the Land of Israel.

Eucharist: in Christianity, the sacrament of Holy Communion, when wine and a wafer, symbolic of the blood and body of Jesus Christ, are consumed.

Gelt: money customarily given on Hanukkah.

Goy: slang term for a non-Jew.

Gut yontif: Yiddish for "happy holiday."

Haftorah: a selection from the books of Prophets that is read following the weekly *Torah* portion. There is a *Haftorah* for each *Torah* portion.

Hagaddah, haggadah: book of prayers, stories, and songs used on Passover.

Halakha: Jewish law (adjective: *halakhic*).

Hamantashen: fruit-filled pastries traditionally eaten during Purim.

Hametz: food that is not kosher for Passover.

HaShem: name of God.

Hatafat dam brit: in conversion of a previously circumcised man, the ritual taking of a drop of blood.

Havdalah: ceremony marking the end of *Shabbat.*

Heksher: stamp of approval.

Hesed shel emet: "true loving kindness," referring to burial of the dead.

Hesped: eulogy.

Hora: Jewish circle dance.

Kaddish: the prayer extolling God that is said by mourners and those observing a *yahrzeit.*

Kavannah, kavvanah: intention, focus.

Kedusha: holiness.

Ketubah: Jewish marriage contract.

Kevod hamet: respect for the dead.

Kiddush: the blessing sanctifying the Sabbath (or festivals) that is recited over wine.

Kiddushin: marriage.

Kippah (plural: *kippot*): head covering worn by Jews, all the time by some, only during times of particular religious significance by others.

Kissei shel Eliyahu: Elijah's chair, used in *bris* and *brit bat* ceremonies.

Kol Nidre: opening prayer of the evening service of Yom Kippur. Also refers to that service itself.

Kosher: within the bounds of Jewish dietary laws (kashrut).

Kreplach: meat pie cooked in soup.

Kriah: tearing of clothing or torn ribbon denoting a mourner.

Kvatterin, kvatter: godmother and godfather, respectively.

Latkes: Potato pancakes traditionally eaten during Hanukkah.

L'chaim: "to life!"

Maasim tovim: good deeds.

Maror: bitter herbs traditionally eaten during Passover.

Mass: in Christianity, the celebration of the Eucharist (the sacrament of Holy Communion).

Matzah: the unleavened bread eaten during Passover.

Matzah brie: fried matzah, eaten during Passover.

Megillah: usually refers to the Book of Esther read on Purim.

Menorah: religious candelabra with seven candlestick holders. A special one for Hanukkah, the *hanukkiyah*, has nine candlestick holders.

Mezuzah: The vessel that holds the handwritten scroll with the *Sh'ma* and that is affixed to the doorposts of Jewish homes.

Midrash: teaching story.

Mikvah: ritual bath.

Minyan: a quorum of ten adults needed to hold a *Torah* service.

Mi shebeirach: blessing for healing.

Mishnah: the first post-biblical collection of Jewish legal materials, and the primary building block of the *Talmud*, the major collection of rabbinic Jewish law.

Mitzvah (plural *mitzvot*): a religious obligation or commandment; a good deed.

Mohel (feminine *mohelet*): the person trained to perform ritual circumcision.

Motzi, Ha-Motzi: blessing over bread recited before meals.

Neilah: concluding service on Yom Kippur.

Nichum avelim: comforting the mourner.

Oneg Shabbat: "Sabbath joy," refers to the light refreshments served after a *Shabbat* service.

Passover: the spring holiday remembering and celebrating the exodus of the Jews from Egypt.

Pesach: Passover.

Pikuah hanefesh: saving a soul.

Pirkei Avot: Sayings of the Fathers, a book containing wise sayings and aphorisms of rabbis spanning hundreds of years beginning around the time of the beginning of the Common Era.

Purim: the festive holiday celebrating Esther's saving of the Jews from the plans of the evil Haman.

Rosh Hashanah: the Jewish New Year.

Sandek, sandeket (feminine): grandparent who holds the baby for the *bris*.

Seder: literally, order. Refers to the traditional course of events, or service, surrounding the Passover and Tu B'Shevat meals.

Shabbat: the Jewish Sabbath, from sunset on Friday to sunset on Saturday.

Shamash: Hanukkah candle used to light the other candles.

Shanah tovah: a "good year," a typical greeting on Rosh Hashanah.

Shavuot: a holiday commemorating the receiving of the Torah on Mount Sinai, it is also known as the Feast of Weeks, as it comes seven weeks after Passover begins.

Shehecheyanu: "who has given us life." Part of a blessing thanking God for bringing us to a special moment.

Sheva brachot, sheva berachot: the seven wedding blessings.

Shiva: the seven days of mourning following the funeral of a family member.

Shloshim: the thirty days of mourning following the funeral of a family member.

Sh'ma: "hear," the first word and name of the central Jewish prayer and statement of faith.

Shofar: ram's horn that is blown on Rosh Hashanah and Yom Kippur.

Shul: Yiddish word for synagogue.

Simcha: celebration.

Simchat Torah: Joy of the Torah, a celebration of the completion of the yearly *Torah* cycle and the commencement of a new one.

Soofganiyot: jelly doughnuts often eaten in Israel during Hanukkah.

Sukkah: the hut in which Jews dwell and/or eat during the festival of Sukkot.

Sukkot: a harvest festival where wooden booths are built to commemorate the Israelite wandering in the desert and to recall our fragility and dependence on God.

Tallit, Tallis: Hebrew and Yiddish words for a prayer shawl.

Talmud: the major collection of rabbinic Jewish law.

Tashlich: Rosh Hashanah ceremony in which sins are symbolically cast away.

Tefillin: black leather straps with a small box containing the *Sh'ma* prayer.

Tefillot: prayers.

T'shuvah: repentance.

Torah: the first five books of the Hebrew Bible, or the scroll that contains them. Also used more broadly to refer to traditional Jewish learning.

Tikkun olam: repairing the world, a goal of the Jewish covenant with God.

Tisha b'Av: fast day that commemorates the destruction of the Temples.

Tu B'Shevat: a holiday celebrating nature that falls on the fifteenth day of the month of *Shevat*.

Tzedakah: righteous giving, charity.

Tzitzit: fringed garment worn usually by traditional male Jews.

Yahrzeit: memorial.

Yarmulke: a Yiddish word for the head covering worn by Jews, either all the time or during specifically religious occasions. Also known in Hebrew as *kippah*.

Yizkor: "remember," the memorial service in which we remember relatives who have died.

Yom Kippur: the Jewish Day of Atonement, the final day of the ten Days of Awe that begin with *Rosh Hashanah*.

Yontif: Yiddish for "holiday."

Zaida: grandfather.

Resources for Interfaith Families

RECOMMENDED WEBSITES

InterfaithFamily.com is an online magazine for interfaith couples and
their extended families. The magazine offers practical suggestions
by experts and first-person accounts by people who have "been
there," online discussions, and current information about welcoming outreach programs and organizations in local communities.

JewishFamily.com is an online magazine also produced by Jewish
Family & Life! that makes Judaism relevant and fun to incorporate
into everyday life.

Joi.org is the website of the Jewish Outreach Institute, the first Jewish
organization to reach out to and advocate for intermarried families. It offers information on how to celebrate Jewish holidays, as
well as resources and online discussions.

UAHC.org and clickonjudaism.org are websites produced by the
Reform Movement that describe its outreach programs and provide articles and resources.

Convert.org is the website of the Conversion to Judaism Resource
Center, an independent non-profit organization offering extensive
materials about conversion.

Beliefnet.com is an interesting and thoughtful website for people of
all religions.

In the San Francisco Bay Area: Intfaith.org, the website of the Jewish
Community Center's Interfaith Connection, and SFJCF.org, the
website of the San Francisco Jewish Community Federation, offer
information about welcoming outreach programs for interfaith
families.

RECOMMENDED CLASSICS FOR
INTERFAITH FAMILIES

Berkowitz, Allan, and Patti Moskovitz. *Embracing the Covenant: Converts to Judaism Talk about Why & How.* Woodstock, Vt.: Jewish Lights, 1996. The thoughtful and personal stories of twenty converts to Judaism show how they made the decision, and how it has changed their lives and the lives of those close to them.

Cowan, Paul, with Rachel Cowan. *Mixed Blessings: Overcoming the Stumbling Blocks in an Interfaith Marriage.* New York: Penguin USA, 1989. A classic on interfaith marriage and raising children in a home where two different religions are practiced. The Cowans were married for fifteen years before Rachel Cowan converted. She became a rabbi and now directs Jewish Life programs for the Nathan Cummings Foundation.

Crohn, Joel. *Mixed Matches: How to Create Successful Interracial, Interethnic, and Interfaith Relationships.* New York: Fawcett, 1995. Major topics include how to understand the differing points of view between cultures, how a culture shapes and defines its individual members, ways to combine two cultures into a single family unit, raising children in this environment, and managing the demands of family and friends. Illuminating vignettes throughout.

Diamant, Anita. *Bible Baby Names: Spiritual Choices from Judeo-Christian Tradition.* Woodstock, Vt.: Jewish Lights, 1996. Includes nearly 1,000 boys' and girls' names from the Hebrew Bible and Christian Bible. Each listing includes a translation from the original language, a citation of where the name appears in the Bible, and a description of its meaning. A wonderful book for those who want to choose a special, spiritual name for a child.

———. *Choosing a Jewish Life: A Handbook for People Converting to Judaism and for Their Family and Friends.* New York: Schocken, 1977. In a gentle, respectful way, Diamant offers information and guidance for those journeying to conversion. She addresses "how to" issues, including selecting a rabbi and participating in conversion celebrations, and deals with personal issues faced by converts.

———. *The New Jewish Baby Book: Names, Ceremonies, Customs—A Guide for Today's Families.* Woodstock, Vt.: Jewish Lights, 1994. A complete guide to the customs and rituals for welcoming a new child to the world and into the Jewish community. Includes ceremonies you can copy for handouts and a special section for interfaith families.

———. *The New Jewish Wedding.* New York: Simon & Schuster, 1986. A comprehensive resource about Jewish weddings, this book is sensitive to the concerns of interfaith couples.

———. *Saying Kaddish: How to Comfort the Dying, Bury the Dead, and Mourn as a Jew.* New York: Schocken, 1998. This guide to Jewish mourning practices addresses the needs of interfaith couples with wisdom and sensitivity.

Fink, Nan. *Stranger in Our Midst.* New York: Basic Books, 1997. Written by a convert to Judaism, the book describes the difficulties she faced, both inside and outside the Jewish community.

Fuchs-Kreimer, Nancy. *Parenting As a Spiritual Journey: Deepening Ordinary & Extraordinary Events into Sacred Occasions.* Woodstock, Vt.: Jewish Lights, 1998. Interviews with over 100 parents of many faiths show how even the most insignificant moments in a day with a child can be full of spiritual meaning.

Glaser, Gabrielle. *Strangers to the Tribe: Portraits of Interfaith Marriage.* Boston: Houghton Mifflin Co., 1997. Glaser provides interesting, in-depth portraits of interfaith couples.

King, Andrea. *If I'm Jewish and You're Christian, What Are the Kids? A Parenting Guide for Interfaith Families.* Foreword by Rabbi Alexander M. Schindler. New York: UAHC, 1993. This helpful parenting book addresses situations that arise in interfaith families with wisdom and sensitivity.

Lerner, Devon A. *Celebrating Interfaith Marriages: Creating Your Jewish/Christian Ceremony.* New York: Owl, 1999. A comprehensive wedding guide specifically for the Jewish/Christian couple who want to honor both religious traditions in their service, vows, and readings. Lerner is both a rabbi and a social worker.

Levin, Sunie. *Mingled Roots: A Guide for Jewish Grandparents of Interfaith Grandchildren.* New York: B'nai B'rith Women, 1991. This books offers suggestions for strengthening the connection between grandparents and grandchildren.

Matlins, Stuart M., and Arthur Magida. *How to Be a Perfect Stranger, Vols. 1 & 2: A Guide to Etiquette in Other People's Religious Ceremonies.* Woodstock, Vt.: SkyLight Paths, 1999. A wonderfully comprehensive guide to the rituals and celebrations of the major religions and denominations in North America. The unbiased information is presented from the perspective of an interested guest of *any* other faith.

McClain, Ellen Jaffe. *Embracing the Stranger.* New York: Basic Books, 1995. This book encourages the Jewish community to reach out to intermarried families.

Petsonk, Judy, and Jim Remsen. *The Intermarriage Handbook: A Guide for Jews & Christians.* New York: Morrow, 1991. When a Jew marries a Christian, sometimes families, rabbis, ministers, and holidays present turmoil and confusion. This comprehensive, immensely practical self-help book for interfaith households offers suggestions for a relationship at any stage.

Salkin, Jeffrey K. *Putting God on the Guest List, 2nd Ed.: How to Reclaim the Spiritual Meaning of Your Child's Bar or Bat Mitzvah.* Woodstock, Vt.: Jewish Lights, 1996. This book explains the spirituality and meaning of *Bar* and *Bat Mitzvah,* discusses the origin of the ceremony, and suggests ways to incorporate non-Jewish family members into the ceremony.

———. *For Kids—Putting God on Your Guest List: How to Claim the Spiritual Meaning of Your Bar or Bat Mitzvah.* Woodstock, Vt.: Jewish Lights, 1998. This book offers kids suggestions on how to make their *Bar* or *Bat Mitzvah* spiritually meaningful.

HELPFUL BOOKS ON LIVING A JEWISH LIFE

Abramowitz, Yosef I., and Susan Silverman. *Jewish Family & Life: Traditions, Holidays, and Values for Today's Parents and Children.* New York: Golden, 1998. This wonderful introduction to a Judaism that can be integrated into modern life addresses the concerns of young parents today in a tolerant, open, and inclusive fashion.

Diamant, Anita, and Karen Kushner. *How to Be a Jewish Parent: A Practical Handbook for Family Life.* New York: Schocken, 2000. A comprehensive guide that covers all aspects of raising children Jewishly.

Green, Arthur. *These Are the Words: A Vocabulary of Jewish Spiritual Life.* Woodstock, Vt.: Jewish Lights, 1999. A very informative and entertaining book that provides the meaning, history, and origin of the core 149 Hebrew words that are central to Jewish spiritual life, and religious and communal identity. An interesting read for those who don't know any Hebrew and for those who do.

Kushner, Lawrence. *Jewish Spirituality: A Brief Introduction for Christians.* Woodstock, Vt.: Jewish Lights, 2001. In his newest book, Lawrence Kushner clearly and beautifully relates the very essence of Judaism for people who may not be familiar with it. Along the way, he shows how this knowledge of Jewish spirituality and wisdom can enrich their own spirituality.

Matlins, Stuart M., ed. *The Jewish Lights Spirituality Handbook: A Guide to Understanding, Exploring & Living a Spiritual Life.* Woodstock, Vt.: Jewish Lights, 2001. Rich, creative material from fifty spiritual leaders on every aspect of today's Jewish spirituality. From the nuts-and-bolts to the purely divine, it includes simple and not-so-simple ways of understanding what "Jewish spirituality" is...and can be.

Strassfeld, Michael. *The Jewish Holidays: A Guide and Commentary.* New York: HarperCollins, 1985. In addition to an in-depth discussion of each holiday, this book includes commentaries, ideas for family holiday involvement, and suggestions for new traditions.

Telushkin, Joseph. *Jewish Literacy.* New York: William Morrow, 1991. An excellent general resource on Jewish texts.

Wolfson, Ron. *The Art of Jewish Living* series. Woodstock, Vt.: Jewish Lights. Written by a well-known family educator, this series of books includes *The Shabbat Seder* (1996), *The Passover Seder* (1996), *Hanukkah, 2nd Ed.* (2001), and *A Time to Mourn, A Time to Comfort* (1996). The holiday and Shabbat books include recipes, crafts, and family activities to enhance observance.

About InterfaithFamily.com

The mission of InterfaithFamily.com is to welcome interfaith families to the Jewish community, to offer them support and information, and to gently encourage them to make Jewish choices. InterfaithFamily.com also seeks to encourage the Jewish community to be inclusive of interfaith families. The magazine publishes articles, in bi-weekly issues on the Internet, that are welcoming, accessible, informative, and relevant, organized around topics including family relationships, life-cycle events, holidays, and religious life. InterfaithFamily.com features personal stories by members of inter-married families, and the advice of leading outreach professionals. The magazine also offers reviews, interviews, profiles; news; video; and a dialogue and debate section of op-ed pieces. Readers are invited to post comments on bulletin board discussions and to search for outreach programs in their local communities.

InterfaithFamily.com is produced by Jewish Family & Life!, a 501(c)(3) non-profit organization that has been funded by many leading Jewish organizations and foundations. Jewish Family & Life! publishes a series of magazines on the Internet, including JewishFamily.com, JVibe.com, GenerationJ.com, JBooks.com, and SocialAction.com, as well as the print journal *Sh'ma*, and is involved in several exciting new projects, including a print magazine called "BabagaNewz" for religious school students with a companion "Scholastic"-type book club, a distance learning network called "JSkyway," the pre- and post-trip Internet connections for students on Birthright Israel trips, and a partnership with the Jewish Television Network called Jewz.com. More information about Jewish Family & Life! is available at JFLmedia.com.

About JEWISH LIGHTS Publishing

People of all faiths and backgrounds yearn for books that attract, engage, educate and spiritually inspire.

Our principal goal is to stimulate thought and help all people learn about who the Jewish People are, where they come from, and what the future can be made to hold. While people of our diverse Jewish heritage are the primary audience, our books speak to people in the Christian world as well and will broaden their understanding of Judaism and the roots of their own faith.

We bring to you authors who are at the forefront of spiritual thought and experience. While each has something different to say, they all say it in a voice that you can hear.

Our books are designed to welcome you and then to engage, stimulate and inspire. We judge our success not only by whether or not our books are beautiful and commercially successful, but by whether or not they make a difference in your life.

We at Jewish Lights take great care to produce beautiful books that present meaningful spiritual content in a form that reflects the art of making high quality books. Therefore, we want to acknowledge those who contributed to the production of this book.

Stuart M. Matlins, Publisher

PRODUCTION
Tim Holtz & Bridgett Taylor

EDITORIAL
Amanda Dupuis, Martha McKinney,
Polly Short & Emily Wichland

COVER DESIGN
Nancy Belford

INTERIOR TYPESETTING
Kristin Goble, PerfecType, Nashville, Tennessee

COVER / TEXT PRINTING & BINDING
Lake Book, Melrose Park, Illinois

The Way Into... Series

A major 14-volume series to be completed over the next several years, *The Way Into...* provides an accessible and usable **"guided tour" of the Jewish faith, its people, its history and beliefs—in total, an introduction to Judaism for adults that will enable them to understand and interact with sacred texts.** Each volume is written by a major modern scholar and teacher, and is organized around an important concept of Judaism.

The Way Into... will enable all readers to achieve a real sense of Jewish cultural literacy through guided study. Available volumes include:

The Way Into Torah

by *Dr. Norman J. Cohen*

What is "Torah"? What are the different approaches to studying Torah? What are the different levels of understanding Torah? For whom is the study intended? Explores the origins and development of Torah, why it should be studied and how to do it.
6 x 9, 176 pp, HC, ISBN 1-58023-028-8 **$21.95**

The Way Into Jewish Prayer

by *Dr. Lawrence A. Hoffman*

Opens the door to 3,000 years of the Jewish way to God by making available all you need to feel at home in Jewish worship. Provides basic definitions of the terms you need to know as well as thoughtful analysis of the depth that lies beneath Jewish prayer.
6 x 9, 224 pp, HC, ISBN 1-58023-027-X **$21.95**

The Way Into Encountering God in Judaism

by *Dr. Neil Gillman*

Explains how Jews have encountered God throughout history—and today—by exploring the many metaphors for God in Jewish tradition. Explores the Jewish tradition's passionate but also conflicting ways of relating to God as Creator, relational partner, and a force in history and nature.
6 x 9, 240 pp, HC, ISBN 1-58023-025-3 **$21.95**

The Way Into Jewish Mystical Tradition

by *Rabbi Lawrence Kushner*

Explains the principles of Jewish mystical thinking, their religious and spiritual significance, and how they relate to our lives. A book that allows us to experience and understand the Jewish mystical approach to our place in the world.
6 x 9, 224 pp, HC, ISBN 1-58023-029-6 **$21.95**

Or phone, fax, mail or e-mail to: **JEWISH LIGHTS Publishing**
Sunset Farm Offices, Route 4 • P.O. Box 237 • Woodstock, Vermont 05091
Tel: (802) 457-4000 • Fax: (802) 457-4004 • www.jewishlights.com
Credit card orders: **(800) 962-4544** (9AM–5PM ET Monday–Friday)
Generous discounts on quantity orders. SATISFACTION GUARANTEED. Prices subject to change.

Spirituality—The Kushner Series
Books by Lawrence Kushner

The Way Into Jewish Mystical Tradition

Explains the principles of Jewish mystical thinking, their religious and spiritual significance, and how they relate to our lives. A book that allows us to experience and understand the Jewish mystical approach to our place in the world. 6 x 9, 224 pp, HC, ISBN 1-58023-029-6 **$21.95**

Eyes Remade for Wonder
The Way of Jewish Mysticism and Sacred Living
A Lawrence Kushner Reader Intro. by *Thomas Moore*

Whether you are new to Kushner or a devoted fan, you'll find inspiration here. With samplings from each of Kushner's works, and a generous amount of new material, this book is to be read and reread, each time discovering deeper layers of meaning in our lives.
6 x 9, 240 pp, Quality PB, ISBN 1-58023-042-3 **$16.95**; HC, ISBN 1-58023-014-8 **$23.95**

Because Nothing Looks Like God

by *Lawrence and Karen Kushner;* Full-color illus. by *Dawn W. Majewski*

What is God like? The first collaborative work by husband-and-wife team Lawrence and Karen Kushner introduces children to the possibilities of spiritual life with three poetic spiritual stories. Real-life examples of happiness and sadness—from goodnight stories, to the hope and fear felt the first time at bat, to the closing moments of life—invite us to explore, together with our children, the questions we all have about God, no matter what our age. **For ages 4 & up**
11 x 8½, 32 pp, HC, Full-color illus., ISBN 1-58023-092-X **$16.95**

 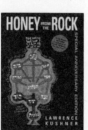   

Invisible Lines of Connection: *Sacred Stories of the Ordinary* AWARD WINNER!
6 x 9, 160 pp, Quality PB, ISBN 1-879045-98-2 **$15.95**; HC, ISBN 1-879045-52-4 **$21.95**

Honey from the Rock: *An Introduction to Jewish Mysticism* SPECIAL ANNIVERSARY EDITION
6 x 9, 176 pp, Quality PB, ISBN 1-58023-073-3 **$15.95**

The Book of Letters: *A Mystical Hebrew Alphabet* AWARD WINNER!
Popular HC Edition, 6 x 9, 80 pp, 2-color text, ISBN 1-879045-00-1 **$24.95**; *Deluxe Gift Edition,* 9 x 12, 80 pp, HC, 2-color text, ornamentation, slipcase, ISBN 1-879045-01-X **$79.95**; *Collector's Limited Edition,* 9 x 12, 80 pp, HC, gold-embossed pages, hand-assembled slipcase. With silkscreened print. Limited to 500 signed and numbered copies, ISBN 1-879045-04-4 **$349.00**

The Book of Words: *Talking Spiritual Life, Living Spiritual Talk* AWARD WINNER!
6 x 9, 160 pp, Quality PB, 2-color text, ISBN 1-58023-020-2 **$16.95**;
152 pp, HC, ISBN 1-879045-35-4 **$21.95**

God Was in This Place & I, i Did Not Know
Finding Self, Spirituality and Ultimate Meaning
6 x 9, 192 pp, Quality PB, ISBN 1-879045-33-8 **$16.95**

The River of Light: *Jewish Mystical Awareness* SPECIAL ANNIVERSARY EDITION
6 x 9, 192 pp, Quality PB, ISBN 1-58023-096-2 **$16.95**

Spirituality

My People's Prayer Book: *Traditional Prayers, Modern Commentaries*
Ed. by *Dr. Lawrence A. Hoffman*

Provides a diverse and exciting commentary to the traditional liturgy, helping modern men and women find new wisdom in Jewish prayer, and bring liturgy into their lives. Each book includes Hebrew text, modern translation, and commentaries *from all perspectives* of the Jewish world.

Vol. 1—*The Sh'ma and Its Blessings*, 7 x 10, 168 pp, HC, ISBN 1-879045-79-6 **$23.95**
Vol. 2—*The Amidah*, 7 x 10, 240 pp, HC, ISBN 1-879045-80-X **$23.95**
Vol. 3—*P'sukei D'zimrah* (Morning Psalms), 7 x 10, 240 pp, HC, ISBN 1-879045-81-8 **$24.95**
Vol. 4—*Seder K'riat Hatorah* (The Torah Service), 7 x 10, 264 pp, ISBN 1-879045-82-6 **$23.95**
Vol. 5—*Birkhot Hashachar* (Morning Blessings), 7 x 10, 240 pp (est), ISBN 1-879045-83-4 **$24.95**
(Vol. 5 avail. Fall 2001)

Becoming a Congregation of Learners
Learning as a Key to Revitalizing Congregational Life by Isa Aron, Ph.D.; Foreword by Rabbi Lawrence A. Hoffman, Co-Developer, Synagogue 2000
6 x 9, 304 pp, Quality PB, ISBN 1-58023-089-X **$19.95**

Self, Struggle & Change
Family Conflict Stories in Genesis and Their Healing Insights for Our Lives
by Dr. Norman J. Cohen 6 x 9, 224 pp, Quality PB, ISBN 1-879045-66-4 **$16.95**; HC, ISBN 1-879045-19-2 **$21.95**

Voices from Genesis: *Guiding Us through the Stages of Life*
by Dr. Norman J. Cohen 6 x 9, 192 pp, Quality PB, ISBN 1-58023-118-7 **$16.95**; HC, ISBN 1-879045-75-3 **$21.95**

God Whispers: *Stories of the Soul, Lessons of the Heart*
by Rabbi Karyn D. Kedar 6 x 9, 176 pp, Quality PB, ISBN 1-58023-088-1 **$15.95**

The Business Bible: *10 New Commandments for Bringing Spirituality & Ethical Values into the Workplace*
by Rabbi Wayne Dosick 5½ x 8½, 208 pp, Quality PB, ISBN 1-58023-101-2 **$14.95**

Being God's Partner: *How to Find the Hidden Link Between Spirituality and Your Work*
by Rabbi Jeffrey K. Salkin; Intro. by Norman Lear **AWARD WINNER!**
6 x 9, 192 pp, Quality PB, ISBN 1-879045-65-6 **$16.95**; HC, ISBN 1-879045-37-0 **$19.95**

God & the Big Bang
Discovering Harmony Between Science & Spirituality **AWARD WINNER!**
by Daniel C. Matt 6 x 9, 224 pp, Quality PB, ISBN 1-879045-89-3 **$16.95**

Soul Judaism: *Dancing with God into a New Era*
by Rabbi Wayne Dosick 5½ x 8½, 304 pp, Quality PB, ISBN 1-58023-053-9 **$16.95**

Finding Joy: *A Practical Spiritual Guide to Happiness* **AWARD WINNER!**
by Rabbi Dannel I. Schwartz with Mark Hass
6 x 9, 192 pp, Quality PB, ISBN 1-58023-009-1 **$14.95**; HC, ISBN 1-879045-53-2 **$19.95**

Spirituality/Jewish Meditation

Discovering Jewish Meditation
Instruction & Guidance for Learning an Ancient Spiritual Practice
by *Nan Fink Gefen*

Gives readers of any level of understanding the tools to learn the practice of Jewish meditation on your own, starting you on the path to a deep spiritual and personal connection to God and to greater insight about your life. 6 x 9, 208 pp, Quality PB, ISBN 1-58023-067-9 **$16.95**

Entering the Temple of Dreams: *Jewish Prayers, Movements, and Meditations for the End of the Day* by *Tamar Frankiel* and *Judy Greenfeld*

Nighttime spirituality is much more than bedtime prayers! Here, you'll uncover deeper meaning to familiar nighttime prayers—and learn to combine the prayers with movements and meditations to enhance your physical and psychological well-being.
7 x 10, 192 pp, Quality PB, Illus., ISBN 1-58023-079-2 **$16.95**

One God Clapping: *The Spiritual Path of a Zen Rabbi* AWARD WINNER!
by *Alan Lew* with *Sherril Jaffe*

A fascinating personal story of a Jewish meditation expert's roundabout spiritual journey from Zen Buddhist practitioner to rabbi. 5½ x 8½, 336 pp, Quality PB, ISBN 1-58023-115-2 **$16.95**

The Handbook of Jewish Meditation Practices
A Guide for Enriching the Sabbath and Other Days of Your Life
by *Rabbi David A. Cooper*

Gives us ancient and modern Jewish tools—Jewish practices and traditions, easy-to-use meditation exercises, and contemplative study of Jewish sacred texts. 6 x 9, 208 pp, Quality PB, ISBN 1-58023-102-0 **$16.95**

Stepping Stones to Jewish Spiritual Living: *Walking the Path Morning, Noon, and Night*
by Rabbi James L. Mirel & Karen Bonnell Werth
6 x 9, 240 pp, Quality PB, ISBN 1-58023-074-1 **$16.95**

Meditation from the Heart of Judaism
Today's Teachers Share Their Practices, Techniques, and Faith
Ed. by Avram Davis 6 x 9, 256 pp, Quality PB, ISBN 1-58023-049-0 **$16.95**;
HC, ISBN 1-879045-77-X **$21.95**

The Way of Flame: *A Guide to the Forgotten Mystical Tradition of Jewish Meditation*
by Avram Davis 4½ x 8, 176 pp, Quality PB, ISBN 1-58023-060-1 **$15.95**

Minding the Temple of the Soul: *Balancing Body, Mind, and Spirit through Traditional Jewish Prayer, Movement, and Meditation*
by Tamar Frankiel and Judy Greenfeld 7 x 10, 184 pp, Quality PB, Illus.,
ISBN 1-879045-64-8 **$16.95**; Audiotape of the Blessings and Meditations (60-min. cassette), JN01 **$9.95**; Videotape of the Movements and Meditations (46-min.), S507 **$20.00**

Life Cycle/Grief

Against the Dying of the Light
A Parent's Story of Love, Loss and Hope
by *Leonard Fein*

The sudden death of a child. A personal tragedy beyond description. Rage and despair deeper than sorrow. What can come from it? Raw wisdom and defiant hope. In this unusual exploration of heartbreak and healing, Fein chronicles the sudden death of his 30-year-old daughter and reveals what the progression of grief can teach each one of us.
5½ x 8½, 176 pp, HC, ISBN 1-58023-110-1 **$19.95**

Mourning & Mitzvah, 2nd Ed.: *A Guided Journal for Walking the Mourner's Path through Grief to Healing* with *Over 60 Guided Exercises*
by *Anne Brener, L.C.S.W.*

For those who mourn a death, for those who would help them, for those who face a loss of any kind, Brener teaches us the power and strength available to us in the fully experienced mourning process. Revised and expanded. 7½ x 9, 304 pp, Quality PB, ISBN 1-58023-113-6 **$19.95**

Grief in Our Seasons: *A Mourner's Kaddish Companion*
by *Rabbi Kerry M. Olitzky*

A wise and inspiring selection of sacred Jewish writings and a simple, powerful ancient ritual for mourners to read each day, to help hold the memory of their loved ones in their hearts. Offers a comforting, step-by-step daily link to saying Kaddish.
4½ x 6½, 448 pp, Quality PB, ISBN 1-879045-55-9 **$15.95**

Tears of Sorrow, Seeds of Hope
A Jewish Spiritual Companion for Infertility and Pregnancy Loss
by Rabbi Nina Beth Cardin   6 x 9, 192 pp, HC, ISBN 1-58023-017-2 **$19.95**

A Time to Mourn, A Time to Comfort
A Guide to Jewish Bereavement and Comfort
by Dr. Ron Wolfson   7 x 9, 336 pp, Quality PB, ISBN 1-879045-96-6 **$18.95**

When a Grandparent Dies
A Kid's Own Remembering Workbook for Dealing with Shiva and the Year Beyond
by Nechama Liss-Levinson, Ph.D.
8 x 10, 48 pp, HC, Illus., 2-color text, ISBN 1-879045-44-3 **$15.95**

Theology/Philosophy

Love and Terror in the God Encounter: *The Theological Legacy of Rabbi Joseph B. Soloveitchik, Vol. 1* by *Dr. David Hartman*

Renowned scholar David Hartman explores the sometimes surprising intersection of Soloveitchik's rootedness in halakhic tradition with his genuine responsiveness to modern Western theology. An engaging look at one of the most important Jewish thinkers of the twentieth century. 6 x 9, 240 pp, HC, ISBN 1-58023-112-8 **$25.00**

These Are the Words: *A Vocabulary of Jewish Spiritual Life*
by *Arthur Green*

What are the most essential ideas, concepts and terms that an educated person needs to know about Judaism? From *Adonai* (My Lord) to *zekhut* (merit), this enlightening and entertaining journey through Judaism teaches us the 149 core Hebrew words that constitute the basic vocabulary of Jewish spiritual life. 6 x 9, 304 pp, Quality PB, ISBN 1-58023-107-1 **$18.95**

Broken Tablets: *Restoring the Ten Commandments and Ourselves*
Ed. by *Rabbi Rachel S. Mikva*; Intro. by *Rabbi Lawrence Kushner* **AWARD WINNER!**

Twelve outstanding spiritual leaders each share profound and personal thoughts about these biblical commands and why they have such a special hold on us.
6 x 9, 192 pp, HC, ISBN 1-58023-066-0 **$21.95**

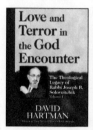  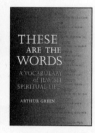 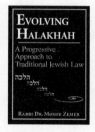 

A Heart of Many Rooms: *Celebrating the Many Voices within Judaism* **AWARD WINNER!**
by Dr. David Hartman 6 x 9, 352 pp, HC, ISBN 1-58023-048-2 **$24.95**

A Living Covenant: *The Innovative Spirit in Traditional Judaism* **AWARD WINNER!**
by Dr. David Hartman 6 x 9, 368 pp, Quality PB, ISBN 1-58023-011-3 **$18.95**

Evolving Halakhah: *A Progressive Approach to Traditional Jewish Law*
by Rabbi Dr. Moshe Zemer 6 x 9, 480 pp, HC, ISBN 1-58023-002-4 **$40.00**

The Death of Death: *Resurrection and Immortality in Jewish Thought* **AWARD WINNER!**
by Dr. Neil Gillman 6 x 9, 336 pp, Quality PB, ISBN 1-58023-081-4 **$18.95**

The Last Trial: *On the Legends and Lore of the Command to Abraham to Offer Isaac as a Sacrifice* by Shalom Spiegel 6 x 9, 208 pp, Quality PB, ISBN 1-879045-29-X **$17.95**

Tormented Master: *The Life and Spiritual Quest of Rabbi Nahman of Bratslav*
by Dr. Arthur Green 6 x 9, 416 pp, Quality PB, ISBN 1-879045-11-7 **$18.95**

The Earth Is the Lord's: *The Inner World of the Jew in Eastern Europe*
by Abraham Joshua Heschel 5½ x 8, 128 pp, Quality PB, ISBN 1-879045-42-7 **$14.95**

A Passion for Truth: *Despair and Hope in Hasidism* by Abraham Joshua Heschel
5½ x 8, 352 pp, Quality PB, ISBN 1-879045-41-9 **$18.95**

Your Word Is Fire: *The Hasidic Masters on Contemplative Prayer* Ed. by Dr. Arthur Green and Dr. Barry W. Holtz 6 x 9, 160 pp, Quality PB, ISBN 1-879045-25-7 **$14.95**

Healing/Wellness/Recovery

Jewish Paths toward Healing and Wholeness
A Personal Guide to Dealing with Suffering
by *Rabbi Kerry M. Olitzky*; Foreword by *Debbie Friedman*

Why me? Why do we suffer? How can we heal? Grounded in personal experience with illness and Jewish spiritual traditions, this book provides healing rituals, psalms and prayers that help readers initiate a dialogue with God, to guide them along the complicated path of healing and wholeness. 6 x 9, 192 pp, Quality PB, ISBN 1-58023-068-7 **$15.95**

Healing of Soul, Healing of Body
Spiritual Leaders Unfold the Strength & Solace in Psalms
Ed. by *Rabbi Simkha Y. Weintraub, CSW,* for The National Center for Jewish Healing

A source of solace for those who are facing illness, as well as those who care for them. Provides a wellspring of strength with inspiring introductions and commentaries by eminent spiritual leaders reflecting all Jewish movements.
6 x 9, 128 pp, Quality PB, Illus., 2-color text, ISBN 1-879045-31-1 **$14.95**

Jewish Pastoral Care
A Practical Handbook from Traditional and Contemporary Sources
Ed. by *Rabbi Dayle A. Friedman*

Gives today's Jewish pastoral counselors practical guidelines based in the Jewish tradition.
6 x 9, 464 pp, HC, ISBN 1-58023-078-4 **$35.00**

Twelve Jewish Steps to Recovery: *A Personal Guide to Turning from Alcoholism & Other Addictions . . . Drugs, Food, Gambling, Sex . . .* by Rabbi Kerry M. Olitzky & Stuart A. Copans, M.D. Preface by Abraham J. Twerski, M.D.; Intro. by Rabbi Sheldon Zimmerman; "Getting Help" by JACS Foundation 6 x 9, 144 pp, Quality PB, ISBN 1-879045-09-5 **$13.95**

One Hundred Blessings Every Day: *Daily Twelve Step Recovery Affirmations, Exercises for Personal Growth & Renewal Reflecting Seasons of the Jewish Year* by Rabbi Kerry M. Olitzky 4½ x 6½, 432 pp, Quality PB, ISBN 1-879045-30-3 **$14.95**

Recovery from Codependence: *A Jewish Twelve Steps Guide to Healing Your Soul* by Rabbi Kerry M. Olitzky 6 x 9, 160 pp, Quality PB, ISBN 1-879045-32-X **$13.95**; HC, ISBN 1-879045-27-3 **$21.95**

Renewed Each Day: *Daily Twelve Step Recovery Meditations Based on the Bible* by Rabbi Kerry M. Olitzky & Aaron Z. *Vol. I: Genesis & Exodus; Vol. II: Leviticus, Numbers and Deuteronomy*
Vol. I: 6 x 9, 224 pp, Quality PB, ISBN 1-879045-12-5 **$14.95**
Vol. II: 6 x 9, 280 pp, Quality PB, ISBN 1-879045-13-3 **$14.95**

Women's Spirituality / Ecology

Torah of the Earth: *Exploring 4,000 Years of Ecology in Jewish Thought*
In 2 Volumes   Ed. by *Rabbi Arthur Waskow*

Major new resource offering us an invaluable key to understanding the intersection of ecology and Judaism. Leading scholars provide us with a guided tour of ecological thought from four major Jewish viewpoints.
Vol. 1: *Biblical Israel & Rabbinic Judaism*, 6 x 9, 272 pp, Quality PB, ISBN 1-58023-086-5 **$19.95**
Vol. 2: *Zionism & Eco-Judaism*, 6 x 9, 336 pp, Quality PB, ISBN 1-58023-087-3 **$19.95**

Ecology & the Jewish Spirit: *Where Nature & the Sacred Meet* Ed. and with Intros.
by Ellen Bernstein 6 x 9, 288 pp, Quality PB, ISBN 1-58023-082-2 **$16.95**;
HC, ISBN 1-879045-88-5 **$23.95**

The Jewish Gardening Cookbook: *Growing Plants & Cooking for Holidays & Festivals*
by Michael Brown 6 x 9, 224 pp, Illus., Quality PB, ISBN 1-58023-116-0 **$16.95**;
HC, ISBN 1-58023-004-0 **$21.95**

 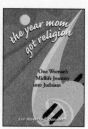   

Moonbeams: *A Hadassah Rosh Hodesh Guide*

Ed. by *Carol Diament, Ph.D.*

This hands-on "idea book" focuses on *Rosh Hodesh,* the festival of the new moon, as a source of spiritual growth for Jewish women. A complete sourcebook that will initiate or rejuvenate women's study groups, it is also perfect for women preparing for *bat mitzvah*, or for anyone interested in learning more about *Rosh Hodesh* observance and what it has to offer. 8½ x 11, 240 pp, Quality PB, ISBN 1-58023-099-7 **$20.00**

The Women's Torah Commentary: *New Insights from Women Rabbis on the 54 Weekly Torah Portions* Ed. by *Rabbi Elyse Goldstein*

For the first time, women rabbis provide a commentary on the entire Five Books of Moses. More than 25 years after the first woman was ordained a rabbi in America, these inspiring teachers bring their rich perspectives to bear on the biblical text. In a week-by-week format; a perfect gift for others, or for yourself. 6 x 9, 496 pp, HC, ISBN 1-58023-076-8 **$34.95**

Lifecycles, in Two Volumes   AWARD WINNERS!
V. 1: *Jewish Women on Life Passages & Personal Milestones*
Ed. and with Intros. by Rabbi Debra Orenstein
V. 2: *Jewish Women on Biblical Themes in Contemporary Life*
Ed. and with Intros. by Rabbi Debra Orenstein and Rabbi Jane Rachel Litman
V. 1: 6 x 9, 480 pp, Quality PB, ISBN 1-58023-018-0 **$19.95**; HC, ISBN 1-879045-14-1 **$24.95**
V. 2: 6 x 9, 464 pp, Quality PB, ISBN 1-58023-019-9 **$19.95**

ReVisions: *Seeing Torah through a Feminist Lens* AWARD WINNER!
by Rabbi Elyse Goldstein 5½ x 8½, 224 pp, Quality PB, ISBN 1-58023-117-9 **$16.95**;
208 pp, HC, ISBN 1-58023-047-4 **$19.95**

The Year Mom Got Religion: *One Woman's Midlife Journey into Judaism*
by Lee Meyerhoff Hendler 6 x 9, 208 pp, Quality PB, ISBN 1-58023-070-9 **$15.95**

Children's Spirituality

In Our Image
God's First Creatures
by *Nancy Sohn Swartz*
Full-color illus. by *Melanie Hall*

For ages 4 & up

A playful new twist on the Creation story—from the perspective of the animals. Celebrates the interconnectedness of nature and the harmony of all living things. "The vibrantly colored illustrations nearly leap off the page in this delightful interpretation." —*School Library Journal*

9 x 12, 32 pp, HC, Full-color illus., ISBN 1-879045-99-0 **$16.95**

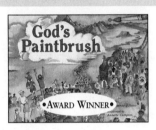
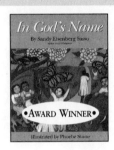
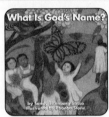

God's Paintbrush
by *Sandy Eisenberg Sasso;* Full-color illus. by *Annette Compton*

For ages 4 & up

Invites children of all faiths and backgrounds to encounter God openly in their own lives. Wonderfully interactive; provides questions adult and child can explore together at the end of each episode.
11 x 8½, 32 pp, HC, Full-color illus., ISBN 1-879045-22-2 **$16.95**

Also available: A Teacher's Guide: **A Guide for Jewish & Christian Educators and Parents**
8½ x 11, 32 pp, PB, ISBN 1-879045-57-5 **$8.95**

God's Paintbrush Celebration Kit 9½ x 12, HC, Includes 5 sessions/40 full-color Activity Sheets and Teacher Folder with complete instructions, ISBN 1-58023-050-4 **$21.95**

In God's Name
by *Sandy Eisenberg Sasso;* Full-color illus. by *Phoebe Stone*

For ages 4 & up

Like an ancient myth in its poetic text and vibrant illustrations, this award-winning modern fable about the search for God's name celebrates the diversity and, at the same time, the unity of all the people of the world.
9 x 12, 32 pp, HC, Full-color illus., ISBN 1-879045-26-5 **$16.95**

What Is God's Name? (A Board Book)

For ages 0–4

An abridged board book version of the award-winning *In God's Name.*
5 x 5, 24 pp, Board, Full-color illus., ISBN 1-893361-10-1 **$7.95** A SKYLIGHT PATHS Book

The 11th Commandment: Wisdom from Our Children
by *The Children of America*

For all ages

"If there were an Eleventh Commandment, what would it be?" Children of many religious denominations across America answer this question—in their own drawings and words. "A rare book of spiritual celebration for all people, of all ages, for all time."—*Bookviews*
8 x 10, 48 pp, HC, Full-color illus., ISBN 1-879045-46-X **$16.95**

Children's Spirituality

Because Nothing Looks Like God
by *Lawrence and Karen Kushner*
Full-color illus. by *Dawn W. Majewski*

For ages 4 & up

MULTICULTURAL, NONDENOMINATIONAL, NONSECTARIAN

What is God like? The first collaborative work by husband-and-wife team Lawrence and Karen Kushner introduces children to the possibilities of spiritual life. Real-life examples of happiness and sadness—from goodnight stories, to the hope and fear felt the first time at bat, to the closing moments of life—invite us to explore, together with our children, the questions we all have about God, no matter what our age.

11 x 8½, 32 pp, HC, Full-color illus., ISBN 1-58023-092-X **$16.95**

Where Is God?
What Does God Look Like?
How Does God Make Things Happen? (Board Books)

For ages 0–4

by *Lawrence and Karen Kushner*; Full-color illus. by *Dawn W. Majewski*

Gently invites children to become aware of God's presence all around them. Three board books abridged from *Because Nothing Looks Like God* by Lawrence and Karen Kushner.
Each 5 x 5, 24 pp, Board, Full-color illus. **$7.95**   SKYLIGHT PATHS Books

Sharing Blessings
Children's Stories for Exploring the Spirit of the Jewish Holidays
by *Rahel Musleah* and *Rabbi Michael Klayman*
Full-color illus. by *Mary O'Keefe Young*

For ages 6 & up

What is the spiritual message of each of the Jewish holidays? How do we teach it to our children? Many books tell children about the historical significance and customs of the holidays. Through stories about one family's preparation, *Sharing Blessings* explores ways to get into the *spirit* of 13 different holidays.
8½ x 11, 64 pp, HC, Full-color illus., ISBN 1-879045-71-0 **$18.95**

The Book of Miracles
A Young Person's Guide to Jewish Spiritual Awareness
by *Lawrence Kushner*

For ages 9 & up

Introduces kids to a way of everyday spiritual thinking to last a lifetime. Kushner, whose award-winning books have brought spirituality to life for countless adults, now shows young people how to use Judaism as a foundation on which to build their lives.
6 x 9, 96 pp, HC, 2-color illus., ISBN 1-879045-78-8 **$16.95**

Children's Spirituality

God Said Amen

by *Sandy Eisenberg Sasso*
Full-color illus. by *Avi Katz*

For ages 4 & up

A warm and inspiring tale of two kingdoms: one overflowing with water but without oil to light its lamps; the other blessed with oil but no water to grow its gardens. The kingdoms' rulers ask God for help but are too stubborn to ask each other. It takes a minstrel, a pair of royal riding-birds and their young keepers, and a simple act of kindness to show that they need only reach out to each other to find God's answer to their prayers.

9 x 12, 32 pp, HC, Full-color illus., ISBN 1-58023-080-6 **$16.95**

For Heaven's Sake

For ages 4 & up

by *Sandy Eisenberg Sasso*; Full-color illus. by *Kathryn Kunz Finney*

Everyone talked about heaven: "Thank heavens." "Heaven forbid." "For heaven's sake, Isaiah." But no one would say what heaven was or how to find it. So Isaiah decides to find out, by seeking answers from many different people.
9 x 12, 32 pp, HC, Full-color illus., ISBN 1-58023-054-7 **$16.95**

But God Remembered

Stories of Women from Creation to the Promised Land

For ages 8 & up

by *Sandy Eisenberg Sasso*; Full-color illus. by *Bethanne Andersen*

A fascinating collection of four different stories of women only briefly mentioned in biblical tradition and religious texts. Vibrantly brings to life courageous and strong women from ancient tradition; all teach important values through their actions and faith.
9 x 12, 32 pp, HC, Full-color illus., ISBN 1-879045-43-5 **$16.95**

God in Between

For ages 4 & up

by *Sandy Eisenberg Sasso*; Full-color illus. by *Sally Sweetland*

If you wanted to find God, where would you look? A magical, mythical tale that teaches that God can be found where we are: within all of us and the relationships between us.
9 x 12, 32 pp, HC, Full-color illus., ISBN 1-879045-86-9 **$16.95**

For ages 4 & up

A Prayer for the Earth: The Story of Naamah, Noah's Wife

by *Sandy Eisenberg Sasso*; Full-color illus. by *Bethanne Andersen*

This new story, based on an ancient text, opens readers' religious imaginations to new ideas about the well-known story of the Flood. When God tells Noah to bring the animals of the world onto the ark, God also calls on Naamah, Noah's wife, to save each plant on Earth.
9 x 12, 32 pp, HC, Full-color illus., ISBN 1-879045-60-5 **$16.95**

Spirituality & More

The Jewish Lights Spirituality Handbook
A Guide to Understanding, Exploring & Living a Spiritual Life
Ed. by *Stuart M. Matlins, Editor-in-Chief, Jewish Lights Publishing*

Rich, creative material from over 50 spiritual leaders on every aspect of Jewish spirituality today: prayer, meditation, mysticism, study, rituals, special days, the everyday, and more.
6 x 9, 456 pp, Quality PB, ISBN 1-58023-093-8 **$18.95**; HC, ISBN 1-58023-100-4 **$24.95**

Six Jewish Spiritual Paths: *A Rationalist Looks at Spirituality*
by *Rabbi Rifat Sonsino*

The quest for spirituality is universal, but which path to spirituality is right *for you?* A straightforward, objective discussion of the many ways—each valid and authentic—for seekers to gain a richer spiritual life within Judaism. 6 x 9, 208 pp, HC, ISBN 1-58023-095-4 **$21.95**

Criminal Kabbalah
An Intriguing Anthology of Jewish Mystery & Detective Fiction
Edited by *Lawrence W. Raphael;* Foreword by *Laurie R. King*

Twelve of today's best known mystery authors provide an intriguing collection of new stories sure to enlighten at the same time they entertain.
6 x 9, 256 pp, Quality PB, ISBN 1-58023-109-8 **$16.95**

 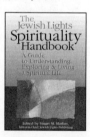 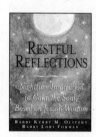  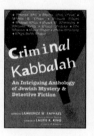

Mystery Midrash: *An Anthology of Jewish Mystery & Detective Fiction* AWARD WINNER!
Ed. by Lawrence W. Raphael 6 x 9, 304 pp, Quality PB, ISBN 1-58023-055-5 **$16.95**

Sacred Intentions: *Daily Inspiration to Strengthen the Spirit, Based on Jewish Wisdom*
by Rabbi Kerry M. Olitzky & Rabbi Lori Forman
4½ x 6½, 448 pp, Quality PB, ISBN 1-58023-061-X **$15.95**

Restful Reflections: *Nighttime Inspiration to Calm the Soul, Based on Jewish Wisdom*
by Rabbi Kerry M. Olitzky & Rabbi Lori Forman
4½ x 6½, 448 pp, Quality PB, ISBN 1-58023-091-1 **$15.95**

The Enneagram and Kabbalah: *Reading Your Soul*
by Rabbi Howard A. Addison 6 x 9, 176 pp, Quality PB, ISBN 1-58023-001-6 **$15.95**

Embracing the Covenant: *Converts to Judaism Talk About Why & How*
Ed. and with Intros. by Rabbi Allan L. Berkowitz and Patti Moskovitz
6 x 9, 192 pp, Quality PB, ISBN 1-879045-50-8 **$15.95**

Wandering Stars: *An Anthology of Jewish Fantasy & Science Fiction* Ed. by Jack Dann; Intro. by Isaac Asimov 6 x 9, 272 pp, Quality PB, ISBN 1-58023-005-9 **$16.95**

Israel—A Spiritual Travel Guide AWARD WINNER!
A Companion for the Modern Jewish Pilgrim
by Rabbi Lawrence A. Hoffman 4¾ x 10, 256 pp, Quality PB, ISBN 1-879045-56-7 **$18.95**

Life Cycle & Holidays

How to Be a Perfect Stranger, 2nd Ed. In 2 Volumes
A Guide to Etiquette in Other People's Religious Ceremonies
Ed. by *Stuart M. Matlins* & *Arthur J. Magida* **AWARD WINNER!**

*What will happen? What do I do? What do I wear? What do I say? What are their basic beliefs?
Should I bring a gift?* Explains the rituals and celebrations of North America's major religions/denominations, helping an interested guest to feel comfortable. Not presented from the
perspective of any particular faith. SKYLIGHT PATHS Books
Vol. 1: *North America's Largest Faiths,* 6 x 9, 432 pp, Quality PB, ISBN 1-893361-01-2 **$19.95**
Vol. 2: *Other Faiths in North America,* 6 x 9, 416 pp, Quality PB, ISBN 1-893361-02-0 **$19.95**

Celebrating Your New Jewish Daughter
Creating Jewish Ways to Welcome Baby Girls into the Covenant—
New and Traditional Ceremonies
by *Debra Nussbaum Cohen;* Foreword by *Rabbi Sandy Eisenberg Sasso*

Features everything families need to plan a celebration that reflects Jewish tradition, including a
how-to guide to new and traditional ceremonies, and practical guidelines for planning the joyous
event. 6 x 9, 272 pp, Quality PB, ISBN 1-58023-090-3 **$18.95**

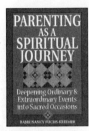    

The New Jewish Baby Book **AWARD WINNER!**
Names, Ceremonies & Customs—A Guide for Today's Families
by Anita Diamant 6 x 9, 336 pp, Quality PB, ISBN 1-879045-28-1 **$18.95**

Parenting As a Spiritual Journey
Deepening Ordinary & Extraordinary Events into Sacred Occasions
by Rabbi Nancy Fuchs-Kreimer 6 x 9, 224 pp, Quality PB, ISBN 1-58023-016-4 **$16.95**

Putting God on the Guest List, 2nd Ed. **AWARD WINNER!**
How to Reclaim the Spiritual Meaning of Your Child's Bar or Bat Mitzvah
by Rabbi Jeffrey K. Salkin 6 x 9, 224 pp, Quality PB, ISBN 1-879045-59-1 **$16.95**

For Kids—Putting God on Your Guest List
How to Claim the Spiritual Meaning of Your Bar or Bat Mitzvah
by Rabbi Jeffrey K. Salkin 6 x 9, 144 pp, Quality PB, ISBN 1-58023-015-6 **$14.95**

Bar/Bat Mitzvah Basics, 2nd Ed.: *A Practical Family Guide to Coming of Age Together*
Ed. by Cantor Helen Leneman 6 x 9, 240 pp, Quality PB, ISBN 1-58023-151-9 **$18.95**

Hanukkah: The Art of Jewish Living
by Dr. Ron Wolfson 7 x 9, 192 pp, Quality PB, Illus., ISBN 1-879045-97-4 **$16.95**

The Shabbat Seder: The Art of Jewish Living
by Dr. Ron Wolfson 7 x 9, 272 pp, Quality PB, Illus., ISBN 1-879045-90-7 **$16.95**

The Passover Seder: The Art of Jewish Living
by Dr. Ron Wolfson 7 x 9, 352 pp, Quality PB, Illus., ISBN 1-879045-93-1 **$16.95**

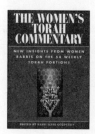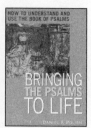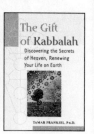